College-Path.com

COLLEGE BOUND

Proven Ways to Plan & Prepare for Getting into the College of Your Dreams

Over 1,200 links to verified college-related resources including financial aid and scholarships

Special admissions information for the artist, the athlete, the military-minded and the home-schooled

100+ minority scholarship websites

Resources for students with disabilities, alternative lifestyles and so much more!

"Using this book is like having your high school college counselor with you all day, every day!"

Christine Hand Gonzales, Ed.D.

PROFESSIONAL COLLEGE COUNSELOR

STUDENT, PARENT, AND EDUCATOR GUIDE TO
OVER 1,200 VERIFIED LINKS TO COLLEGE-
RELATED RESOURCES INCLUDING FINANCIAL
AID AND SCHOLARSHIPS

COLLEGE BOUND

College Path, LLC

Sumter, South Carolina 29154

SM College-Path.com is a service mark of College Path, LLC

ISBN-13: 978-1491203781

ISBN-10: 1491203781

Author: Christine Hand Gonzales, Ed.D

Cover and Book Design: Amy Lorenti

2014 Edition

COLLEGE BOUND:
Proven Ways to Plan and Prepare For Getting Into the College of Your Dreams

PRAISE FROM STUDENTS

*"'College Bound' has everything! The first place I researched was a major. The links to O*NET and the career and major profiles really helped. Then I used the link to College Navigator to match majors with colleges. Testing, essay ideas, asking for letters of recommendation, and finding money are all important topics to me. There's so much in this book. No matter what I needed, I found it in College Bound! There's nothing else like it – and I know it helped me get into USC."*

JESSICA, UNIVERSITY OF SOUTH CAROLINA FRESHMAN

"I learned a lot! 'College Bound' really helped me understand how to figure out exactly what I needed to do college-wise. Now that I'm a senior, I'm many steps ahead of some of my friends! In 'College Bound' everything I need is just a click away! It's amazing!"

MICHELLE, HIGH SCHOOL SENIOR - CONNECTICUT

"'College Bound' is awesome! I began my search for a college my junior year when I was interested in playing sports at the Division II or III level, and Dr. Chris's book helped a lot. Step-by-step instructions made the process easy to understand for a student-athlete. It also answered all my other questions about visits, the interviews, and the application process."

BRIAN, HIGH SCHOOL SENIOR - CONNECTICUT

PRAISE FROM PARENTS

"'College Bound' by Dr. Christine Hand Gonzales is the ultimate reference guide for the college application process. It is filled with essential checklists and links that cover all the necessary bases. If you have a question about applying to college, the answer can be found here. This organized and practical guide not only imparts the techniques needed to survive the process, but also it offers a collective wisdom that will make students and their families feel more in control of the experience, allowing them to make better informed decisions regarding that all important college choice."

GIGI MEYERS, DEVELOPMENT DIRECTOR AND MOTHER OF A RECENT GRADUATE

"It is so refreshing to find a guide that takes you from the very beginning, from middle school to the acceptance to college and beyond. 'College Bound' is well organized, simple to digest, and thorough - covering all areas from special interests to general eventualities, e.g., Naval Academy to Ivy League schools to state institution information. Also the links for financial aid and scholarship information are absolutely essential to families in this financial climate. We are very fortunate to have someone of Dr. Gonzales's caliber walking us through this complicated journey!"

MAUREEN G. MARTIN, LCSW, LMFT, THERAPIST, MOTHER'S CLUB PRESIDENT; MOTHER TO A SENIOR

"College Bound' has been an amazing resource for our family! With one child in college and another who will graduate in two years, this book is a wealth of information! We are using it to help our daughter prepare for getting into the right school, and we're using it to find additional financing for our son. I would have loved to have had this book when he was in high school."

ROSE MAIRE, MOTHER TO A HIGH SCHOOL JUNIOR AND COLLEGE SOPHOMORE

PRAISE FROM EDUCATION PROFESSIONALS

"As a high school college counselor and a private consultant, 'College Bound' and the 'My College Bound Plan' workbook have become essential tools in working with my students. The step by step process details every piece of important information needed for your student to be successful in the college search and with the challenge of applications. I use the workbook with my students and have 'College Bound' on my iPad as an instant resource. I have recommended both of these books to my students and their parents."

CHRISTINE CARRIUOLO, M.S., COLLEGE COUNSELOR

"This is the ultimate guide to the college search process! It is very well researched and informative with an expansive list of current web resources. This guide has everything you ever wanted to know about the college application process with an emphasis on special admission topics such as students with disabilities, benefits of women's colleges and diverse populations, to name a few. After sixteen years in the field as an Assistant Director of Admission and High School College Counselor, I can actually say that I learned something new from reading the up-to-date, real-time information 'College Bound' provides."

LEPRÊT DICKINSON WILLIAMS, DIRECTOR OF DIVERSITY AND EDUCATIONAL CONSULTANT

"'College Bound' goes beyond other guidebooks in providing an abundance of information about how to afford college, in addition to how to approach the selection process by putting the student first. This top-notch, time saving resource helps readers move through the maze of websites and search engines in a well-organized fashion. I would highly recommend any college-bound student and parent read this guide."

DR. HAROLD GONZALES, PROFESSOR, AUTHOR OF, "HOW TO IMPRESS YOUR ONLINE INSTRUCTOR: QUICK TIPS TO SUCCESS FOR THE VIRTUAL STUDENT"

"The Author hits the nail on the head! Dr. Chris provides invaluable advice for students and parents in 'College Bound.' She starts with a timeline and leads you through the college search and application process all the way through finding money for college. And for parents, she addresses discussions parents should have with their children revolving around this transition to college life. I'll be sure to share this thorough and comprehensive guide with my students and their families."

DR. TERESA WILBURN, LONGTIME COUNSELOR, SCHOOL ADMINISTRATOR, COLLEGE PROFESSOR, AND GATES MILLENNIUM SCHOLARS CONSULTANT

"What a wonderful resource for prospective college students of all ages, as well as for parents! If I were planning to go back to school, I would certainly use this tremendous resource. The fact that it is an eBook makes it that much easier to use! For middle school and high school students who are so technologically savvy, this makes sense. There is such an abundance of resources; I truly believe you could not have written a better title. With 'College Bound,' how can one not get into the college of his/ her choice! Bravo!"

KAREN DESSABLES, EXECUTIVE DIRECTOR, REACH FOR EXCELLENCE PROGRAM

ABOUT THE AUTHOR – "DR. CHRIS"

 Dr. Christine Hand Gonzales, author of "College Bound: Proven Ways to Plan and Prepare for Getting into the College of Your Dreams," the companion workbook, "My College Bound Plan," "Your College Planning Survival Guide: Smart Tips From Students, Parents, and Professionals Who Made It Through,"and "Paying For College Without Breaking e Bank" is a professional college planning consultant, instructor, a high school college counselor, and registered therapist with more than twenty years of experience. Her work with high school juniors and seniors has focused on career exploration and college counseling. Dr. Gonzales earned a Doctorate in Counseling Psychology from Argosy University, a Master's in Counseling Education from the University of Bridgeport, and a Bachelor's in Art Education and Economics from St. Lawrence University.

To contact Dr. Gonzales or to learn more about her consulting practice, books, or her college planning blog, College-Path.com, see the College Path website at http://www.college-path.com.

MORE

The 2013-2014 Edition of "My College Bound Plan" – the companion workbook to this edition of College Bound, with updated forms and checklists – is now available at College-Path.com, http://www.college-path.com/college-path-store and in paperback through Amazon.com.

Follow Dr. Chris's College Planning Blog via Facebook, Twitter and RSS Feed:

Friend the College Path Fan Page on Facebook:
http://www.facebook.com/pages/College-Pathcom/74842441589

Follow Dr. Chris on Twitter ID:
http://twitter.com/drchristinehand

Subscribe to the College-Path.com RSS Feed:
http://feeds.feedburner.com/CollegePath

ACKNOWLEDGEMENTS

First and foremost, I will always be grateful to my late parents, John and Dorothy Sarosky, for instilling in me the strength and fortitude it took to complete this project. I was able to pursue my education because of their constant encouragement and selfless sacrifice. Without their farsightedness, this book would never have seen the light of day. It is every bit as much their accomplishment as it is mine.

Many thanks go to my siblings, in particular my sister Val Sarosky, who believed in my endeavor. Her love, support, and encouragement helped me to continue writing. And to my husband, Dr. Hal Gonzales; thank you for taking the time to offer suggestions and – when my to-do list piled up higher and higher and there was no end in sight – talked me through the stressful times.

To my editor, Jim Stelljes, who possesses an abundance of talent and patience – thank you. I trusted him to read my drafts, identify my grammatical errors, and advise me of sections that needed rewriting for clarity. Jim understood my message and helped me to say what I wanted to say.

Year after year I am blessed to work side by side with a talented group of professionals who have a vast bank of knowledge regarding the college search and application process – thank you for sharing your perspectives. I would like to acknowledge the contributors to this book: U.S. Department of Education, Common Application, ACT, Sally Chopping of Acting for Business, and NACAC.

Lastly, a special acknowledgement goes to Amy Lorenti, whose marketing expertise and forward thinking were the inspiration for this project. Without you, this book would never have been published.

Christine M. Hand Gonzales, Ed.D.

AUTHOR, COLLEGE BOUND: PROVEN WAYS TO PLAN AND PREPARE FOR GETTING INTO THE COLLEGE OF YOUR DREAMS; YOUR COLLEGE BOUND PLAN WORKBOOK, YOUR COLLEGE PLANNING SURVIVAL GUIDE: SMART TIPS FROM STUDENTS, PARENTS, AND PROFESSIONALS WHO MADE IT THROUGH, AND PAYING FOR COLLEGE WITHOUT BREAKING THE BANK.

A LETTER FROM DR. CHRIS

Dear Parents and Students,

I wrote "College Bound: Proven Ways to Plan and Prepare for Getting Into the College of Your Dreams" as a guide to help parents and students prepare for what comes after graduation. "College Bound" is written so it will be like having a professional college counselor beside you every step of the way.

The "2013-2014 Edition of College Bound" guides you through the college planning timeline, the search and application process, and campus visits, with additional tips and resources. It will show ways to approach counselors, teachers, or moderators to request an effective letter of recommendation, give tips on self-marketing through the college essay, provide suggestions for a top-notch resume of extracurricular activities, and offer advice for taking standardized tests.

- ✓ If you are a budding artist, a competitive athlete, or interested in a military career, or transitioning from being homeschooled to college, this book is for you.

- ✓ If you have special needs or a disability, this book is for you.

- ✓ If you are thinking about learning a trade or attending community college, this book is for you.

- ✓ Interested in understanding the "nuts and bolts" of financial aid and where to find scholarships? This book is for you.

- ✓ Looking for an extensive list of publications and internet resources that is beyond compare? "College Bound" is for you – giving you all these resources and more.

I hope you will find this must-read guide helpful and informative, and I wish you all the best as you plan a path to an exciting future.

Sincerely,

Dr. Chris

Christine Hand Gonzales, Ed.D., Author *"Knowledge is Power"*

HOW TO GET THE MOST OUT OF THIS BOOK

1. Be sure you have an Internet connection with a browser window open. There are over 1,200 live links (shown in full URL format) that you will want to open and bookmark for future reference. If you have the Interactive Digital edition of *College Bound*, you will be able to click on the embedded links and go directly to that particular website.

2. Start with the Table of Contents. It offers an organized format to learn more about various topics. The chapters proceed in an orderly fashion, covering subjects from how to approach the college search and application process, to finding financial aid, and heading off to college. If you have the Interactive Digital edition of *College Bound*, you will be able to click on a topic in the contents and go directly to that page.

3. Follow the blog on the College Path website at http://www.college-path.com for weekly tips on the college planning process, and view updates and special offers for readers.

A Note about Links, Email Addresses, and Telephone Numbers

Within these pages, live links, email addresses, and telephone numbers to hundreds of resources have been provided to help you find the information you need simply by clicking, typing or calling. They have been checked as of August 1, 2013. However, we cannot guarantee the links will always work, as the World Wide Web changes constantly, nor can we guarantee all email addresses or telephone numbers are up to date. If you find a link, email address or telephone number that does not take you to the intended page, person or organization, simply type the organization name into your search engine and you should find what you're looking for. We apologize ahead of time for any inconvenience.

TABLE OF CONTENTS

COLLEGE BOUND:

Proven Ways to Plan and Prepare for Getting into the College of Your Dreams

Christine M. Hand Gonzales, Ed.D.

2013 - 2014 Edition

The Timeline: "Where Do I Start?"

Are you thinking about attending college or training in a particular field? It is never too early to start the process even if college is still a few years away. Begin now to position yourself to get into the college of your dreams by using this planning timeline and the hundreds of resources in this guide.

GRADES 6-8 - MIDDLE SCHOOL YEARS

Talk with a school counselor about:

- Taking courses required for entrance into high school and developing strong study habits.

- Reviewing college preparatory courses you plan on taking in high school including English, math, history, science, and modern and classical languages.

- Participating in summer enrichment programs or community-based extracurricular activities that may be available in your county or school.

- Read magazines, newspaper articles, and books of interest.

- Doing well on standardized tests by developing test-taking strategies.

- Developing organization and time-management skills.

- Getting extra tutoring to improve skills as needed.

- Researching options after high school related to careers, training and college.

- Exploring new topics and discover what subjects and activities really excite you.

- Attending career days, talking to college students, teachers, and counselors.

GRADE 9 - FRESHMAN YEAR

Talk to your guidance counselor (or teachers, if you don't have access to a guidance counselor) about the following:

- Attending a four-year college or university

- Establishing your college preparatory classes; and a schedule which should consist of at least four college preparatory classes per year, including:

  - 4 years of English
  - 4 years of Math (through Algebra II or Trigonometry)
  - 2 years of Foreign Language, minimum
  - 3 to 4 years of Natural Science (two lab sciences such as Chemistry and Biology; Physical Science or Physics)
  - 3 years of History/Social Studies (World and United States History, Economics/Government)
  - 1 elective of Art
  - 1 year of electives from the list above
  - Physical Education/Health

- Each student should check with his or her State Department of Education to verify college preparatory course requirements.

- Create a file of the following documents and notes:

  - Copies of report cards
  - List of awards and honors
  - List of school and community activities in which you are involved, including both paid and volunteer work, and descriptions of tasks or activities.

- Start thinking about the colleges you want to attend. Search for additional campus facts using the Department of Education School

Search Tool — College Navigator.
http://nces.ed.gov/collegenavigator/

- Study! The higher your grades, the more options you will have.

- Keep NCAA eligibility requirements in mind. Certain grades in core classes are necessary to be eligible to play sports in college. Review information on NCAA website – www.eligibilitycenter.org.

- Record statistics.

- Attend summer camps. Summers provide a block of time to focus on your sport(s) and connect with others.

GRADE 10 - SOPHOMORE YEAR

Talk to your guidance counselor (or teachers, if you do not have access to a guidance counselor) about the following:

- Reviewing the high school curriculum needed to satisfy the requirements of the colleges you are interested in attending.

- Finding out about Advanced Placement courses.

- Understanding what courses are available and whether or not you are eligible for the classes you want to take.

- How to enroll in them for your junior year.

- Updating your file, or start one if you have not already. "See Grade 9" for a list of what it should contain.

- Continuing extracurricular activities; admissions officers look at students' extracurricular activities when considering them for admission.

- Continuing participation in academic enrichment programs, summer workshops, and camps with specialty focuses such as music, arts, science, etc.

- Taking the PSAT in October; the scores will not count for National Merit Scholar Program consideration in your sophomore year, but it is valuable practice for when you take the PSAT again in your junior year (when the scores will count). Taking the PSAT is excellent practice for the SAT Reasoning Exam, which you should also be taking in your junior year. PSAT results are received in December.

http://www.collegeboard.com/student/testing/psat/about.html
http://www.collegeboard.com/student/testing/sat/about.html

- Many sophomores take the PLAN, the preliminary test to the ACT that is also used in the college admissions process.

  http://www.actstudent.org/plan/
  http://www.act.org/

- In April, registering for the SAT for any subjects you will be completing before June.

  http://www.collegeboard.com/student/testing/sat/about.html

- Taking the SAT Reasoning test.

- Taking Subject Test(s) in June. If students are interested in a military career, they should begin to research the options.
  http://www.todaysmilitary.com/futures

- The student athlete may begin reviewing information on the NCAA Eligibility Center requirements.
  https://web1.ncaa.org/eligibilitycenter/common/

- Begin researching career and college options by using the Internet, attending college fairs, and visiting college campuses.

GRADE 11 - JUNIOR YEAR

Fall Semester

- Maintaining your grades during your junior year is especially important. You should be doing at least two hours of homework each night and participating in study groups. Using a computer can be a great tool for organizing your activities and achieving the grades you want.

- Talk to your guidance counselor (or teachers, if you don't have access to a guidance counselor) about the following:

  - Availability of and enrollment in Advanced Placement classes

  - Schedules for the PSAT, SAT Reasoning Test and SAT Subject Test, ACT with Writing, and AP exams

  - Discuss reasons to take these exams and ways they could benefit you.

- Determine which exams to take. (You can always change your mind.)
- Sign up and prepare for the exams you've decided to take.
- Ask for a preview of your academic record and profile; determine what gaps or weaknesses there are, and get suggestions on ways to strengthen your candidacy for the schools in which you are interested.
- Determine what it takes to gain admission to the college(s) of your choice, in addition to grade point average (GPA) and test score requirements.
- Continue to explore career options using the Internet, interviewing professionals, shadowing people with a job that interest you, and think about an internship next year to learn details about jobs.

August
- Obtain schedules and forms for the SAT Reasoning Test, SAT Subject Test, ACT with Writing, and AP exams.

September
- Register for the PSAT exam offered in October. Remember that when you take the PSAT in your junior year, the scores will count towards the National Achievement Program and the National Merit Scholarship Program (and it is good practice for the SAT Reasoning Test).

October
- Take the PSAT. Narrow your list of colleges to include a few colleges with requirements at your current GPA, a few with requirements above your current GPA, and at least one with requirements below your GPA. Your list should contain approximately 8 - 12 schools you are seriously considering. Start thinking about the colleges you want to attend. Search for additional campus facts using the Department of Education School Search Tool — College Navigator. Start researching your financial aid options as well starting with the FAFSA4caster.
  http://nces.ed.gov/collegenavigator/
  http://www.fafsa4caster.ed.gov/F4CApp/index/index.jsf

- Begin scheduling interviews with college admissions counselors. If possible, schedule tours of the campus grounds on the same days. You and your parent(s) may want to visit the colleges and universities during spring break and summer vacation so that you do not have to miss school. Some high schools consider a campus visit an excused absence; however, if need be, you may be able to schedule interviews and visits during the school year without incurring any penalties.

November

- Review your PSAT results with your counselor in order to identify your strengths to determine the areas that you may need to improve in.

December

- You will receive your scores from the October PSAT. Depending on the results, you may want to consider signing up for an SAT preparatory course. Many high schools offer short-term preparatory classes or seminars on the various exams, which tell the students what to expect, and ways to potentially boost their scores.

SPRING SEMESTER

January

- Take campus tours online or in-person to further narrow your list of colleges to match your personality, interests, GPA, and test scores.

February

- Register for the March SAT and/or the April ACT with Writing Tests. Find out from each college the deadlines for applying for admission and which tests to take. Make sure your test dates give the college ample time to receive test scores. It is a good idea to take the SAT and/or ACT with Writing in the spring to allow you time to review your results and retake the exams in the fall of your senior year, if necessary.

March

- Take the March SAT Reasoning Test.
- If you are interested in taking any AP exam(s), you should sign up for the exam(s) at this time. If your school does not offer the AP exams, check with your guidance counselor to determine schools in

the area that do administer the exam(s), as well as the dates and times that the exam(s) you are taking will be offered. Scoring well on the AP exam can sometimes earn you college credit.

April

- Take the April ACT with Writing test.

- Talk to teachers about writing letters of recommendation for you. Think about what you would like included in these letters (how you would like to be presented) and politely ask your teachers if they can accommodate you.

- Create a resume of activities for those writing letters of recommendations on your behalf.

May

- Take SAT Reasoning Tests, SAT Subject Test, and AP exams.

June

- Add any new report cards, test scores, honors, or awards to your file. Visit colleges. Call ahead for appointments with financial aid, admissions, and academic advisors at the college(s), which most interest you. While there, talk to professors, sit in on classes, spend a night in the dorms, and speak to students. Doing these things will allow you to gather the most information about the college and the atmosphere in which you would be living, should you choose to attend. Some colleges have preview programs that allow you to do all of these; find out which of the schools that you will be visiting offer these programs and take advantage of them.

- Take SAT Reasoning Test, SAT Subject Tests (if required for admission to specific colleges on your list), and ACT with Writing Test.

- If you go on interviews or visits, do not forget to send thank-you notes.

SUMMER IN BETWEEN JUNIOR AND SENIOR YEARS

- Practice writing online applications by filling out rough drafts of each application without submitting them. Focus on the essay portions of these applications, deciding how you would like to present yourself. Do not forget to mention your activities outside of school.

- Check your applications, especially the essays. Have family, friends, and teachers review them for grammar, punctuation, readability, and content.

- Decide whether you are going to apply under a particular college's early decision or early action programs. This requires you to submit your applications early, typically between October and December of your senior year, but offers the benefit of receiving the college's decision concerning your admission early, usually before January 1. If you choose to apply early, you should do so to the college/university that is your first choice to attend. Many early decision programs are legally binding, requiring you to attend the college you are applying to, should they accept you.

  - Read your college mail and email, send reply cards or electronic response cards to your schools of interest.

  - If you are interested in the military, begin the application process.

GRADE 12 - SENIOR YEAR - FALL SEMESTER

September

- Check your transcripts to make sure you have all the credits you need to get into your college(s) of choice. Find out from the colleges to which you are applying whether or not they need official copies of your transcripts (sent directly from your high school) at the time of application.

- Register for October/November SAT Reasoning Test, SAT Subject Tests (if required for admission), and ACT (with Writing) tests.

- Take another look at your list of colleges, and make sure that they still satisfy your requirements. Add and/or remove colleges as necessary.

- Make sure you meet the requirements (including any transcript requirements) for all the colleges to which you want to apply. Double-check the deadlines, and apply.

- Give any recommendation forms to the appropriate teachers or counselors with stamped, college-addressed, envelopes making certain that your portion of the form is filled out completely and accurately. Be sure to give them a resume of your activities. Some of these may be done electronically, so be sure you have the correct email address.

- Most early decision and early action applications are due between October 1 and November 1. Keep this in mind if you intend to take advantage of these options and remember to request that your high school send your official transcripts to the college to which you are applying.

October

- Make a final list of schools that interest you, and keep a file of deadlines and required admission items for each school.

- Begin to request that transcripts be sent to schools to which you are applying Early Decision (a binding agreement between the college and you, stating that if you are admitted, you will attend their institution of higher learning –notification for Early Decision is mid-December), Early Action (a non-binding agreement between you and the college to enter after your senior year if you are accepted– notification is in mid-December), or Rolling Admission (colleges will make decisions 3-6 weeks after receiving all application documentation).

- Complete applications for Early Admission or Rolling.

- Take SAT Reasoning Test and/or ACT test with Writing. Have the official scores sent by the testing agency to the colleges/universities that have made your final list of schools. Register for December or January SAT Reasoning Test and/or SAT Subject Tests, if necessary.

- Continue thinking about and beginning writing (if you have not already started) any essays to be included with your applications.

November

- Submit your college admission application for Regular Admission.

- If you are applying for scholarships, research deadlines, write essays for applications, and request transcripts as needed.

- Some private colleges may request the CSS Profile or other financial forms be completed. Check your applications for further information.
  https://profileonline.collegeboard.com/prf/index.jsp

December

- Early Decision replies usually arrive between December 1st and December 31st.

- If you have not already done so, make sure your official test scores are being sent to the colleges to which you are applying.

- Schedule any remaining required interviews.

SENIOR YEAR - SPRING SEMESTER

January

- Submit the Free Application for Federal Student Aid (FAFSA) on or after January 1st. Contact the Financial Aid Office to see if you need to complete additional financial aid forms and check into other financial aid options. In order to be considered for financial aid, you will need to submit these forms even if you have not yet been notified of your acceptance to the college(s) to which you applied. http://www.fafsa.ed.gov/

- Go to the FAFSA now to complete the form. Or complete a paper FAFSA. http://www.fafsa.ed.gov/

- Request that your high school send your official transcripts to the colleges to which you are applying.

- Make sure your parents have completed their income tax forms in anticipation of the financial aid applications. If they have not completed their taxes, providing estimated figures is acceptable.

- Contact the admissions office of the college(s) to which you have applied to make sure that your information has been received and that they have everything they need from you.

February

- If you completed the FAFSA, you should receive your Student Aid Report (SAR) within 2-3 weeks if you applied via paper. If you applied online, you can receive results via email by the next business day after electronic submission. If corrections are needed, correct and return it to the FAFSA processor promptly. http://www.fafsa.ed.gov/FOTWWebApp/studentaccess.jsp

- Complete your scholarship applications.

- Contact the financial aid office of the college(s) to which you have applied to make sure that your information has been received and that they have everything they need from you.

March/April

- If you have not received an acceptance letter from the college (s) to which you applied, contact the admissions office.

- Compare acceptance letters, and financial aid and scholarship offers.

- When you choose a college that has accepted you, you may be required to pay a non-refundable deposit for freshman tuition (this should ensure your place in the entering freshman class).

May

- Take Advanced Placement (AP) exams for AP subjects studied in high school.
  http://www.collegeboard.com/student/testing/ap/about.html

- You should make a decision by May 1st as to which college you will be attending. Notify the school by mailing your commitment deposit check. Many schools require your notification letter be postmarked by this date.

- If placed on a waitlist for a particular college and you decide to wait for an opening, contact the college, and let them know you are still very interested.

June

- Have your school send your final transcripts to the college you will be attending.

- Thank your counselors and teachers for their assistance along the way.

- Contact your college to determine when fees are due for tuition, and room and board are due, and how much they will be.

SUMMER AFTER SENIOR YEAR

- Participate in any summer orientation programs for incoming freshmen.

- Now that you know you will be attending college in the fall, decide whether to get student health insurance. How will you handle unforeseen emergencies? Will your family's insurance coverage be sufficient?

Source: U.S. Department of Education

NOTES

Glossary of Terms for the College Search

ACT with Writing

The American College Testing Program test is divided into four parts: English usage, mathematics usage, social science reading, and science reasoning. Score range is 1-36. The national average is 21. The ACT Writing test is a 30-minute essay that measures writing skills.

Admission Decisions

Colleges usually reply in one of five ways: (1) accept, (2) deny, (3) defer (You have not been accepted or denied as an Early Decision or Early Action candidate; therefore, your application will be reviewed in the regular pool of applicants.) (4) waitlist, or (5) admit/deny. (You are admitted but denied financial aid.)

A.P.

Advanced Placement courses are considered college-level courses offered in high school for possible college credit. National exams given in May are graded on a scale of 1 (low) to 5 (high).

B.A.

Bachelor of Arts is the traditional degree awarded by a liberal arts college or university following the completion of a degree program. You may receive a B.A. in the humanities or the social and natural sciences.

B.S.

Bachelor of Science is usually awarded at the completion of a vocationally oriented program like business, nursing, or education.

Candidate's Reply Date

May 1 is the date a student must give all accepting colleges a definite "yes" or "no," and send a deposit to the final-choice college.

CLEP Exams

Developed by the College Board, the people behind AP and SAT, the College-Level Examination Program (CLEP) has been the most widely trusted credit-by-examination program for over 40 years, accepted by 2,900 colleges and universities and administered in over 1,700 test centers. CLEP exams test mastery of college-level material acquired in a variety of ways — through general academic instructions, significant independent study, or extracurricular work. CLEP exam-takers include adults just entering or returning to school, military service members, and traditional college students.

College Board

An association of 2,700 high schools, colleges, universities, and educational systems, the College Board is a major provider of essential educational services and information to students, families, high schools, and colleges. In conjunction with Educational Testing Service (ETS), the College Board sponsors the ATP (Admission Testing Program – PSAT, SAT, SAT Subject Tests, and AP).

Common Application

A universal application accepted by over 400 private and public colleges in lieu of their own applications. An applicant fills out one Common Application and then may mail photocopies to any of the colleges that subscribe to the service.

College Scholarship Service (CSS)

A clearinghouse for the Financial Aid Form (FAF). CSS Profile evaluates each FAF, determines the family contribution (what the family can afford to pay), and forwards that analysis to the college Financial Aid Offices and scholarship programs designated by the applicant.

College Work-Study Program

CWSP is a federal program, which allows students to pay some of their college expenses by working part time on campus. Eligibility is determined by FAFSA.

Credit Hour

The value of a college course according to its level of difficulty. A four-credit course would be more demanding than a three-credit course. Most colleges require a certain number of credit hours for graduation.

Deferred Admission

A student applied early or rolling admission to a school, and the college has postponed its decision until a later date in order to receive more data that could include grades, other essays, achievements, or recommendations.

Deferred Entrance

A deferred entrance is an admission plan that allows an accepted student to postpone entrance to college for a year while retaining a guarantee of enrollment. During that year the student may work or travel but may not enroll at another college.

Degree

There are three basic degrees: Associate's Degree awarded by two-year colleges; Bachelor's Degree awarded by four-year colleges and universities, Master's and other graduate degrees offered by universities.

Demonstrated Need

Cost of attending a college or university, minus the family's estimated contribution (as determined by federal or institutional methodology).

Demonstrated Interest

A term used during the admissions process that encourages a student to express a great deal of interest in the institution in order to possibly receive a favorable admission decision.

Early Action (EA)

Early Action is an admission plan offered by some highly selective colleges that allow the most qualified students the chance to earn a letter of acceptance in December. The student does not have to withdraw other applications and does not have to accept or refuse the EA offer of admission until May 1.

Early Admission

Early Admissions is an admission plan that allows a student to enter college at the end of the junior year in high school. Admission requirements are usually as stringent as or more so than usual.

Early Decision

Early Decision is a binding admission plan that requires an early application (typically October or November) and promises a reply by December or January. There are two types of ED plans: (1) Single Choice, in which the student is allowed to apply to only one college and (2) First Choice, in which the student may apply elsewhere but agrees to withdraw other applications if accepted by the ED school. This plan is recommended only if the applicant is absolutely sure of his or her college choice. If accepted, the student is ethically obligated to attend if sufficient financial aid is offered.

Early Notification

Is an admission plan that promises an early reply to an early application. If accepted, the student is not obligated to attend.

Educational Testing Service (ETS)

The people responsible for the PSAT, SAT, SAT Subject Tests, and A.P. Exams.

Enrollment Deposit/Matriculation Deposit

This non-refundable deposit reserves a place in the entering freshman class. Send this in by the date specified in the admission materials (usually but not always May 1).

Financial Aid Profile (formerly the FAP)

The application to the College Scholarship Service is similar in function to the Federal Financial System. The profile is required by some colleges, universities, and scholarship programs to award their own private funds.

Free Application for Federal Student Aid (FAFSA)

An application form for need-based and federal aid.

GPA

Grade Point Average is the average of all student grades from freshman year through senior year in high school.

Gapping

Gapping occurs when an admitted student is awarded a financial aid package that meets less than his or her full-demonstrated need.

Liberal Arts

An introduction to a wide variety of subjects including the social sciences, humanities, fine arts, and natural sciences. The liberal arts do not include such technical majors as engineering, business, allied health, or architecture.

Merit-based Financial Aid

Financial aid, including scholarships, that is awarded based on a candidate's merit (i.e., academic ability, special talent, competition /audition) excluding athletic aid. It may or may not take into consideration the financial need of the candidate. This does not have to be paid back.

Need-based Financial Aid

Aid offered by colleges and the federal government to bridge the gap between college costs and the family's ability to pay as determined by the profile FFS, FAFSA, and/or the college Financial Aid Office. A typical aid package is divided into three parts: grant (gift money you do not pay back), loan, and work-study (campus job).

Need-blind Admission

Students are admitted based on academic and personal criteria, regardless of ability to pay. This does not include international students.

Need-conscious (Need-aware, Need-sensitive) Admission

Financial need might be a factor in the admission decision.

Pell Grants

Federal grants (gifts, not loans) designed to help students with college costs. Eligibility is determined by the FAFSA.

Preferential/differential Packaging

The awarding of financial aid packages of differing attractiveness based upon the desirability of the candidates to the admitting institution.

PSAT/NMSQT

Preliminary Scholastic Assessment Test/National Merit Scholarship Qualifying Test, a shorter version of the SAT given to sophomores and juniors in preparation for the SAT. The PSAT is used to determine eligibility for National Merit and National Achievement Scholarship Programs.

Rolling Admission

An admission plan in which applications are evaluated very soon after they are completed in the Admission Office. The applicant can receive a decision very quickly but is not obligated to attend.

Regular Decision

The decision process does not begin until a college accepts applications from prospective students but delays the admission decision until all applications from the entire applicant pool have been received. Decision letters are mailed or emailed to applicants, all at once, traditionally in late March or early April.

SAT Reasoning Test

The Scholastic Assessment Test is designed to measure a student's verbal and mathematical aptitude as well as writing skills. The score ranges 200-800 on each section. The national average is in the 500 range on each part.

SAT Subject Tests

Formerly called Achievement Tests, these were developed by the College Board to measure a student's knowledge or skills in a particular area and the ability to apply that knowledge. Each test is multiple-choice and takes one hour. Many colleges require the SAT Subject Tests for admission.

SAT Score Choice

This option allows the test taker to review his or her SAT test scores and select the scores they want sent to colleges.

Scholarships

Some colleges use the term "scholarship" to mean a grant, need-based aid that does not have to be repaid. Other colleges reserve the term "scholarship" for awards given for high academic achievement or special talent, regardless of demonstrated need.

Student Search

A College Board service that allows the colleges to receive the names of students who have taken the PSAT or SAT and have indicated their willingness to receive mailings from colleges.

TOEFL

Test of English as a Foreign Language is a verbal aptitude test for non-native speakers of English.

Transcript

A transcript, an official grade report, shows the final grade you received in each of your courses. It contains personal information: name, address, social security number, date of birth, graduation date, cumulative GPA, total credits earned, courses taken each term, and the signature and seal of the registrar at the high school.

Waitlist

The Waitlist is a list of qualified students who may be offered admission by a college at a later date, if space becomes available. Waitlisted students should initially accept another offer of admission and discuss with their college counselor various ways to handle the waitlist situation.

The College Search

1. How Do I Figure Out What To Major In?

2. Whom Do I Ask and Where Do I Look For College Information?

3. What Post High School Program Makes Sense to Me?

4. Finding the Right College Fit – A Self-Assessment

5. What Colleges Look For in Student Applicants

6. How to Email a College Admissions Counselor – Check Your Email Address First

7. Admissions Representatives Visit With Students

8. College Visits and College Fairs!

9. Can't Get to a College Campus? Why Not Visit from Home?

10. College Visit Comparison Charts

11. College Ranking Issues

12. Publications to Peruse During the College Search

13. 90 Best Education Advice College Planning Blogs

14. Internet Resources for Career Exploration and the College Search

Even before a student begins the college search, he or she needs to think about what would make a college the right fit, the perfect match. Start by answering these questions. Why would you continue an education? Do you want to fulfill your dreams? Have fun? Meet new people and exercise your mind? What about learning more about what you love to do and learning how to get paid doing it? To do this, the student should understand his or her strengths, weaknesses, and interests. He or she will need to think about his or her potential to succeed by reviewing his or her grade point average, his or her standardized test scores and coursework, while verifying what the admissions requirements are for specific colleges.

This chapter addresses the many choices students have regarding career opportunities, choosing a major, and finding a college that offers that major. The student should ask him or herself, what type of post- high school program makes sense – a technical or trade school, or a 2-Year (community college) or 4-Year college or university? The next question to answer is what am I looking for in a college, as well as, what exactly are colleges looking for in a student-applicant? He or she can complete a self-assessment to find out what aspects of a college or university will be most important to him or her. Visiting a campus, a college fair, or taking a virtual tour online are other ways to gather information on colleges that will help the student build the initial list of schools. Lastly, the student may want to peruse the extensive list of publications or Internet resources created for the college search. These are posted at the end of the chapter. So, let's get started with the college search!

1 - HOW DO I FIGURE OUT WHAT TO MAJOR IN?

Some students know what they would like to major in, and others do not. For those who are still searching for the area of study that piques their interest, don't panic! A majority of students in many colleges and universities change their majors at least once in their college careers.

Take Your Time to Explore. Try new courses you never had the opportunity to take while in high school. Talk with professors about what you can do with a major in the specific course area. Enjoy the variety of options before you make a decision. Who knows, maybe you will invent your own major!

Don't Judge a Course Too Quickly. Just like the saying, "don't judge a book by its cover," you should give each class a chance. You may end up loving the subject and course content.

Consider Your Current Interests and Hobbies. You probably already know what you like to do with your time. There is a major related to your interests.

What Do You Value? When you graduate, do you want a job that has security, and offers the chance to make a lot of money, or feeds your creativity and personal growth? Do you thrive on pressure and deadlines, or would you prefer a low pressure experience? What type of work environment would make you the happiest – working outdoors or inside? Would you like to help people and work in a hospital or school? Would you find it exciting to "fly the friendly skies" and see the world? How much money do you need to live on after graduation? Are you an independent worker, or would you rather be a member of a team? Would you rather work with people or things? Are you seeking stability or is adventure necessary? Rank your values.

Read the Course Catalogs and Syllabi. Though the course catalog might not be the most exciting material to read, you can gain a glimmer of what the course will cover and what the class requirements will be.

Talk to Your Advisor. You will be assigned an advisor when you start college. These individuals can be very helpful in answering questions about various majors. They are experts in their own discipline. Your advisor can offer you suggestions based on your interests and academic strengths. These professionals know what it takes to succeed in certain subjects. Let them help you by offering their insights.

Ask an Upperclassman! Upperclassmen have been where you are. They had to make difficult decisions about their major as well. Many are willing to answer your questions and offer advice about the process. These students will tell you the truth from their perspective about what it will take to excel.

Network with Marketplace Professionals. Set appointments for informational interviews with professionals in your field of interest. Ask if you can job-shadow for a day to see what the job entails. Investigate the work environment, the job schedule, and responsibilities. Most professionals will answer questions about their educational degrees, how they got started in their field, and offer tips about the paths you may need to take to reach your goal.

You Can Major in More than One Subject. Yes, this is true! Many schools will allow you to double major. Some allow you to develop a major or choose a major and minor combination. Talk with your advisor and the chairpersons of the departments to see if this is possible. Your major will not necessarily determine your career. Follow your passions!

Co-op Programs Grow in Popularity Along with Internships. Cooperative education or internships are a great way to test drive a career and major. Virginia Tech notes their Career Service Cooperative Education/Internship Program is an undergraduate academic program which incorporates real world work experience and learning into the student's college academic experience. The program is a partnership among the undergraduate student, the employer and the college with the program. Co-ops and internships give students educationally-related work and learning experience that integrates theory learned in the classroom with practical application and skill development on the job, and contributes to the development of personal and professional maturity and ethics. Co-ops and internships give employers the opportunity to assist in the student's development, supplement their workforce with emerging talent, and enhance their long-range recruiting efforts by evaluating students' potential for employment at graduation.

Here are some easy steps to take to narrow down your choices of majors:

- Complete the O*NET Interest Profiler by downloading the program. It is one of the most researched and accepted career exploration tools used by counselors. It uses the Holland Typology code.
  http://www.onetcenter.org/IP.html
  http://www.mynextmove.org/
  http://www.roguecc.edu/counseling/hollandcodes/test.asp

- Conduct a self-assessment and ask yourself these questions: What are your strengths? What are your weaknesses? What are your best subjects and what courses do you like the best in high school? What motivates you?

- Check a college course catalogue and register for classes you are interested in.

- Complete the Career Interest Game. This is a game designed to help you match your interests and skills with similar careers. Holland codes are realistic, investigative, artistic, social, enterprising, and conventional.
  http://career.missouri.edu/students/majors-careers/skills-interests/career-interest-game/

- Search majors aligned with your codes through the University of Oklahoma's Career Services.
  http://www.ou.edu/career/Students/CareerExploration/HollandCodes.html

- Check out major and career profiles through College Board.
  http://www.collegeboard.com/csearch/majors_careers/profiles/

- Use College Navigator to find the college that has the major related to your career interest. http://nces.ed.gov/collegenavigator/

- Volunteer for an organization for which you think you might like to work.

- Observe an adult who has a job that seems interesting to you.

- Participate in an internship to see what the job is all about.

- Find a summer or part-time job to "test the waters" in a career area.

- Talk to people including classmates, instructors, employers, friends, and family members.

2 - WHOM DO I ASK AND WHERE DO I LOOK FOR COLLEGE INFORMATION?

Check the following resources:

- Talk with your guidance counselor.

- Review guidebooks like Peterson's, Barron's, or College Board.

- The Internet is a great source of information (see the list of Internet resources at the end of each chapter of this resource guide).

- Visit the individual websites of the colleges in which you are interested.

- Attend college fairs and meetings at your high school scheduled with admissions representatives.

- Thumb through college catalogues, view videos, and read brochures.

- Chat with friends, relatives, neighbors, coaches, teachers about college. Maybe they attended the one you would like to attend. Maybe they have some new ideas.

- Stay organized by making files of those colleges on your list.

3 - WHAT POST HIGH SCHOOL PROGRAM MAKES SENSE TO ME?

Types of Schools: Technical, 2-Year, 4-Year, College & University

- Most post-secondary schools can be described as public or private, 2- or 4-year.

- Public institutions are state supported. Private for-profit institutions are businesses. Private not-for-profit institutions are independent – for instance, the school might have been established by a church or through local community donations rather than by the state government.

- Four-year institutions offer bachelor's degrees, and some offer advanced degrees. Two-year institutions offer associate's degrees. Less-than-two-year institutions offer training and award certificates of completion.

- You can use the U.S. Department of Education's search tool to find information about schools in all these categories. http://nces.ed.gov/ipeds/cool/

Here is a more detailed description of the kinds of schools you might hear about as you plan for your post-high-school education:

College – A four-year college grants bachelor's degrees (Bachelor of Arts; Bachelor of Science). Some colleges also award master's degrees.

University – A university grants bachelors and masters degrees, and sometimes includes a professional school such as a law school or medical school. Universities tend to be larger than colleges, focus more on scholarly or scientific research, and might have larger class sizes.

Community college – A public two-year college granting associate's degrees and sometimes certificates in particular technical (career-related) subjects. Many students start their postsecondary education at a community college and then transfer to a four-year school, either because a community college tends to be more affordable than a four-year college, or because of the open admissions policy at community colleges.

Junior college – A Junior College is similar to a community college, except that a junior college is usually a private school.

Career school, Technical school, Vocational/Trade school – These terms are often used interchangeably. These schools may be public or private, two-year or less-than-two-year. Career schools offer courses that are designed to prepare students for specific careers, from welding to cosmetology to medical imaging, etc. The difference between technical schools and trade schools is that technical schools teach the science behind the occupation, while trade schools focus on hands-on application of skills needed to do jobs.

Source: U.S. Department of Education

4 - FINDING THE RIGHT COLLEGE FIT – A SELF-ASSESSMENT

What are your priorities for choosing a college? What would make a college a "perfect fit" for you? You may change your mind over the course of four years of high school, so you may need to revise your wish list.

Using the list below, check off the top ten characteristics that are of greatest importance to you.

- ☐ Size of college
- ☐ Location (small town or large city)
- ☐ Distance from home
- ☐ Class size
- ☐ Co-ed or single sex enrollment
- ☐ College's reputation
- ☐ Athletics (Division I, II, III or intramural)
- ☐ Cost (after financial aid and scholarship)
- ☐ Academic entrance requirements (GPA, coursework, test scores)
- ☐ Selectivity– easy, moderate, difficult
- ☐ Major you want is offered
- ☐ Resources – library, research opportunities
- ☐ Safety of campus
- ☐ Social activities and student involvement
- ☐ Greek life (fraternities and sororities)
- ☐ Student to faculty ratio
- ☐ Endowment (financial resources)
- ☐ Graduation rate
- ☐ Retention rate
- ☐ Graduate school placement
- ☐ Job placement
- ☐ Career Services
- ☐ Alumni satisfaction
- ☐ Friends and family attended (legacy factor)

☐ Campus appearance

☐ Religious affiliation

☐ Curriculum – liberal arts, vocational, technical, engineering, etc.

☐ Internship opportunities

☐ Computer support in labs and rooms

☐ Student diversity – geographic, economic, racial, ethnic, etc.

☐ Honors or Special Programs

☐ Friendliness of students and faculty

☐ Extracurricular activities

☐ Residential or commuter campus

☐ Food quality – meal plans

☐ Cultural opportunities

☐ Classroom environment– large or small, discussion or lecture, lab or research

☐ Housing options

☐ Tuition, room and board (meal plan) cost

☐ Military opportunities – ROTC, academies, enlistment

5 - WHAT COLLEGES LOOK FOR IN STUDENT APPLICATIONS

What are the factors that affect the decisions of the college admissions committee? Some carry more weight in the application process than others; the following are ranked from the most influential to the least.

- Challenging Schedule

- Academic Performance

- Standardized Test Scores Consistent with Grades

- Rank in Class

- Passionate involvement in Extracurricular Activities

- Contribution to Community through Volunteer Activities

- Application Essay/Personal Statement (authenticity, reflective, impact-oriented)

- Letters of Recommendation – Counselor/Teacher

"Tipping factors" that can play a role in admissions:

- Interview

- Family Ties and Legacy

- Internships/Portfolios/Jobs – Out of School Activities

- Geographic Diversity

- Academic Diversity

- Extracurricular Diversity

- Ethnic/Racial Diversity

- Socioeconomic Diversity

6 - HOW TO EMAIL A COLLEGE ADMISSIONS COUNSELOR – CHECK YOUR EMAIL ADDRESS FIRST

Yes, you were given a formal name at birth and you may be a creative individual who wants to express yourself with a unique email address, but suddenly you realize hotmama@mail.com might not be the most appropriate email address to use. Who is your audience? What impression will you leave on the admissions officer? Every bit of information you reveal tells the college admissions office something about you. I often ask students to think about how their grandparents might react to the address. It may be safer and more appropriate to use your school email address or create one that will be used for all your college correspondence.

Next, are you taking the time to create an email message that will make a good impression and get your questions answered? After all, you don't want to hurt your chances of getting into the school.

You might be writing an email message to an admissions counselor to ask for advice, check the status of an application, or just to get a bit more information. Here's how to compose it in a way that will not cause the counselor to hit the delete button, or worse, make the counselor reconsider your acceptance to the college.

- Check for typos and grammatical errors.

- Use standard and proper English, and never use text message abbreviations.

- Consider the following two examples:

  1. *"hi i am interested in ur school can u send me more info plz."*

2. *"Dear (Name of Counselor), I am interested in your school and would like to receive more information. I appreciate your time and assistance. Best Regards/Sincerely, Your Name".*

Or, if communication has been slightly more informal, a simple message like this may be sufficient.

1. *"Dear (Name of Counselor), Thank you very much for the information! (Your Name)"*

Which one would impress the reader? The first one requires decoding, the second is straightforward and in plain English. It's better to avoid using abbreviations entirely, unless relevant to the school (Bachelor of Arts, for example, can be abbreviated to B.A.)

The simpler, the better, so be straightforward and to the point.

Maintain contact and always follow up with the admissions counselors.

The moral of this story is this; remember that while you may have fantastic talents and skills to share, you may never even get a foot in the door with a "freaky" or funny email name like "shedevil" or "studmuffin." While you never know how an admissions counselor perceives you before he or she meets you, you can control some of the variables used to evaluate you. "Goofy" e-mail names are just fine with your Yahoo buddy list but he or she are not appropriate during a college application process. Put yourself in the counselor's place and think twice before you send that email!

7 - ADMISSIONS REPRESENTATIVE VISIT WITH STUDENTS

College admissions representatives begin their fall visits in August and conclude sometime in November. Your high school counselor is probably busy scheduling these visits right now. The representatives share information with prospective applicants and allow students time to ask pertinent questions about the search and application process. This is a great time for seniors and juniors, who are interested in gathering data, to meet the representatives face-to-face. The admissions officer may be the one who will eventually read your college application.

Here is a list of events and places where you may be able to meet with admissions representatives:

- College fairs at nearby schools
- College night information programs

- High school visits

- Recruitment events at local hotels

- PROBE fairs at local malls

- Admissions events on campus

- Online at College Week Live
  http://www.collegeweeklive.com/en_CA/guest/college_events

- Speak with an Admission Counselor on Skype – Using Skype and a webcam, prospective undergraduate students applying as freshman, transfer, or adult students can speak from home or school directly with an admission counselor. Many schools allow students to make appointments during the day. Check with the admissions office to see if the college or university has this set-up.

You can also contact the admissions officers directly to see when the representative will be in your neighborhood. If you know when he or she will be visiting your area, drop the officer a note or email introducing yourself sharing your plan to meet at the specific location. This is also a great time to let the representative know some interesting information about your school community. If you are playing in a game or are involved in a school play, let them know the dates and times. Sometimes the representatives have time between destinations and would love to know more about your area.

Remember to prepare for the meeting by doing some homework. Gather information about the college and create a list of questions you want answered. Maintain eye contact, offer a firm handshake, and complete their information card. The following day write them a thank you for the opportunity to meet.

One last note, campus tours and overnight visits are another way to meet with a representative. Many colleges offer these sessions throughout the year, so be sure to check the school's website for details. Once you get on campus, sign in at the admissions office. You want them to know you have arrived!

8 - COLLEGE VISITS AND COLLEGE FAIRS

Visiting the campus is probably one of the most important steps in actually choosing a college. After all, you may be choosing where you would like to live for the next four years. A visit to the campus will indicate to the admissions representatives that you are interested in their program of study. If you do not get a chance to visit, you may have a chance to meet an admissions officer at a college fair in your hometown. Either way, it will be important for you to be prepared.

- Do your research about the college ahead of time.

- Know your own goals and what questions you would like answered.

- Know your PSAT, SAT and/or ACT scores, and GPA.

- Be able to talk about your strengths in the academic arena as well as in extracurricular activities.

- Avoid the obvious questions – focus more on academic and student life opportunities.

- Be yourself, be honest, and be prepared.

- Never underestimate the value of the meeting.

When planning a visit to a campus:

- Call ahead to schedule the visit, take a tour, and attend an information session.

- Arrive on time for your tour.

- Dress appropriately – you may be meeting with the admissions representative who may be reviewing your application for admission.

- Interact with students, faculty, coaches, and admissions staff.

- Pick up a school newspaper.

- Attend a class or lecture if possible.

- Eat a meal in the dining hall.

- View the library and the labs.

- Visit a dorm and stay overnight if allowed.

- Collect a business card from the admissions person you meet.

After a college visit or a **college fair** meeting:

- Make notes of your reactions, and other important data you may need to consider later in the process.

- Ask yourself if the college was a "good fit" for you and your interests.

- Send a thank-you note to those with whom you had an appointment.

9 - CAN'T GET TO A COLLEGE CAMPUS? WHY NOT VISIT FROM HOME?

Visiting the campus is probably one of the most important steps in actually choosing your college. After all, you may be choosing where you would like to live for the next four years. If you do not have the opportunity to visit, or have a chance to meet an admissions officer at a college fair in your hometown, it will be important for you to take a virtual visit:

- Do your research about the college online.

- Know your own goals and what questions you would like answered.

- Know your PSAT, SAT and/or ACT scores, and GPA.

- Understand your own strengths in the academic arena as well as in extracurricular activities.

- Focus more on academic and student life opportunities.

- Be honest with yourself and what you are looking for.

- Never underestimate the value of a tour whether online or in person.

When planning a **virtual visit** to a campus:

- Listen to students, faculty, coaches, and admissions staff presentations online.

- Read the school newspaper online through Campus Newspapers by State
http://newslink.org/statcamp.html.

- View the academic buildings, dorms, the library, the labs, the recreational facilities offered online.

- Read the school's website and learn about your admissions representative and the informational tours.

- Learn more about the community and cultural venues.

Choose from the following by using one of the following websites:

- Campus Virtual Tours - Virtual tours of college campus. http://www.campustours.com/

- Channel One Virtual College Tours - Student virtual discussions online on campus topics. http://www.channelone.com/news/virtual_college_tours/

- College Week Live-Virtual College Fair - Interact with college admissions representatives online. http://www.collegeweeklive.com/

- Virtual Campus Tours: Tour the Campus of 25 Top Colleges and Universities http://diplomaguide.com/articles/Virtual_Campus_Tours_Tour_the _Campus_of_25_Top_Colleges_and_Universities.html

- Your Campus 360 - A walking virtual tour of college campuses. http://www.yourcampus360.com/index.php

- YOUniveristy - Review virtual college video tours and students' interviews about campus. http://www.youniversitytv.com

- You Tube Education - Search, tour, and watch student and faculty interviews online. http://www.youtube.com/education?b=400

- Youvisit - View virtual college tours. http://www.youvisit.com/

After the **online visit** or **online college fair** meeting:

- Make notes of your reactions, and other important data you may need to consider later on in the process.

- Ask yourself if the college was a "good fit" for you and your interests.

- If they offer an interactive blog with students, take part and get your questions answered.

Though virtual visits should not be a replacement for actual college tours and information sessions on campus, they can be a great way to start gathering important information and gauge the makeup of the school community.

10 - COLLEGE VISIT COMPARISON CHARTS

Using the charts on the following pages, objectively compare the colleges you are interested in.

College Comparison Checklist

	College 1	College 2	College 3	College 4	College 5
Undergrad Student Body Size					
Faculty / Student Ratio					
Distance from Home					
Urban / Rural / Suburban					
Numbers of Majors					
Is my major offered here? Yes / No					
Technology					
Special Support Offerings					
Facilities: dorms, dining, laboratories, recreation, etc.					
Research for Undergrads					
Study Abroad Opportunities					
Specific Questions Per College					

Notes

Financial Considerations

	College 1	College 2	College 3	College 4	College 5
Is Financial Aid available?					
Are there jobs on campus or Federal Work-Study Programs available?					
Annual In-state Tuition / Out-of-state Tuition & Fees					
Annual Housing Cost					
Annual Meal Plan Cost					
Round-trip Travel Cost					

Notes

Financial Consideration Criteria

	College 1	College 2	College 3	College 4	College 5
Can you double major? Will that make you more marketable after graduation?					
Career Placement and Planning: Do you need an advanced degree? Will jobs in your area be sent overseas or available in the U.S.? Does the college hold recruitment fairs?					
Are students accepted to Graduate School and placed satisfactorily?					
Review alumni support and networking opportunities.					
Major Fits / Passion for Study: Internships, research, Co-Op programs, summer work with faculty, and study abroad opportunities.					
Level of credentials of professors teaching your major.					
Environment fits me Best: Accessibility to home, city, suburb or rural, college-town feel.					
Size of Student Population – Is it what I'm looking for?					
Financial Check: School matches my budget/offers financial aid, and scholarship possibilities all four years.					
Level of satisfaction with living space.					
Extracurricular activities fit needs.					
Rate Programs by FSP Index (Faculty Scholarly Productivity) The Chronicle of Higher Education http://chronicle.com/stats/productivity/ and research productivity, grants, publications and academic awards. – Talk with others, but make your own decision – Go with your "gut feeling" in the end – Don't stress – students do change their minds and transfer					

- Talk with others, but make your own decision

- Go with your "gut feeling" in the end

- Don't stress – students do change their minds and transfer

11 - COLLEGE RANKING ISSUES

Time and time again articles are printed in magazines and newspapers about college rankings. A particular college may be rated number one by a group, but that does not mean it is the best match for the student. Each student will need to look at his or her interests and college characteristics to see if it is a good fit. These rankings hold different meanings for each person, just as the Oscars rate movies, and the Grammys rank music, not everyone will agree with the outcome. It is okay to read the college ranking magazines as long as the student and his or her family review other sources of information to make his or her decision.

12 - PUBLICATIONS TO REVIEW DURING THE COLLEGE SEARCH

There are many guides, books, and publications students and parents may find valuable as they search for the ideal school. Below are independent resources that can be of use in the college search process. Many are available in high school career centers or college counseling offices. These publications and more can be found online and in your local bookstores.

Comprehensive guides include:

- *Barron's Best Buys in College Education*
- *Barron's Profiles of American Colleges*
- *Peterson's Guide to Four Year Colleges*
- *Peterson's Colleges in New England, Middle Atlantic, West, Midwest, New York, the South*
- *College Board: The College Handbook*
- *The Big Book of Colleges – by College Prowler*
- *U.S. News and World Report Ultimate College Directory*

Guides to **"selective" colleges** are as follows:

- *Barron's Profiles of the Most Prestigious Colleges*
- *Peterson's Competitive Colleges*
- *The Princeton Review: America's Elite Colleges*
- *The Princeton Review: America's Best Value Colleges*
- *The Best 371 Colleges*

- *The Fiske Guide to Colleges*
- *The Insider's Guide to the Colleges*

Guides with **great college lists** can be found in:

- *America's Best Colleges for B Students*
- *College Prowler Series*
- *College Navigator*
- *Colleges that Change Lives*
- *Cool Colleges*
- *Harvard Schmarvard: Getting Beyond the Ivy League to the College that is Best for You*
- *100 Colleges Where Average Students Can Excel*
- *Looking Beyond the Ivy League*
- *Rugg's Recommendations on the Colleges*
- *The College Finder: Choosing the School That's Right for You*
- *The Templeton Guide: Colleges that Encourage Character Development*
- *Treasure Schools: America's College Gems*

Guides for **students with special interests**:

- *College Bound Sports: The High School Athlete's Guide to College Sports*
- *ARCO The Performing Arts Major's College Guide*
- *College Guide for Students with Learning Disabilities*
- *Community College: Is It Right For You?*
- *Creative Colleges: A Guide For Student Actors, Artists, Dancers, Musicians, and Writers*
- *100 Best Colleges for African American Students*
- *Historically Black Colleges and Universities Resource Book*
- *NACAC Early College Application Directory*

- *Peterson's Colleges with Programs for Students with Learning Disabilities or ADD*

- *Peterson's Nursing Programs: Find the Right Program for You*

- *Peterson's Professional Degree Programs in the Visual and Performing Arts*

- *The Princeton Review: Catholic Colleges Guide to College Visits*

- *Peterson's Nursing Programs*

- *Student Guide to Catholic Colleges and Universities*

- *The Black Student's Guide to Colleges*

- *The K & W Guide to Colleges for Students with Learning Disabilities or ADD*

- *The Official Catholic College & University Guidebook*

- *Television, Film, and Digital Media Programs*

- *Guide to Service – Learning College & Universities*

College Majors:

- *90 Minute College Major Matcher*

- *College Board's Book of Majors*

- *The Princeton Review: Guide to College Majors*

- *100 Best Careers for the 21st Century*

- *What Can I Do with a Major in …?*

Books known for **strong tips on essay writing**:

- *College Board – The College Application Essay*

- *Conquering the College Admission Essay in 10 Easy Steps*

- *How to Write a Winning College Application Essay*

- *Writing a Winning Essay*

- *The College Application Essay*

- *Peterson's: Best College Admission Essays*

Books for understanding **more about financial aid**:

- *Barron's Best Buys in College Education*
- *College Board – Getting Financial Aid*
- *College Board – Meeting College Costs*
- *College Board – Scholarship Book*
- *FastWeb – College Gold: A Step by Step Guide to Paying For Jobs*
- *The A's & B's of Academic Scholarships*
- *College Board – Scholarship Handbook*
- *Peterson's: College Money Handbook*
- *Peterson's: Scholarships, Grants & Grants*
- *Peterson's: Sports Scholarships & College Athletic Program*
- *Sallie Mae How to Pay for College: A Practical Guide for Families*
- *The Princeton Review: Paying For College*

College guides that are unique and offer **perspectives on "hot" topics**:

- *College Bound: Proven Ways to Plan and Prepare for Getting Into the College of Your Dreams*
- *Your College Planning Survival Guide: Smart Tips From Students, Parents, and Professionals Who Made It Through*
- *The College Advisor*
- *The Best Resources*
- *Reading Lists for College Bound Students*
- *Summer on Campus*
- *Campus Pursuit – How to Make the Most of the College Visit & Interview*
- *Gatekeepers*
- *Creating Your High School Resume*
- *Your First Resume*

Career Counseling:

- *What Color Is Your Parachute?*

- *Occupational Handbook*

- *O*Net Career Values and Interest Inventories*

- *Barron's ASVAB-Armed Services Vocational Aptitude Battery*

- *Peterson's – Exploring Careers*

- *150 Best Jobs for Your Skills*

- *Best Jobs in the 21st Century*

- *Top 300 Careers*

- *100 Fastest Growing Careers*

- *300 Best Jobs Without a Four-Year Degree*

- *Great Careers in Two Years*

ACT/SAT Prep:

- *Barron's: ACT*

- *Cliffs Test Prep: ACT*

- *College Board: The Official SAT Study Guide*

- *The Princeton Review: Cracking the SAT*

- *The Princeton Review – Cracking the ACT*

"Empty Nest" resources for parents about to send a child off to college:

- *I'll Miss You Too: An Off-to-College Guide for Parents and Students*

- *The Launching Years: Strategies for Parenting from Senior Year to College Life*

- *Almost Grown: Launching Your Child from High School to College*

- *You're On Your Own (But I'm Here if You Need Me): Mentoring Your Child During the College Years*

- *Letting Go: A Parents' Guide to Understanding the College Years*

- *On Losing a Son (to College) - from "I'm a Stranger Here Myself"*

** Dr. Chris's Pick!

1. **College-Path.com**** – The ultimate college planning blog with timely tips about topics like the college search and application process, finding money for college and much, much more. A must read for students and parents interested in the process and beyond. http://www.college-path.com

2. **myUsearch** – "myUsearch.com exists to provide honest, unbiased information to help students make the right college choice, get into college, pay for college and live a happy and healthy college life," write the authors. "Our founder was working for a college that was spending millions of dollars trying to recruit students who really had no interest in attending their college…It was out of this frustration that myUsearch.com, the Honest College Matchmaker, was born." http://myusearchblog.com/

3. **College Thrive** – "I have always enjoyed writing, and I figured since I was going to be in college for the next four or so years, why not help others out and write about all of the tips and resources I come across as I go," writes blogger Dan Northern. "I hope [my readers] find ways to make college a little less stressful, as well as find useful information and resources along the way. http://collegethrive.com/

4. **Homework/Study Tips** – From About.com, educational writer Grace Fleming posts countless articles which provide great advice for high school and college students. Some topics include how to use verbs in an essay, time management, and how to improve your home homework and studying habits. http://homeworktips.about.com/

5. **Study Hacks** – This site is not only a great starting point for students in need of educational advice; it's also a popular resource for education bloggers. The articles cover everything from must-read books, writing advice, and the college admissions process. http://calnewport.com/blog/

6. **Parents Countdown to College Coach** – "I started writing [my blog] when I began my parent coaching business about a year ago," explains Suzanne Shaffer. "I have been coaching parents on college admissions for about 10 years and felt my expertise in this area would be helpful. My site is geared mostly toward the "parents" of the students, but often they pass them along to their kids. I hope they learn that college admissions is not as daunting as some might think if you have the right

tools and gather all the information."
http://www.parentscountdowntocollegecoach.com/

7. **Top Test Prep** – If you're struggling with test anxiety or you're worried about your upcoming SAT exams, author Ross Blankenship writes numerous tips for students concerning SAT math problems and writing scores, as well as background information on the SAT exam.
http://toptestprep.com/blog/

8. **Great College Advice** – Written by a group of education consultants who provide expert advice on choosing majors, avoiding debt, applying for college, and improving grades.
http://toptestprep.com/blog/

9. **Sharp Brains** – If you're a student, who is struggling to get back into the back-to-school mode, then try this site on for size. These articles cover numerous brain exercise activities as well as memorization tools, tips on multi-tasking, and treatment for ADHD.
http://www.sharpbrains.com/

10. **The Fat Envelope** – "I've been an SAT tutor off and on for over 10 years," writes Jenn Cohen, President & Chief Word-Nerd. "My husband Gary and I started Word-Nerd because I wasn't happy with what was available to my students for vocabulary prep, so we did it ourselves! We hit a range of topics from SAT prep tips to college admissions to general rambling about the state of education, all with the aim of not taking ourselves (or college prep) too seriously."
http://www.word-nerd.com/pt/blog/

11. **Jeannie's FYI College Admission Blog** – Jeannie Borin, M.Ed., has appeared on Fox News and MSNBC and was interviewed for *Time Magazine*, CNN and numerous other major publications. She has been on talk radio and written for *The Wall Street Journal*. It is Jeannie's hope that students and families will "garner the information necessary to assist them in navigating any of their educational needs from career assessment, financial planning, athletic recruitment, art and performing art portfolios, academic tutoring, test preparation, college searches, resume and essay writing to making their final decisions."
http://jeanniesfyi.wordpress.com/

12. **The Admission Game** – This award-winning blog provides great advice on improving your test scores, applying for college, and preparing for college admissions interviews. Blogger Peter Van Buskirk is an author, motivational speaker, educational advocate, and a 25-year veteran of

the selective college admissions process.
http://www.theadmissiongame.com/blog/

13. **The Huffington Post's College Blog** – Not only does this blog cover various political and educational issues, some articles also touch on how to improve your grades, the transition from college to your career, or how to get bed bugs out of your dorm.
http://www.huffingtonpost.com/college/the-blog/

14. **College Candy** – "Having just graduated from college, I felt there was a major void in the media world when it came to college students," writes Lauren Herskovic, the site's Editor in Chief. "We have 100 student writers contributing, giving the most thorough and varied advice out there. I want students to come to CollegeCandy to learn everything from study tips to tips on how to make the most of their experience. Mostly, though, I want them to enjoy themselves on the site, laugh a lot and learn in the process. http://collegecandy.com/

15. **Hack College** – "Lectures are boring and inefficient," write the authors, "HackCollege is educating the students of the world about effective, open source software, putting techno-political arguments in everyday language, and creating a cult of 'Students 2.0.' If we can change the way one percent of college students and faculty in the world view education and technology, we've done our job."
http://www.hackcollege.com/

16. **Student Branding Blog** – These posts provide insight as to how students can brand themselves as employees making them attractive for the college market after graduation.
http://studentbranding.com/category/high-school/

17. **Knowledge Points** – These articles provide great tips for junior and/or high school students concerning reading comprehension, test anxiety, as well as ACT and SAT tests. Many of the articles are written from the perspective of a parent who are looking for tips on how to help their children with their education.
http://info.knowledgepointslearning.com/

18. **College Counseling Culture** – "My site is actually geared more toward adults who work with students. Willard M. Dix, the President of College Access Counseling, Ltd. "I've always been interested in how much college, college counseling, and college admission are linked to American ideas about class, status, education, economics, and many other cultural aspects, but I've never seen much written about them. I have over 30 years experience with teaching, college admissions, and

college counseling, so I've experienced just about everything except having a child of my own to go through the process." http://funnyhamlet.wordpress.com/

19. **Allen's College Admissions Blog** – From About.com, the articles on this site have a combination of both educational advice and the latest in education news. Author Allen Grove has a Ph.D. in English, and used to work as a college professor and director of a program for new college students. http://collegeapps.about.com/b/

20. **College Basics** – "I am a retired high school college counselor with over 35 years of experience, and my business partner is a retired English teacher who has taught more than 25 years and is a certified writing consultant," writes Maureen Hodge. "We both wanted to continue helping students, so we came up with the idea of creating a website with all of the information needed to successfully navigate the college application process from the freshman year in high school through the first year of college. We devoted special attention to writing the college essay, selecting a college, interviewing, and paying for college." http://www.collegebasics.com/blog/

21. **Reading, Writing & Math Help for Dyslexia, LD & ADHD** – Blogger Bonnie Terry is a Board Certified Educational Therapist as well as a best-selling author. Her posts include numerous case studies and articles to help educate parents, students, homeschoolers, and teachers on how to address a child's learning problems. http://bonnieterry.com/blog/

22. **Admitted Blog** – This is the official blog of the National Association for College Admission Counseling organization. The articles are packed full of statistical information written for students, parents, and high school counselors. hthttp://www.nacacnet.org/learning/communities/admitted/default.aspx

23. **My College Guide** – This entertaining-yet-still-educational blog advises college students on how to prepare for college. Categories include choosing a college and/or a major, college applications and interviews, or transferring to a different school. http://mycollegeguide.org/blog/

24. **How to Get In** – This Edvisors Company is one of the top online providers to help students with their college search and preparation. Categories include college admissions, tips college counselors, financial aid, online courses, and much more. http://blog.howtogetin.com/

25. **College Admissions Partners** – This website has numerous resources for students which provide advice on the college application and transferring process, as well as background information on college preparation, admissions, and rankings. http://www.collegeadmissionspartners.com/blog/

26. **Student Positioning Blog** – "The whole idea of student positioning is to make students as attractive as possible, as they are marketing themselves to businesses called colleges," writes Jeffrey Sonnergren, a College Planning and Funding Specialist. "It is a lot of fun when students realize that they can play offense and create leverage for merit-based scholarships, as opposed to doing well in school and SAT/ACT tests, picking a few good schools, crossing their fingers, and hoping for the best. I would hope that students realize that this is a high stakes situation and they can truly help themselves by applying to the best fit colleges for themselves and they can absolutely play offense. By necessity and sheer competition, there are multi-level strategies to employ in the college application process, but careful planning is the key." http://studentpositioningblog.com/

27. **ProfHacker** – From the Chronicle of Higher Education, this site is a great tool for students who want to see into the minds of their professors. Even though the target audience for this blog is generally teachers, the authors provide great advice for students from a professor's perspective. http://chronicle.com/blogs/profhacker/

28. **Get Schooled** – This site is full of articles for both high school grads and college students. The posts entertain readers on financial advice, packing for college, employment after graduation, and the latest in educational news. http://www.getschooled.com/

29. **College Advice** – "When I was an undergraduate in college, I used to wish there was someone who could advise me or tell me what their experience has been like with many college related topics," writes blogger Sam S. "Getting help from the college advisement center is great, but it's limited; moreover, firsthand experience of other students is really something one can relate to. It is my hope that students will walk away with something that they can really implement throughout college, instead of just a momentarily intake of information. If from reading my blog one student will save $400 on textbooks or one student will be ahead of the game when applying to grad school, then really that's enough for me." http://www.collegeadviceblog.com/

30. **Perfect Essay** – If you're a student who despises writing essays or is currently suffering from writer's block, this site offers great tips on everything essay-related: from methodology, organizations, and conclusions. http://perfectessay.net/blog/

31. **Study Prof** – "I have taught college, high school, and elementary school students," writes Cody Blair. "In addition, I've always been interested in how our brains learn (and don't learn). Both of those things played their part in getting me started writing my studyprof.com blog. I hope students will find out how they can succeed in their school work, even if they find learning difficult. Students often struggle with procrastination, focus, and the memorization of large amounts of material. I try and give students concrete ways of overcoming those difficulties." http://studyprof.com/blog/

32. **Campus Grotto** – This site has been featured in several publications like *The New York Post*, *The Huffington Post*, and CNBC.com. Their articles cover a wide variety of different educational topics such as college rankings, tips for studying or employment, and how to finance for college. http://www.campusgrotto.com/news/index.php

33. **The Thesis Whisperer** – "I work in a graduate school helping Ph.D. students from all over with 'generic skills' training – such as writing and presentation skills," explains Dr. Inger Mewburn who works at the School of Graduate Research. "I like to read broadly – which is a luxury many Ph.D. students cannot afford. This enables me to act as an information filter for students, in drawing research on other areas such as motivation and relationship management – even addiction behavior – which might be relevant. A lot of the advice out there in books for completing a Ph.D. or dissertation is pretty one dimensional – like giving lists of dos and don'ts (my pet hate). The problem with lists and the 'do this, don't do that' sort of advice that is very hard to put into practice. Instead, I like to get at the meaning behind the advice, unpack it, and encourage discussion about what works and what doesn't." http://thethesiswhisperer.wordpress.com/

34. **ProtoScholar** – "I felt that there were a lot of things about productivity that didn't really address the student population, particularly the graduate student population," explains blogger/author Rebecca, a Ph.D student in Education Policy. "I wanted to offer some thoughts about how to make that better. Tips, tricks, and sometimes just a different perspective. Plus a bit about what graduate school means and is all about, particularly for those who are considering it." http://protoscholar.com/

35. **To Do: Dissertation** – "When I started writing my dissertation, I didn't see the kinds of blogs that would be helpful to my writing," explains Katie Linder. "There are plenty of spaces for dissertation writers to talk about how they are struggling, but I didn't come across many places that offered supportive and encouraging suggestions for getting the dissertation done. My hope is that this blog will be that space. The goal of ToDo is to talk realistically about practical steps that dissertation writers can take to finish their writing and take satisfaction and pride in their process and the final product. I hope that dissertation writers can find tips on the site that will help them through writer's block, being overwhelmed by a large writing project, and other common obstacles for dissertation writers." http://tododissertation.wordpress.com/

36. **College News** – These posts cover everything from sex and relationship advice, the latest in educational news, top movies at the box office, and sports updates. But most importantly, this blog also touches on crucial educational advice every college student should be aware of. http://www.collegenews.com/

37. **My College Calendar** – This site is written by numerous authors who have experience working in the educational field. There are also various resources available on the site such as individual planning outlines for freshmen, sophomores, juniors, seniors, or even parents. http://blog.mycollegecalendar.org/

38. **Notes on Student Success** – This site is the "companion blog" to MyCollegeSuccessStory.com. These posts are full of academic tips that could help inspire students to become more successful throughout their educational journey. http://www.studentsuccessblog.com/Blog/Blog.html

39. **Her Campus** – "My co-founders and I met at Harvard through running Harvard's lifestyle and fashion magazine," writes Stephanie Kaplan, co-founder, CEO and Editor-in-Chief of Her Campus Media LLC. "...girls from all over were telling us they wished their school had a magazine like this, because their only writing outlet was the campus newspaper. Our site is an online hub for everything college women need to know – a student's guide to life. In addition to our national content, we also provide local content from teams of students at 50+ schools across the country, so readers can also gain insight into what college life is like at different schools by visiting Her Campus." http://www.hercampus.com/

40. **Inside College** – Although this blog has more entertainment value than educational value, it still provides some great tips for students who need more information on scholarships, or tips on the college admissions process. The majority of the articles are lists of recommendations students should check out before applying for college. http://www.insidecollege.com/reno/home.do

41. **Kaarme: The High School Counselor Week Blog** – Kaarme's motive is to expand college opportunities for all students and protect their personal data at the same time. "A college education is not an option; it is required so try EVERYTHING you can to identify and earn one," writes Mark North, CEO of Kaarme. "The best quality tools for finding an education should be easy to get and free to use so everyone has a chance and our world educates as many people as possible. If you search for an education, your efforts should not be exploited or your personal information sold to third parties. Seeking an education should not be risky." http://kaarme.com/hscounselorweek

42. **Why Boys Fail** – Richard Whitmire, former editorial writer for USA Today, writes on how males can improve their productivity in the classroom. Majorities of the posts are summaries of other educational articles he found on the web, and cover topics like minority teachers and students, college gender gaps, and single sex education. http://blogs.edweek.org/edweek/whyboysfail/

43. **Study Successful** – The topics on this blog cover everything from electronic books, to how to get motivated for school and productivity. The site's author is a 19-year-old medical student who is studying at the University of Groningen in the Netherlands. http://studysuccessful.com/

44. **In Like Me** – Lynn Radlauer Lubell is the founder of Admission by Design, (an educational consultancy), and is also a graduate of MIT and Harvard Business School. Her posts are packed full of statistical information to help college-bound students with the admissions process. http://admissionscoop.com/

45. **Student on Campus** – This site is full of unique and informative articles about student finances, the latest technological tools for students, and social media. Some of the most entertaining posts cover popular YouTube videos, college drinking games, and how to design your dorm room. http://www.studentoncampus.com/

46. **College Blogaversity** – "I write my blog to take a different twist to what everyone else in my field is saying," explains Paul Hemphill. "The fact

that I have videos with my blog makes my point. Videos are easier to do and easier to receive from the perspective of the viewer. As a result, students will more likely view my message than someone else's who doesn't use video." http://collegevideos.wordpress.com/

47. **Teen College Education** – "I started my blog originally because I wanted some sort of a summer job as a sophomore going on vacation," writes Andy S. "Then after I wrote a few articles, I started to really enjoy the topic and now I hope to spread education information to everyone I can. I feel that as a teen living through everything, I can provide unique insight into my topics. I hope that students will learn from my experiences and research so that they can have the best educational experience possible. I also hope to give students a different perspective on the daily school routines that they are used to." http://www.teencollegeeducation.org/

48. **Pre-Med Hell** – Specifically for medical school students, the posts on this site are written by a group of authors who are all undergraduate students, and they describe their articles as "rants of neurotic pre-meds." Book reviews and interviews with their fellow classmates or doctors are also included in the articles." http://www.premedhell.com

49. **College and University Blog** – This unique blog is full of entertaining articles which touch on why students drop out of school, the use of social media in classrooms, and the most common myths about college. http://www.stateuniversity.com/blog/

50. **The Mad Grad** – These posts are a combination of educational and personal reflections and are written by two former college students who experienced the "after-college crisis" first hand. Their site was also listed as one of the "Top 10 Gen Y Blogs" by Ryan Stephens Marketing in 2009. http://themadgrad.com/

51. **Cammy Bean's Learning Visions** – Cammy Bean works as an eLearning instructional designer as well as a writer, project manager, and multimedia producer. The majority of her posts are directed towards students who are pursuing a career in technology, and they reflect her own insights on how students can become more successful through eLearning. http://cammybean.kineo.com/index.html

52. **Not Just Your Average Admissions Blog** – Blogger Andrew Flagel is the current Dean of Admissions and Associate Vice President for Enrollment Development at George Mason University. His posts cover everything about the college admissions process and how students can

get the most out of their education.
http://www.mycollegeoptions.org/Core/SiteContent/Students/Advice/PrepTalkHome.aspx

53. **University of Venus** – This is a site which was recently launched in January 2010. With a mixture of personal experiences, opinions, and reflections, these authors update their readers on reading and writing tips as well as the latest in educational news. http://www.insidehighered.com/blogs/university_of_venus

54. **Smart College Visit** – The specific goal of this blog is to help college-bound students prepare for their future campus visit. Parents could also find some helpful advice from these articles, which range from academic programs, travel tips, and how to become a successful entrepreneur. http://www.smartcollegevisit.com/

55. **NextStepU** – Next Step Magazine's blog is an "award-winning college-planning resource for teens, adult learners, and school counselors." Post categories include financial aid tips, how to plan a timeline for college, as well as themed posts like "Tuesday Tour Day" and "Wanna Win Wednesday." http://nextstepu.wordpress.com/

56. **College Times** – The posts on this blog range from politics, science, finance, relationships, employment, humor and most of all ... controversy. The topics are so diverse they cover everything from how to build a perfect playlist for your iPod, how to last longer in bed, or the latest movie and book reviews. http://collegetimes.us/

57. **Find Your College Card** – "Find College Cards blog is a blog dedicated to those currently going to college, and those preparing for college," writes the author. "Here, you're going to find great money saving tips, education advice, and many other articles." http://www.findcollegecards.com/blog/

58. **Life After College** – Author Jenny Blake is a UCLA graduate who currently works as a Career Development Manager and Life Coach. She is also the author of "Life After College: The Complete Guide to Getting What You Want" which is set for release next March. http://www.lifeaftercollege.org/

59. **Dissertation Research** – From the Regents Center Library at the University of Kansas, this blog is full of advice for students who need help with their research papers. Post topics include statistical abstracts, trans-literacy, or sites to help you with your business research. http://dissertationresearch.blogspot.com/

60. **Get Into College Blog** – Author Steve Schwartz works as a professional college counselor in New York City, and posts his expert advice on how students can get into college. Post topics range extra-curricular activities and recommendations, to SAT's and the college essay. http://www.getintocollegeblog.com/

61. **University Parent Connection** – "Our site is intended to help parents navigate their student's college and local community," writes Sarah Schupp. "[Our mission is to provide] comprehensive information that will easily help you navigate the university and its surrounding community during your visit, as well as provide you with helpful tips and resources when you are back home!" http://www.universityparent.com/topics/college-admissions

62. **College Puzzle** – Dr. Michael W. Kirst is a professor of Education and Business Administration at Stanford University. He has also written ten books, two of which are "The Political Dynamics of American Education" (2005) and "From High School to College" (2004). http://collegepuzzle.stanford.edu/

63. **Surviving College** – "Surviving college life is every student's guide to the ins and outs of college," writes blogger Jamie, a recent UC San Diego graduate. "Here you'll find tips about relationships, finances, productivity, studying, health, and beginning your life as an adult." http://www.survivingcollegelife.com/

64. **Google Student Blog** – "Jessica Bagley and I started this blog to keep students informed about products, tools, tips, programs and opportunities at Google that are relevant for them on and off campus," explains Miriam Schneider. "We hope that students will learn about Google products that will make their lives easier and find out about ways and opportunities to get involved with our efforts." http://googleforstudents.blogspot.com/

65. **Cramster Blog** – This site is essentially an online community of study groups for schools, courses, or even textbooks. Users can generate their own customized quizzes or search for practice problems in subjects like math, physics, computer science, chemistry, and much more. http://www.cramster.com/blog

66. **Stay Out of School** – "StayOutOfSchool.com investigates why one of the greatest, albeit hard-headed, creative thinkers of our time advises young, creative college graduates to stay out of graduate school," writes author Elizabeth King, who is also the President of Elizabeth King Coaching Inc., a test preparation company. Her post topics touch on

art, pop culture, creativity, music, and much more. http://stayoutofschool.com/blog/

67. **iStudent Advisor** – This "interactive international higher education guide" has great advice for students who are interested in studying abroad. There are also study guide resources for those who are interested in studying in Australia, Canada, Europe, Ireland, the UK, and New Zealand. http://www.i-studentadvisor.com/news

68. **Admissions Hook** – Categories include how to find scholarships, and tips and tricks from experts in the educational industry. Numerous essay editing tips are included on the site, and students can also read various writing samples. http://www.admissionhook.com/Blog/

69. **College Admissions** – "Blogger Jeannie Borin, M.Ed., has an extensive educational background having served as counselor, school administrator, admissions director, teacher and curriculum supervisor for over twenty years in both the public and private sectors. Her affiliation with the National and Western Association of College Admissions Counselors as well as the Higher Educational Consultants Association keeps her on the forefront of innovative and current trends in college admissions and education." http://college-connections.blogspot.com/

70. **Graduated and Clueless** – "I was inspired to write my blog based on my inability to find or create the life I wanted after I graduated and moved to Boston," writes blogger Jeff Sanders. "I hope students and graduates will learn that college is not a real-world preparatory institution. By that I mean college is designed to teach you how to learn, not to qualify you for any specific job. The real world is a completely different beast that requires completely different skills than what you learned to master in the classroom. Some skills do carry over, but the big stuff (personal finances, finding a job, office politics) is only learned through experience on the job, not in school. Take your education into your own hands and learn what you need to on your own. Don't rely on a school, job, or another person to hand you success. You have to create it for yourself." http://graduatedandclueless.com/

71. **Head4College** – "I started my blog as a complement to my college planning business, McLaughlin Education Consulting," explains Sharon McLaughlin. "Through my college planning service, I assist clients with both the admissions process and the financial aid planning process for undergraduate and graduate school. Having worked as a college administrator in admissions and financial aid for over twenty years, I

knew that students and parents are frequently making college planning decisions with outdated information. Trends are changing with college entrance testing; the economy has led to changes in financial aid funding policies and increased the competitiveness of college admissions. It is important to educate families on the current trends and issues in college admissions and financial aid, so that they make informed decisions when choosing a college and comparing financial aid awards." http://head4college-ne.blogspot.com/

72. **A Better Education** – "I am a former teacher but found I didn't enjoy teaching," writes blogger Tracy Stevens. "I left education for many years but when my son had a hard time starting in kindergarten, it reignited my passion for it. It was my quest to find the best model and school fit so he would thrive, I found myself researching, reading and thinking about education all the time. I thought I might open my own school so I applied for a "Building Excellent Schools" fellowship and was denied because my application wasn't about college prep and had an arts focus. I wrote to Daniel Pink after reading his book 'A Whole New Mind,' telling him about my experience, asking 'what's a girl to do?' It was his suggestion that I write a blog about education." http://head4college-ne.blogspot.com/

73. **Creative Learning Systems** – "I have children of my own, and they attend school in New Zealand, which is totally different from the schools I knew when growing up," writes Dr. Yvonne Eve Walus. "I was born and raised in communist Poland, where the standard of education was extremely high. As a 9-year old, I learned about non-decimal forms of arithmetic operations (binary and hex and others), two years later the syllabus included trigonometry (sine, cosine, tan etc.) In other subjects the standard was as high: discursive essays, laws of motion, ancient history, detailed biology." Her advice for students? "You have a unique learning style, a 'best for me' way of learning. Find out what it is and homework will be a breeze." http://yvonnewalus.blogspot.com/

74. **Fragment/Framework** – "I began blogging about my teaching strategies, practices, experiences, and theories a few months after I first started teaching Introductory Composition as a Master's student at the University of Cincinnati," writes Kathryn Trauth Taylor. "I continue my blog today as a doctoral student at Purdue. In my field of Rhetoric and Composition, many scholars have studied and encouraged reflective practices – it is one of the core values of the field, as I see it. Through blogging, I hope to connect with other Composition instructors—especially graduate student instructors who are forming their teaching persona for the first time alongside me. My site is not

really geared towards my students, specifically. Rather, I share it with peers, professors, family members, and other friends in academia."
http://trauthke.wordpress.com/

75. **Improve Your Learning and Memory** – "As a faculty member who has seen students struggle inefficiently for some 47 years, I realized that I knew a lot about learning they did not," writes W. R. (Bill) Klemm, a Professor of Neuroscience at Texas A&M University. "So I wanted to share this information, hope they will recognize their counterproductive learning behaviors, and as a result, make what I say are 'better grades, with less effort.'"
http://thankyoubrain.blogspot.com/

76. **Kapp Notes** – "The blog turned out to be the perfect place for me to keep my ideas in one place and to share with my students and others in the field," writes Karl Kapp, who works as an educator, consultant, speaker, as well as an author of several educational books. "I want [students] to learn about the industry and to gain a perspective about what it takes to be a practicing professional in the field of e-learning and instructional technology. The second thing I want students to learn is to use and become comfortable with Web 2.0 tools."
http://karlkapp.blogspot.com/

77. **Grad Hacker** – "I found that productivity blogs geared towards grad students lacking [when I started my blog]," writes the Grad Hacker. "I may or may not have been wrong as, in hindsight, [but I] found that a lot of people had these ridiculous habits that made them seem productive, but I felt were in the end, simply ridiculous. That's what started the How to Act Productive Series, which in the end brought over a lot of traffic to my site." So what does the Grad Hacker want students to learn from their posts? "That keeping a list or two and doing work goes a long ways. And that there are alternatives to traditional career paths after you get a Ph.D."
http://www.gradhacker.com/

78. **My Montessori Journey** – "I started writing the blog to document my transition from teaching elementary special education in a public school setting to teach Montessori preschool in a private setting," writes blogger Laura L. "At the time I started the blog (May 2008) there were only a few blogs that featured Montessori education and I had been inspired by those few quite a bit. Now there are lots more bloggers writing about their experiences incorporating Montessori principles into a variety of settings, which is really exciting. I hope that my blog readers will come away with new ideas and new ways of

thinking about how to present activities to young children."
http://mymontessorijourney.typepad.com/

79. **GradSpot** – "After graduating from college, I was surprised at how unprepared we (grads) were to confront many of the issues that were confronting us at the start of our independent adulthood, ranging from career to financial to healthcare and other issues," writes Stuart Schultz, co-founder and CEO of Grad Spot. "In order to make sure that future classes of graduating college students had all of the information and tools to help them not only transition to life after college but thrive in the real world, we created Gradspot.com. I hope that from Gradspot.com and our book, "Gradspot.com's Guide to Life After College," students will learn how to tackle the major issues they'll confront in their first year or two out of college, from securing a job, to finding a place to live, to understanding health care, to getting their credit and finances in order, and more."
http://www.gradspot.com/blog

80. **Academic Remediation** – This author works with elementary school children who are struggling to keep up with their fellow classmates. The categories on this blog include ADHD, autism, learning disabilities, and advice for students who are struggling in math, reading, and writing. http://lizditz.typepad.com/academic_remediation/

81. **Omniac Education** – This blog is a great resource for parents or students who need advice on exams, the college admissions process, or writing a college essay. The articles touch on various topics such as financial aid, SAT or ACT exams, and test anxiety.
http://www.omniaceducation.com/education-blog

82. **Learning Circuits** – This blog is "dedicated to sharing ideas and opinions about the state of learning and technology." The main feature of this blog is its "Question of the Month" series where other educational bloggers can respond to a question posted in an article, which is then re-posted in the LC blog post. http://learningcircuits.blogspot.com/

83. **StuVu** – The blog otherwise known as Student View allows college students to post their own photos, videos and reviews of their college experiences to other students. Some of the posts provide entertaining advice like how to cure a hangover, or tips on how to get into the college spirit. http://blog.stuvu.com/

84. **Algebra Homework** – The authors of this blog write about the different online resources that are available for students who are struggling with their algebra homework." http://www.algebrahomeworkhelp.org/

85. **College and University Search** – From the College Bound Network, these articles provide expert information on everything related to the college admission process, such as high school transcripts, application deadlines, and recommendation letters. http://www.collegebound.net/content/cat/college-admissions/77/

86. **Playing Your A Game** – Author Kantis Simmons is an "educational guru" who delivers "content rich information through books, articles, keynotes, seminars, e-mails, consulting, and conferences." His tag line is "helping students play their 'A' game in school and life," and he has been invited to speak at many schools and conferences to talk about how students can achieve academic success. http://kantissimmons.com/

87. **StudentStuff** - This unique blog provides numerous tips which cover everything from Diet Coke and long-distance relationships, or how to work out to music. Post categories include health and fitness, career and money, activism and awareness, or studying abroad. http://www.studentstuff.com/cgi-sys/defaultwebpage.cgi

88. **The Ivy Coach** – Bev Taylor, the Ivy Coach's founder and president, has been featured in numerous broadcasts and publications like the *US News & World Report*, *The Wall Street Journal*, *The New York Times* and many more. She provides expert advice on how to find the right college, letters of recommendations, and issues that are facing educational counselors. http://www.theivycoach.com/the-ivy-coach-blog/

89. **College Jolt** – The articles on this blog provide background information on the different types of college majors, as well as campus politics, what students should bring to college, and the perks of being a student at a community college. http://collegejolt.com/?cat=5

90. **eduFire** – Even though updates are scarce, this entertaining blog writes about a variety of different topics like homeschooling, educational technology, tips for teachers, and the latest in educational news and politics. http://blog.edufire.com/

14 - INTERNET RESOURCES FOR CAREER EXPLORATION AND THE COLLEGE SEARCH

Career Search Websites

Source: Website descriptions are taken directly from the individual website.

- **America's Job Bank** - Lists thousands of jobs and includes links to state and local employment service sites. Job Bank
  http://www.ajb.dni.us/
  http://www.jobbankinfo.org/

- **ASVAB Career Program** - This program is designed to help students learn more about themselves and the world of work.
  http://www.asvabprogram.com/

- **Career Builder** - The largest career search tool on the web.
  http://www.careerbuilder.com/

- **Career Center Missouri State** - Helpful information for students seeking career information.
  http://careercenter.missouristate.edu/

- **Career Experience** - *The New York Times* career site with a large selection of jobs in the sports and recreation industry. Includes profiles of many different jobs so you can find out what a particular career is like. http://www.careerexperience.com/

- **Career City** - Post your resume. Helpful segments on resumes, interview questions, and negotiation techniques. True Careers
  http://www.careercity.com/ - http://www.truecareers.com/

- **Career Mosaic** - Large industry database, including job openings overseas. "The College Connection" site is set up for recent college graduates. http://www.careermosaic.org/

- **CareerOneStop** - Is a U.S. Department of Labor-sponsored website that offers career resources and workforce information to job seekers, students, businesses, and workforce professionals to foster talent development in a global economy. http://www.acinet.org/

- **Career Site** - Set up a confidential profile that companies can access. Includes a wide variety of companies.
  http://www.careersite.com/

- **Career Zone** - Online career exploration and planning system designed for today's high-tech youth in New York state. Career Zone presents current and relevant occupational and labor market Information in a clear and interesting way, making career exploration and planning fun and easy.
  http://www.nycareerzone.org/

- **College Navigator**- Explore majors and perform a college search via the National Center for Educational Statistics. http://nces.ed.gov/collegenavigator/

- **College Prowler** – Provides answers to questions on all aspects of the school environment. http://collegeprowler.com/

- **Creighton University's Career Center** - Plenty of tips for resume writing and the career search. http://www.creighton.edu/careercenter/students/resumescoverletters/resumewritingtips/index.php

- **Delaware State** - Majors - Links academic majors to career paths and job titles with a short bibliography. Connect your major with a career. http://archives.desu.edu/special/majors/default.php

- **Employer Locator** - Search for jobs/companies by state and zip code. http://www.servicelocator.org/default.asp?

- **Engineer Your Life** - A guide to engineering for high school girls http://www.engineeryourlife.org/

- **Index of Learning Styles Questionnaire** - The Index of Learning Styles is an online instrument used to assess preferences on four dimensions (active/reflective, sensing/intuitive, visual/verbal, and sequential/global) of a learning style model formulated by Richard M. Felder and Linda K. Silverman. The instrument was developed by Richard M. Felder and Barbara A. Soloman of North Carolina State University. http://www.engr.ncsu.edu/learningstyles/ilsweb.html

- **JobSmart** - Contains helpful links to information about a variety of careers with resume and salary tips included. http://www.jobsmart.org/ - http://jobstar.org/index.php

- **Jung Typology** - Complete the questionnaire, obtain a formula according to Carl Jung and Isabel Myers-Briggs typology with the strengths of the preferences, the description of your personality type, the list of occupations and educational institutions for relevant degree or training most suitable for your personality type - Jung Career Indicator™. http://www.humanmetrics.com/cgi-win/JTypes2.asp

- **Mapping Your Future** - Helps students and their parents plan careers, search for college, and manage money. http://www.mappingyourfuture.org/downloads/MYFParentsFlyer.pdf

- **Monster Board** - Post resumes, view the online bulletin board, and search for jobs. Includes some listings of government jobs. Salary information and relocation hints, too. http://www.monster.com/

- **MonsterTrak** - The college arm of monster.com contains salary information and job search tips. You can post your resume and search for full-time jobs and internships listed by employers specifically for UNCG students. http://www.monstertrak.monster.com/

- **My Next Move** - Find out about your interest by taking a quick assessment. http://www.mynextmove.org/

- **My Road** - Major and career search, career assessments, and interest inventories. http://apps.collegeboard.com/myroad/navigator.jsp

- **Quintessential Careers** - Career exploration, articles on careers, resume building, links, and resources. http://www.quintcareers.com/

- **O*NET** - The government website that includes free self-inventories, interest profiler, career information, and job profiles. http://online.onetcenter.org/

- **Occupational Handbook** - The handbook gives you job search tips, links to information about the job market in each state, and more. http://www.bls.gov/oco/home.htm

- **The Princeton Review Career Quiz** - This website is an introduction to how you need to know yourself before you can find that career that you really love. It's free and quick (only 24 "choose A or B" questions), but it will give you an idea of the concepts. Once you understand the basics, you can move on to a detailed survey for career assessment that is even more specific. http://www.princetonreview.com/CareerQuiz.aspx

- **ThinkTalk** - Career TV for College - ThinkTalk is Career TV for college students. ThinkTalk creates dynamic, interactive programming where students interview high profile professionals about their career paths. Guests include actors, authors, CEOs, directors, entrepreneurs, journalists and politicians. http://www.thinktank.com/about

- **University of North Carolina Wilmington** provides a resource for finding careers related to specific college majors. http://www.uncwil.edu/stuaff/career/Majors/

- **What Color is Your Parachute?** - Many links to sites with extensive info on all aspects of career development, including resumes, interviews, and job search strategies. http://www.jobhuntersbible.com/

- **WetFeet** - Advice about careers, resumes, job interviews, internships and much more. http://www.wetfeet.com

- **You Tube Education** - Find information about many topics including the college search, college tours, and watch student and faculty interviews online. http://www.youtube.com/education?b=400

College Search Websites

Source: Website descriptions are taken directly from the individual websites.

- **2-Year Community Colleges** - List of all community colleges by state. http://www.utexas.edu/world/comcol/state/

- **4-Year Universities and Colleges** - All universities and colleges by state. http://www.utexas.edu/world/univ/state/

- **A to Z College Search** - A college search website. http://www.a2zcolleges.com/

- **Academic Common Market** - For more than fifty years, the SREB Academic Common Market has enabled students to pursue out-of-state college majors at discounted tuition rates, through agreements among the states and colleges and universities. http://www.sreb.org/programs/acm/acmindex.asp

- **Adult Student Center** - The Adult Student Center is your resource for inspiration and information on returning to and succeeding in

college – at any age!
http://www.adultstudentcenter.com/

- **All About College** - A search engine for the college search process. http://www.allaboutcollege.com/

- **All About Universities** - Around the World. http://www.allaboutuni.com/index.php

- Five reasons to review your university:

  1. Helps future students around the world

  2. It only takes five minutes

  3. Fun and free

  4. Your independent feedback matters

  5. It can be very therapeutic

- **All Engineering Schools** - A list of schools of engineering in the states. http://www.allengineeringschools.com/

- **American Universities** by state. http://www.globalcomputing.com/university.htm

- **Association of American International Colleges and Universities** - AAICU is a leadership organization of American international universities, whose members provide responsible delivery and quality assurance of American higher education outside the United States. http://www.aaicu.org/

- **BrainTrack** - BrainTrack is the oldest and most complete online directory of the world's universities and colleges. The website is an index of international links and an information reference for more than 10,000 higher education institutions in 194 countries. BrainTrack is regularly updated and has been operating continuously since 1996. http://www.braintrack.com/

- **British Colleges** - A complete list of homepage links for higher education institutions in England, Ireland, Scotland, and Wales. http://www.studyoverseas.com/universitiesuk.htm

- **Canadian Colleges** - A list of high school, universities, community college, and colleges in Canada. http://www.4icu.org/ca/

- **Catholic Colleges Online** - Catholic college search website. http://www.catholiccollegesonline.org/

- **Christian College Guide** - List of Christian Colleges. http://christiancollegeguide.net/

- **College Answer** - The "Going-to-College" process from preparation to getting loans, including interactive tools to analyze the affordability of schools, compare financial aid award letters, and search for scholarships. http://www.collegeanswer.com/

- **College Board** - An organization that connects students to colleges and opportunities. Register here online for the SAT. http://www.collegeboard.com/splash

- **College Fairs** - A national parade of 40+ National College Fairs sponsored throughout the year by the National Association for College Admission Counseling. Find out which institutions have registered for each fair. http://www.nacacnet.org/college-fairs/Pages/default.aspx

- **College.gov** - College options and how to pay for school. http://www.college.gov/

- **College Navigator** - This site is a free consumer information tool designed to help students, parents, high school counselors, and others get information about nearly every college in the United States. http://nces.ed.gov/collegenavigator/

- **College Net** - A guide to colleges and universities. http://www.collegenet.com/about/index_html

- **College Prowler** - View the schools that rank among the best in the areas of campus life that matter the most to you; narrow the search based on cost, majors, city setting, student body size, and religious affiliation. http://collegeprowler.com/colleges/

- **Colleges That Change Lives** - A non-profit dedicated to the advancement and support of a student-centered college search process. http://www.ctcl.org/

- **College View** - View pictures of over 3,300 campuses. Send email from here to request additional information. http://www.collegeview.com/

- **College Visits** - Tours cover all aspects of college life- include small, medium and large schools, rural and urban, public and private. http://www.college-visits.com/

- **College Week Live-Virtual College Fair** - Interact with college admissions representatives online. http://www.collegeweeklive.com/

- **Combined BA-MD Programs** - A list of schools that offer a combined degree of a bachelors and medical degree. http://www.medicalhelpnet.com/content/view/28/46/

- **Fiske Guide Books** - From the author of the reliable and popular guidebooks comes a full array of admission-related resources. http://www.fiskeguide.com/

- **Historically Black Colleges and Universities** - HBCU's website and be used for a college search and database. http://www.american-school-search.com/colleges/hbcu?gclid=CO2RhtacvbICFQQ3nAodA1sACw

- **IIE Passport** - A list of study abroad programs. http://www.iiepassport.org/

- **International Association of Universities** - A complete listing of universities around the world. http://www.unesco.org/iau/onlinedatabases/index.html

- **Jesuit Colleges and Universities** - 28 member institutions. http://www.ajcunet.edu/

- **Jewish College List** - A list of Jewish Colleges. http://www.campusexplorer.com/colleges/religions/jewish/

- **Know How 2 Go** - Find excellent information for under-represented students. http://www.knowhow2go.org/

- **Mapping Your Future** - A general information website which includes sign-up for monthly email reminders and newsletter. http://mappingyourfuture.org/CollegePrep

- **NACAC** - The National Association for College Admission Counseling (NACAC), founded in 1937, is an organization of more than 11,000 professionals from around the world dedicated to serving students

as they make choices about pursuing postsecondary education.
http://www.nacacnet.org/

- **Peterson's Guide** - Everything you need to stay on top of planning for private school, college, grad school, continuing education, or a vocational program. Search and save lists of schools; find financial aid; learn everything you need to know about admission tests. It's the easiest way to stay organized, and, best of all, it's free!
http://www.petersons.com/

- **Princeton Review** - Helps students, parents, and educators achieve the best results at every stage of their educational careers. By focusing on preparation and practice, we help students improve their performance in the classroom and on standardized tests. Our website helps parents, teachers, students and schools navigate the complexities of school admissions.
http://www.princetonreview.com/home.asp

- **Students Review** - Welcome to Students Review! Uncensored college reviews. Informative and awesome.
http://www.studentsreview.com/

- **Study USA** - An education guide with helpful information for international students studying in the United States.
http://www.studyusa.com/

- **U-Can College Search** - College search website. Browse hundreds of private college and university profiles.
http://www.ucan-network.org/

- **US Colleges with Foreign Campuses** - U.S. colleges to set-up branches in foreign countries.
http://www.pbs.org/now/shows/420/foreign-campuses.html

- **US News: America's Best Colleges** - Be wary of rankings, but much to learn from this site. The "school comparison" feature is great.
http://www.usnews.com/sections/rankings

- **Visa** - Information about types of visas available for international students and how to apply for the appropriate visa.
http://travel.state.gov/visa/temp/types/types_1268.html

- **Women's Colleges** - The Women's College Coalition – complete list of schools. http://womenscolleges.org/

The College Application Process

How many schools should you apply to? When should you apply? Is it more beneficial to apply online or fill out a paper application? This chapter will cover all aspects of the college application process from completing forms, discussing standardized test options, building a substantial resume of activities, offering ways to improve chances of admission, and more. Each section takes you step-by-step through the application process.

1 - ADMISSION PROCEDURES: WHICH ADMISSION OPTION IS RIGHT FOR YOU?

Each individual is unique; therefore, the number of schools the student chooses to apply to will vary. Most students will pare down their foundation list of colleges to the final five to seven schools. There should be a long shot — a **stretch school** — a reach — a college where the student's chances of gaining admission are less than 50/50 based upon his or her academic profile when compared to the students the admission office admitted in the previous year.

A reasonable reach — 50/50 or better – colleges are likely to admit within the student's range of grade point average, standardized test scores, and course curriculum. Other factors that enhance admission status could include activities, an interview, special talents, recommendations, essays, etc.

Target schools — sure shots — these are colleges where a student is confident that he or she will be admitted. However, be sure it is a school where your academic and personal needs will be met should you enroll. Be sure to include a **financial safety** in this category.

The best way to create this list is to research colleges by visiting the campus, taking tours, and speaking with admissions representatives. Review what is required to apply to the colleges including grade point average, high school course requirements, standardized test scores, resume of activities, essays, and recommendations. We will go into detail on each of these subjects and more. But before we start, review important *application jargon* and *deadlines.*

The **application deadline** is the date by which all completed applications are due to the college. In some cases the date will be a postmark date; in others it will be a date by which all material must be *received*. It will be helpful to read the section, called "How to Apply," on each college's website.

Early Action – Early Action is an admission plan offered by some highly selective colleges allowing the most qualified students the comfort of a letter of acceptance in December. The student does not have to withdraw other applications and does not have to accept or refuse the EA offer of admission until May 1.

Early Decision – Early Decision is a binding admission plan that requires an early application (typically October or November) and promises a reply by December or January. There are two types of ED plans: Single Choice, in which the student is allowed to apply to only one college; First Choice, in which the student may apply elsewhere but agrees to withdraw other applications if accepted by the ED school. This plan is recommended only if the applicant is absolutely sure of his or her college choice. If accepted, the student is ethically obligated to attend if sufficient financial aid is offered.

Rolling Admission – An admission plan in which applications are evaluated very soon after they are completed in the Admission Office. The applicant can receive a decision very quickly but is not obligated to attend.

Regular Decision – is the process whereby a college accepts applications from prospective students and delays the admission decision until all applications from the entire applicant pool have been received. Decision letters are mailed or emailed to all applicants, at once, traditionally in late March or early April.

Waitlist – The Waitlist is a group of qualified students who may be offered admission by a college at a later date, if space becomes available. Waitlisted students should initially accept another offer of admission and discuss with the college counselor ways to handle the waitlist situation.

Candidate's Reply Date – May 1 is the date by a student must give all accepting colleges a definite "yes" or "no," and send a deposit to the final-choice college.

2 - MORE ABOUT EARLY DECISION – A GOOD IDEA OR A BAD IDEA?

It may be a "good idea" if the college is clearly your first choice, you have a strong curriculum your senior year, your grades from junior year were excellent, your standardized test scores are competitive, and you can complete your testing requirements by October of your senior year.

It may be "an idea" if you are on the "bubble" for admissions, you are a traditional candidate for that school, you may be a child of an alumnus, you have a brother or sister at that school, you are an athlete (non-scholarship school), and your test scores and grades are in the middle 50% of accepted students.

It may be a "bad idea" if financial aid is a major concern and want to compare packages, have weak junior year grades, your standardized testing is not complete or not competitive, you not sure if you really have a first choice college, you have not visited the campus, you may not be in the range academically of students who are typically admitted, and admission is an exceptional long shot.

Bottom line, check out statistics on the college's website and speak to a college admissions representative directly about why you are considering Early Decision as an application method.

College Admissions Checklist of Things to Do

CHECKLIST OF THINGS TO DO	College 1	College 2	College 3	College 4
Campus Visit.				
Campus Interview (if required).				
Resumes of activities, academics, and achievements to a counselor and a teacher for letter of recommendation.				
Teacher Recommendation 1 - Date requested - Stamped envelopes addressed to admissions office or email address if recommendations sent electronically.				
Teacher Recommendation 2- Date requested- Stamped envelopes addressed to admissions office or email address if recommendations sent electronically.				
Letters of Recommendation – Peer review or optional writer of letter of recommendation as required by college.				
Counselor recommendation letter/Secondary School Report Form to counselor/thank-you note.				
Follow-up and thank-you notes written.				
Test scores requested and sent from College Board (ETS) or ACT to colleges.				
Transcripts sent from high school(s) to colleges.				
If student-athlete, NCAA Eligibility form submitted and transcript sent				
Auditions scheduled if theater, dance, or music performance student.				
Portfolio completed for students applying to fine arts program.				
Military application completed including physical, letters of nomination, recommendations, and application.				
Application completed.				
Essay(s) completed.				

Financial aid forms from college enclosed				
FAFSA and/or CSS Profile completed by deadlines				
Application fee processed if online, enclosed if paper application				
Postage affixed/copies made/return address on envelopes sent to the college				
Copies made of all forms and documentation enclosed in application packet if applying online				
Letters of acceptance/denial/waitlist received by April 1				
Colleges notified of intent by May 1				
Tuition deposit sent to one college of choice by May 1				
Housing and other forms submitted to chosen college by May 1				
Ask high school to send final transcript to one college				
Orientation scheduled				

4 - COMPLETING THE COLLEGE APPLICATION

Before you begin completing your college applications, it will help you to review the basic tips provided here to prevent "application overload."

Start early! Give yourself plenty of time to produce a stellar final product. You want a winning application, not one that looks harried and rushed.

Have the following information on hand before you start your application. It's not a bad idea to save this information on a card or in a computer file.

Your Social Security Number

Family Information

☐ Father's name, address, date of birth, and occupation
☐ Mother's name, address, date of birth, and occupation
☐ Father's college, degree, and date of graduation
☐ Mother's college, degree, and date of graduation
☐ Sibling(s), name(s), age(s), and college(s) attended

Your Transcript

- ☐ Courses taken
- ☐ Grade Point Average; Class Rank
- ☐ Test Scores (SAT and ACT)
- ☐ Extracurricular Activities in order of importance
- ☐ Honors and Awards

School Information

- ☐ SAT and ACT Code
- ☐ Counselor's phone, fax number, and email address
- ☐ Teacher 's email address

Student Work History

- ☐ Name of employer and dates employed

Common errors on college applications to avoid:

- Be careful not to confuse "country" with "county."

- Do not forget to sign your application.

- When a college asks for your senior year schedule, be sure to submit your schedule for the entire year, not just the first semester.

- For "nickname," include your preferred name. Do not write in names your friends use when they joke with you.

- Watch how you enter dates. Admissions officers have complained of students listing the current year as their birthday (e.g. 8/28/2009 instead of 8/28/1991).

- If there is more than one section on the essay question, be sure to answer every part. Make sure your response answers the question.

If you have written your essays on a separate sheet of paper, do not forget to include them with the application. Place your name and, if they ask, your social security number at the top right corner of each page.

If you are going to use some of responses for more than one school, be sure to replace the name of the school with the correct one. For example, in an application to Brown, do not write,"… and this is why I want to go to Wesleyan."

Decide if you want to complete a paper or online application.

5 - ONLINE AND COMMON APPLICATIONS

Source: CommonApp.org - http://www.commonapp.org

Should you apply online?

Technology provides you with three options when completing your college applications.

1. Fill out the college's standard paper application from the admissions office.

2. Log on to their website, locate the online application, complete it online, print a copy for your files, and submit the online application with the fee. (The student may want a counselor to proofread his or her forms before the final submission)

3. Complete a Common Application or Universal Application online. https://www.commonapp.org/CommonApp/FAQ.aspx; http://www.universalcollegeapp.com/

Some college or universities will offer a waiver of the application fee for applying online. Check with each admissions office regarding its policy. There is no advantage or disadvantage to applying online.

Common Questions for Applicants

GENERAL QUESTIONS

What is the Common Application?

The Common Application is a not-for-profit organization that serves students and member institutions by providing an admission application – online and in print – that students may submit to any of our 520 plus members.

https://www.commonapp.org/
https://recsupport.commonapp.org/ics/support/kbanswer.asp?deptID=33
014&task=knowledge&questionID=794

Why use it?

Once completed online, copies of the Application for Undergraduate Admission can be sent to any number of participating colleges. The same is true of the School Report, Optional Report, Midyear Report, Final Report and Teacher Evaluation forms. This allows you to spend less time on the busywork of applying for admission, and more time on what's really important: college research, visits, essay writing, and senior year coursework.

Is it widely used?

Absolutely! Millions of Common Applications are printed and accepted by members each year. In addition, last year almost 2.5 million applications were submitted via the Common App Online.

Is it treated fairly?

YES! College and university members have worked together over the past 35 years to develop the application. All members fully support its use, and all give equal consideration to the Common Application and the college's own form. Many of our members use the Common Application as their only undergraduate admission application.

Can all colleges participate?

Membership is limited to colleges and universities that evaluate students using a holistic selection process. A holistic process includes subjective as well as objective criteria, including at least one recommendation form, at least one untimed essay, and broader campus diversity considerations. The vast majority of colleges and universities in the United States use only objective criteria – grades and test scores – and therefore are not eligible to join. If a college or university is not listed on this website, they are not members of the consortium. Sending the Common Applications to non-members are prohibited.

What is the Common App Online School Forms System?

As part of the application process, schools require a variety of information to be provided by teachers and guidance counselors who have interacted with you in the high school environment. Until last year, those forms were only available as PDF files that could be printed, copied, and mailed to the appropriate colleges. Now each teacher and counselor will have the option to complete the forms online via the Common App Online School Forms system if they desire. There is no cost to you or high schools, and using the online system is completely optional for your teachers and counselor.

When you create an account on the Common App Online, you must first indicate what high school you attend. Once this information has been saved, you can access a "School Forms" section of the Common App where teachers and counselors can be identified. By adding a teacher or counselor to the list of school officials, an email is triggered to the teacher or counselor with information about how to log into the Online School Forms system or how to opt for the "offline" or paper process. You are then able to track the progress of your various teachers and counselors via a screen within the Common App Online.

What if I'm a transfer student?

There's a Common Application for Transfer Admission as well as First-Year Admission. The Transfer Application is available primarily for online submission - https://www.commonapp.org/

TECHNICAL QUESTIONS

How do I get help?

If you are experiencing technical difficulties with the Common App Online, if you need to request your username or password, or if you have a general question about the Common Application (including access to our numerous FAQs), please submit a request to the online Support Center. All email you receive from technical support will be sent from this email address: appsupport@commonapp.net. Please be sure to add this email address to your address book and/or safe list to prevent the messages from being blocked as "SPAM." This is particularly important for AOL users.

Is phone support available?

No. In order to maintain the Common App Online as a free service to students and high schools, all tech support is provided via a much more cost-efficient email system.

- Applicants: Please click here to access the Application Support Center. Please do NOT submit support requests on behalf of a school official; the school official should submit those directly in order to avoid confusion and speed the resolution of problems.

- School Officials (counselor/teachers): Please click here to access the School Official Support Center. Please do NOT submit support requests on behalf of a student; the student should submit those directly in order to avoid confusion and speed the resolution of problems.

TIPS FOR COMPLETING THE COMMON APP ONLINE

What browser should I use?

PC (Windows XP/Vista/7)

- Internet Explorer 7 or higher

- Firefox 4 or higher

Mac (OS X Tiger / Leopard / Snow Leopard)

- Safari 4 or higher

While the majority of its features will work with other browsers, we cannot guarantee complete compatibility or offer support for other browsers. Users have reported significant issues with the following browsers, and we do not recommend you use them:

- AOL browser

Regardless of browser, use the following browser settings:

- Javascript must be enabled.

- Cookies must be enabled.

- Popup blockers must be disabled.

How can I prevent my spam filter from blocking Common App emails?

All email you receive from technical support will be sent from "appsupport@commonapp.net." Please be sure to add this email address to your address book and/or safe list to prevent the messages from being blocked as "SPAM." This is particularly important for AOL users.

Do you have any tips for viewing and submitting online?

- Save your work often.

- Logout after each session.

- Use a word processor to type your writing samples before cutting and pasting or uploading them into the online forms.

- Use Print Previews to view your forms before submitting. (You will need to install Adobe Acrobat Reader. It's free.)

- Adobe Acrobat Reader Download Page:

- http://get.adobe.com/reader/

For a complete list of Common Application members, deadlines for applications, fees, supplement information, test policy, and school forms required, search Membership Requirements.

https://www.commonapp.org/Login

Common Application – All Members

There are now 520 Common Application members in 46 states and the District of Columbia, as well as in Germany and Italy. They represent an enormously diverse variety of institutions: small and large, public and private, coed and single-sex, highly selective and relatively open enrollment. However, they all share a commitment to the mission of promoting access through holistic admission.

https://www.commonapp.org/CommonApp/Members.aspx
https://www.commonapp.org/CommonApp/Mission.aspx

Common Application

We strongly encourage you to consider applying online. It's quick, easy, and secure. However, if you prefer to print a hard copy, complete it by hand, then mail it in, you can find copies of all our forms in PDF format below. Note: Please do not mix-and-match your application, supplement, and payment between online and paper submission. Either submit the application, supplement and payment (or fee waiver) online, or submit them all by mail.

https://www.commonapp.org/

Some Changes in Application, but Essay Questions Remain the Same

There have been some new items added to the application itself but the essay questions remain the same. In 250 to 500 words, students should respond to one of these prompts:

1. Evaluate a significant experience, achievement, risk you have taken, or ethical dilemma you have faced and its impact on you.

2. Discuss some issue of personal, local, national, or international concern and its importance to you.

3. Indicate a person who has had a significant influence on you, and describe that influence.

4. Describe a character in fiction, a historical figure, or a creative work (as in art, music, science, etc.) that has had an influence on you, and explain that influence.

5. A range of academic interests, personal perspectives, and life experiences adds much to the educational mix. Given your personal background, describe an experience that illustrates what you would bring to the diversity in a college community or an encounter that demonstrated the importance of diversity to you.

6. Choose a topic of your choice.

Forms & Downloads

https://recsupport.commonapp.org/ics/support/kbanswer.asp?deptID=33014&task=knowledge&questionID=794

To download a form, just click its' link. You will need Adobe Acrobat Reader to open all files below. With the exception of the Application (student form), you can type data into any of the forms below before printing, though you cannot save that data into a PDF unless you purchased Adobe Acrobat Professional.

http://www.adobe.com/products/acrobat/readstep2.html

A sample 2013-14 Common App is on shown on pages 78 through 86.

NOTES

 **COUNSELOR GUIDE TO THE APPLICATION**

This guide displays the sections and pages within The Common Application. It is designed to familiarize students with the information they will be asked to report and is not intended to be a comprehensive collection of all questions within the application.

PROFILE	**Contacts** *Email address, phone number, mailing address* **Demographics** *Religion, military service, race/ethnicity (all optional)* **Geography** *Birthplace, countries lived in, language proficiency, citizenship*
FAMILY	**Household** *Parent marital status, parent(s) with whom you reside* **Parent and/or Guardian** *Name, birthplace, occupation, education, stepparent information* **Siblings** *Age, grade, education*
EDUCATION	**School** *Current school, dates attended; counselor name, phone, and email* **History** *Previous schools, dates attended, past/pending education interruptions (e.g. time off, early graduation, gap year, etc.), college courses, college assistance programs* **Academic Information** *GPA, class rank, current year courses, honors and awards*
TESTING	**College Entrance** *ACT and SAT* **English For Non-Native Speakers** *TOEFL, IELTS, PTE Academic* **Academic Subjects** *AP, IB, SAT Subject Tests, A-Levels* **Other** *Optional reporting for other relevant 9-12 testing*
ACTIVITIES	**Principal Activities/Work** *Years of participation, hours per week, weeks per year, position/leadership held (50 characters), brief description (150 characters). 10 activities maximum.*

ESSAY	**Select One, 650 Words Maximum**
	• *Some students have a background or story that is so central to their identity that they believe their application would be incomplete without it. If this sounds like you, then please share your story.*
	• *Recount an incident or time when you experienced failure. How did it affect you, and what lessons did you learn?*
	• *Reflect on a time when you challenged a belief or idea. What prompted you to act? Would you make the same decision again?*
	• *Describe a place or environment where you are perfectly content. What do you do or experience there, and why is it meaningful to you?*
	• *Discuss an accomplishment or event, formal or informal, that marked your transition from childhood to adulthood within your culture, community, or family.*
EXPLANATIONS	**Required Responses**
	Explanations regarding school discipline[1], criminal history[2], education interruption, veteran discharge status
ADDITIONAL INFO	**Optional Responses**
	Relevant circumstances or qualifications not reflected elsewhere in the application
COLLEGE PAGE 1	**General**
	Entry term, degree status, housing preference, test-optional preference, scholarship and financial aid preference
	Academics
	Academic interest, program(s) applying to
	Contacts
	Interactions with the institution (campus visit, off-campus interview, etc.)
	Family
	Family members who have attended or been employed by the institution
	Evaluations
	Names of classroom teachers, coaches, other recommenders
	Residence
	Required by some public institutions to determine in-state status
	Signature
	Acknowledgments and affirmations
	(Not all member colleges will ask all questions.)
COLLEGE PAGE 2	**Writing Supplement**
	Additional short answer or essay responses if requested by institution

1. Have you ever been found responsible for a disciplinary violation at any educational institution you have attended from the 9th grade (or the international equivalent) forward, whether related to academic misconduct or behavioral misconduct, that resulted in a disciplinary action? These actions could include, but are not limited to: probation, suspension, removal, dismissal, or expulsion from the institution.

2. Have you ever been adjudicated guilty or convicted of a misdemeanor, felony, or other crime? Note that you are not required to answer "yes" to this question, or provide an explanation, if the criminal adjudication or conviction has been expunged, sealed, annulled, pardoned, destroyed, erased, impounded, or otherwise ordered by a court to be kept confidential.

THE COMMON APPLICATION

FY RD Fall 2014 01/01/1995 CEEB: 000000 CAID: **0000000**

LastName, FirstName
FERPA Waived

SCHOOL REPORT

CONTACTS

Official Name / Title	Name and contact info for official completing form
Email / Phone	
Website / Profile	
School / CEEB	
Address	

Identifying information prints from the student's account. FERPA will show as Waived or Not Waived depending on student's online selection.

SCHOOL PROFILE School Profile data should be completed to the extent possible.

College Bound	_____ % Four-Year _____ % Two-Year
Ethnicity	_____ % Asian _____ % Black _____ % Latino _____ % White _____ % Native
First Gen	_____ % First-Generation
International	_____ % US Citizens _____ % Non-US Citizens
Socioeconomic	_____ % Receive Free or Reduced Lunch
Financial Aid	_____ % Receive Financial Aid (Independent Schools)
Setting	☐ Rural ☐ Suburban ☐ Urban
Curriculum	Total Offered/Yearly Limit AP _____ / _____ Honors _____ / _____ IB _____ / _____ IB Diploma Candidate? ☐ Yes ☐ No Block Schedule ☐ Yes ☐ No
Attached Grades	☐ 11: Final ☐ 12: 1st Quarter ☐ 12: 2nd Quarter/1st Semester ☐ 12: 1st Trimester ☐ 12: 2nd Trimester ☐ 12: 3rd Quarter ☐ 12: Final
Graduation	_____ (m/d/y)

"Attached Grades" refers to the most recent grades reflected on the accompanying transcript.

TO BE COMPLETED BY INTERNATIONAL SCHOOLS THAT DO NOT USE AN AP CURRICULUM

Language of Instruction _____

Promotion based on a state or national exam? ☐ Yes ☐ No

If so, has student taken leaving exams? ☐ Yes ☐ No

These questions replace the International School Supplement.

Grading/Marking Scale	A	B	C	D	F
	Excellent	Very Good	Average	Poor	Failing

If applicable, please attach an official copy of this student's lower secondary examination results. If the student has already taken senior secondary leaving exams, please include an official copy of the results. If this applicant's senior secondary leaving exam results are not yet available, please attach predicted results.

SR *FirstName LastName RD FY Fall 2014 01/01/95 CEEB: 000000 CAID: **0000000***

HOME SCHOOL SUPERVISORS SHOULD ATTACH AND EXPLAIN:

• Name of homeschooler's association, if applicable:  These questions replace the Home School Supplement.
• Any information about the applicant's home school experience and environment that you believe would be helpful to the reader (e.g. educational philosophy, motivation for home schooling, instruction setting, etc.).
• Grading scale or other methods of evaluation.
• Any distance learning, traditional secondary school, or higher education coursework not included on the transcript. List the course title and content, sponsoring institution, instruction setting and schedule, and frequency of interactions with instructors and fellow students (once per day, week, etc.).
• Standardized testing beyond what is collected in the Common Application.

ACADEMICS

Class Rank _____ Class Size _____ Covering a period from (m/y) _____ to _____

The rank is ☐weighted ☐unweighted. How many additional students share this rank? _____

Cumulative GPA: _____ on a _____ scale, covering a period from (m/y) _____ to _____

This GPA is ☐weighted ☐unweighted. The school's passing mark is: _____

Highest GPA in class _____

In comparison with other college preparatory students at your school, the applicant's course selection is:
☐Most demanding ☐Very demanding ☐Demanding ☐Average ☐Below average

---

RATINGS

No Basis		Below Average	Average	Good (above average)	Very Good (Well above average)	Excellent (top 10%)	Outstanding (top 5%)	Top few (top 1%)
	Academic achievement							
	Extracurricular Accomplishments							
	Personal qualities and character							
	OVERALL							

THE COMMON
APPLICATION

EVALUATION

How long have you known this student, and in what context? _____

_____

What are the first words that come to your mind to describe this student? _____

_____

COMMENTS

Please provide comments that will help us differentiate this student from others. Feel free to attach an additional sheet or another reference you have prepared for this student. Alternatively, you may attach a reference written by another school official who can better describe the student.

Has the applicant ever been found responsible for a disciplinary violation at your school from the 9th grade (or the international equivalent) forward, whether related to academic misconduct or behavioral misconduct, that resulted in a disciplinary action? These actions could include, but are not limited to: probation, suspension, removal, dismissal, or expulsion from your institution.
☐Yes ☐No ☐School policy prevents me from responding

To your knowledge, has the applicant ever been adjudicated guilty or convicted of a misdemeanor, felony, or other crime?
☐Yes ☐No ☐School policy prevents me from responding.
Note that you are not required to answer "yes" to this question, or provide an explanation, if the criminal adjudication or conviction has been expunged, sealed, annulled, pardoned, destroyed, erased, impounded, or otherwise ordered to be kept confidential by a court.

If you answered "yes" to either or both questions, please attach a separate sheet of paper or use your written recommendation to give the approximate date of each incident and explain the circumstances.

Applicants are expected to immediately notify the institutions to which they are applying should there be any changes to the information requested in this application, including disciplinary history.

☐ Check here if you would prefer to discuss this applicant over the phone with each admission office.

I recommend this student: ☐No basis ☐With reservation ☐Fairly strongly ☐Strongly ☐Enthusiastically

Signature _____

Please mail this form and accompanying documents directly to the each college/university admission office. Do not mail this form to The Common Application offices.

THE COMMON
APPLICATION

TEACHER EVALUATION

Identifying information prints from the student's account. FERPA will show as Waived or Not Waived depending on student's online selection.

CONTACTS

Official Name / Title   Name and contact info for official completing form

Email / Phone

School / CEEB

Address

EVALUATION

In what subject did you teach this student?

How long have you known the student, and in what context?

What are the first words that come to mind to describe this student?

In which grade level(s) was the student enrolled when you taught him/her?   9☐   10☐   11☐   12☐

Other

List the courses in which you have taught this student, including the level of course difficulty (AP, IB, accelerated, honors, elective; 100-level, 200-level; etc.)

COMMENTS

Please attach additional comments that address what you think is important about this student, including a description of academic and personal characteristics, as demonstrated in your classroom. We welcome information that will help us to differentiate this student from others. (Feel free to attach another reference you may have already prepared on behalf of this student.)

TE *FirstName LastName RD FY Fall 2014 01/01/95*
*CEEB: 000000 CAID: **0000000***

FY RD Fall 2014 01/01/1995 CEEB: 000000 CAID: **0000000**

LastName, FirstName

FERPA Waived

RATINGS

No Basis		Below Average	Average	Good (above average)	Very Good (Well above average)	Excellent (top 10%)	Outstanding (top 5%)	Top few (top 1%)
	Academic Achievement							
	Intellectual Promise							
	Writing							
	Creativity							
	Class Discussion							
	Faculty Respect							
	Work Habits							
	Maturity							
	Motivation							
	Leadership							
	Integrity							
	Resilience							
	Collaborative							
	Self-confidence							
	Initiative							
	OVERALL							

Signature _____

Please mail this form and accompanying documents directly to the each college/university admission office. Do not mail this form to The Common Application offices.

TE *FirstName LastName RD FY Fall 2014 01/01/95*
*CEEB: 000000 CAID: **0000000***

COMPLETE FIRST YEAR APPLICATION PACKET

Instructions and Application

https://www.commonapp.org/Login

For Contact Information; Arts Supplement; Athletic Supplement, Early Decision Agreement, Teacher Evaluation, Secondary School Report, and Essay Prompts

https://recsupport.commonapp.org/ics/support/kbanswer.asp?deptID=33014&task=knowledge&questionID=794

6 - WHAT IS FERPA? THE FAMILY EDUCATIONAL RIGHTS AND PRIVACY ACT (FERPA)

Family Policy Compliance Office (FPCO) Home
http://www2.ed.gov/policy/gen/guid/fpco/index.html

Source: U.S. Department of Education

The Family Educational Rights and Privacy Act (FERPA) (20 U.S.C. § 1232g; 34 CFR Part 99) is a Federal law that protects the privacy of student education records. The law applies to all schools that receive funds under an applicable program of the U.S. Department of Education.

FERPA gives parents certain rights with respect to their children's education records. These rights transfer to the student when he or she reaches the age of 18 or attends a school beyond the high school level. Students to whom the rights have transferred are "eligible students."

- Parents or eligible students have the right to inspect and review the student's education records maintained by the school. Schools are not required to provide copies of records unless, for reasons such as great distance, it is impossible for parents or eligible students to review the records. Schools may charge a fee for copies.

- Parents or eligible students have the right to request that a school correct records which they believe to be inaccurate or misleading. If the school decides not to amend the record, the parent or eligible student then has the right to a formal hearing. After the hearing, if the school still decides not to amend the record, the parent or eligible student has the right to place a statement with the record setting forth his or her view about the contested information.

- Generally, schools must have written permission from the parent or eligible student in order to release any information from a student's education record. However, FERPA allows schools to disclose those records, without consent, to the following parties or under the following conditions (34 CFR § 99.31):

  - School officials with legitimate educational interest;

  - Other schools to which a student is transferring;

  - Specified officials for audit or evaluation purposes;

  - Appropriate parties in connection with financial aid to a student;

  - Organizations conducting certain studies for or on behalf of the school;

  - Accrediting organizations;

  - To comply with a judicial order or lawfully issued subpoena;

  - Appropriate officials in cases of health and safety emergencies; and

  - State and local authorities, within a juvenile justice system, pursuant to specific State law.

Schools may disclose, without consent, "directory" information such as a student's name, address, telephone number, date and place of birth, honors and awards, and dates of attendance. However, schools must tell parents and eligible students about directory information and allow parents and eligible students a reasonable amount of time to request that the school not disclose directory information about them. Schools must notify parents and eligible students annually of their rights under FERPA. The actual means of notification (special letter, inclusion in a PTA bulletin, student handbook, or newspaper article) is left to the discretion of each school.

For additional information, you may call 1-800-USA-LEARN (1-800-872-5327) (voice). Individuals who use TDD may call 1-800-437-0833. Or you may contact:

Family Policy Compliance Office
U.S. Department of Education
400 Maryland Avenue, SW
Washington, D.C. 20202-8520

7 - COLLEGE APPLICATION INFORMATION WEBSITES:

Source: Website descriptions are taken directly from the individual websites.

2-Year/Community Colleges - List of all community colleges by state.

> http://www.utexas.edu/world/comcol/state/

- **4-Year/Universities and Colleges** - Lists all universities and colleges by state.
  http://www.utexas.edu/world/univ/state/

- **Boarding Schools** - Post Grad Opportunities after high school.

  http://boardingschools.com/find-a-school/search-tools/a-z-school-list.aspx

- **Common Application** - The Common Application currently provides both online and print versions of its First-year and Transfer Applications. Our membership of more than 400 institutions now represents the full range of higher education institutions in the US: public and private, large and small, highly selective and modestly selective, and East Coast, West Coast, and every region in between. We have also welcomed our first two international members.
  http://www.commonapp.org/

- **Common Black College Application** - For the low price of $35, students can have their applications submitted to all 33 participating HBCU institutions. Also offers information on employment and scholarships for black students.
  http://www.eduinconline.com/eduweb/

- **Universal Application** - The Universal College Application is an online admissions application consortium for college-bound students.
  http://www.universalcollegeapp.com/

8 - RADIO STATION WEBSITES FOCUSING ON COLLEGE ADMISSIONS

Source: Website descriptions are taken directly from the individual websites.

- **Count Down To College** - Radio show with segments on the college application process.
  http://www.countdowntocollegeradio.com/archive_applications.html

- **LA Talk Radio** - LA Talk Radio sponsors an online podcast every Sunday at 12:00 pm. Elsa Clark and Chris Krzak address various topics that pertain to the college admissions process. Often the team schedules guest speakers to talk to their audiences on subjects from standardized testing to financial aid and everything in between. Each presentation is archived and can be played or downloaded to your computer or iPod. Listen to one podcast on a topic of interest to you.
  http://www.latalkradio.com/College.php

- **NPR-The College Admissions Game** - College admissions, especially at a small group of highly selective colleges, is intense and, according to some college deans, out of control. In a seven-part series, NPR explores the alternatives.
  http://www.npr.org/templates/story/story.php?storyId=7537888

9 - TYPES OF STANDARDIZED TESTS USED IN COLLEGE ADMISSIONS

There are several types of standardized tests used for college admissions. Each one has a purpose, and these tests give the college admissions representatives an idea of a student's college readiness. The admissions committee will often look at these scores in conjunction with the grade point average and rigor of courses taken by the student. The tests are the SAT, SAT Subject Test, ACT with Writing, TOEFL, and AP (Advanced Placement Tests).

SAT Reasoning Test is a standardized test which measures a student's verbal and mathematical aptitude as well as writing skills. Score range is 600-2400.

SAT Subject Tests were developed by the College Board to measure the student's knowledge or skills in a certain area such as math, history, physical science, literature, and foreign language. These tests can be taken at any point in the student's junior or senior year as long as he or she has completed the related course work in that subject area. Check the college's website to see if these tests are needed for the application process.

ACT with Writing is also taken nationally like the SAT Reasoning Test. It focuses on English usage, mathematics usage, social science reading, and science reading. An optional writing section is recommended by most colleges. Score range is 1-36.

TOEFL evaluates non-native English speakers' ability to read, write, speak, and listen to English similar to the way it is used at the university level. The sections covered include Reading, Listening, Speaking and Writing.

AP or advanced placement tests are considered college-level courses given in high school for possible college credit. Scores range from 1-5. Students should check with the colleges they are applying to see if they accept AP credits. Some colleges will offer credit for a score of 3, though most require a 4 or 5.

Students are reminded to submit their scores directly to the colleges they are applying to.

Quick Tips for Prepping for the Test

Start soon enough to make a difference. Students should give themselves enough time to prepare for the various subject areas. Sufficient preparation will leave the student feeling less rushed and reduce their anxiety. Various test preparation tools are available: study guides, flashcards, Internet programs, and CDs produced by the testing companies. Be sure to get enough sleep the night before the test. The student should read a lot to build reading comprehension skills.

On Testing Day

- Eat well and bring a snack for the break
- Bring the right supplies – photo ID, number two pencils
- Get to the test center site early
- Wear comfortable clothes
- Know the procedures
- Review the whole test section before you start
- Answer easy questions first
- In the ACT, answer every question because no deductions are taken for incorrect answers
- Identify key words
- Rephrase difficult questions
- Eliminate answers on multiple choice sections
- Jot down your thoughts
- Write neatly
- Use all of the time given

10 - ACT VS. SAT

Colleges will accept either the ACT or the SAT. Some colleges do not require either but these institutions will place more emphasis on the grade point average and the rigor of the student's coursework (See Fairtest.org for the list of schools).

Students should do practice work on both tests to see which fits their learning style—free sample test questions can be found on Number2.com. Many high schools offer students the opportunity to take the preliminary SAT called the PSAT or the preliminary ACT called the PLAN. These are usually taken during October of the sophomore and junior year. Depending on the student's math level, juniors will begin to take both tests around January of their junior year and continue through their senior year.

Most students will choose to take a standardized test at least two times before applying to college. Those students with diagnosed learning disabilities should check the sites for further information about extended time on standardized test (Special Testing ACT and Special Testing SAT). Test preparation can help those who choose to spend extra time understanding the test questions.

http://www.fairtest.org/
http://www.number2.com/
http://www.act.org/aap/disab/opt3.html
http://professionals.collegeboard.com/testing/ssd/accommodations/time

See the comparison chart that follows.

	ACT	SAT
Length of Test	3 hours, 25 minutes (including optional 30-minutes Writing section)	3 hours, 45 minutes
Sections	4 Sections (plus optional Writing section): English, Math , Reading, Science, Writing	10 Sections: 3 Critical Reading, 3 Math, Writing (including Essay) and 1 Experimental section (not scored)
Subjects	English, Math, Reading, Science and Writing (optional)	Critical Reading, Math and Writing
Reading	4 passages, 10 questions per passage	Reading passages with questions pertaining to comprehension, and sentence completion
Science	Science (analysis, knowledge, problem solving)	Not applicable
Math	Arithmetic, Algebra, Geometry, and Trigonometry	Arithmetic, Algebra, Geometry, and Trigonometry
Essay	Optional (final section)	Required
Score Composition	1/4 English, 1/4 Math, 1/4 Reading, 1/4 Science	1/3 Math, 1/3 Reading, 1/3 Writing
Scoring	Based on Composite Score of 1-36 points for each section, 0-12 for Optional Essay	Score of 600-2400 based on total of 3 scores (Reading, Math and Writing) Essay score range from 0-12
Penalties	No penalties for incorrect answers	1/4 point deducted for wrong answers
Sending Scores to Colleges	All scores from the selected test date(s) will be sent. Students can choose which test date to send	Students decide which scores are sent (may use Score Choice option or not)
Websites for More Information	www.act.org	www.collegeboard.com

http://www.act.org/
http://www.collegeboard.com/

11 - SAT/ACT CONCORDANCE CHART

The ACT and SAT are different tests that measure similar but distinct constructs. The ACT Test measures achievement related to high school curricula, while the SAT Reasoning Test measures general verbal, quantitative reasoning, and writing skills.

ACT and the College Board have completed a concordance study that is designed to examine the relationship between two scores on the ACT and SAT, providing a tool for finding comparable scores (Understanding Concordance).
http://www.act.org/aap/concordance/understand.html

ACT If you scored...	CURRENT SAT or...	NEW SAT It's about the same as...
36	1600	2400
35	1560-1590	2340
34	1510-1550	2260
33	1460-1500	2190
32	1410-1450	2130
31	1360-1400	2040
30	1320-1350	1980
29	1280-1310	1920
28	1240-1270	1860
27	1210-1230	1820
26	1170-1200	1760
25	1130-1160	1700
24	1090-1120	1650
23	1060-1080	1590
22	1020-1050	1530
21	980-1010	1500
20	940-970	1410
19	900-930	1350
18	860-890	1290
17	810-850	1210
16	760-800	1140
15	710-750	1060
14	660-700	1000
13	590-650	900
12	520-580	780
11	500-510	750

Download: ACT *(PDF; 2 pages, 30KB)*
ACT/College Board Joint Statement and Tables *(PDF; 4 pages, 69KB)* See also, Estimated Relationship between ACT Composite
Score and SAT CR+M+W Score. © ACT.org

http://www.act.org/aap/concordance/pdf/reference.pdf
http://www.act.org/aap/concordance/pdf/report.pdf
http://www.act.org/aap/concordance/estimate.html

12 - SAT SCORE CHOICE

Score Choice allows the students to forward the scores they choose to the colleges or universities they are applying to. So, what does a student need to know about this policy?

Here are some items to think about:

- SAT Reasoning and Subject test scores can be submitted by test date. If a student does not choose Score Choice, all scores will be sent to the college.

- Score Choice is optional.

- Students should follow the score-reporting requirements of the colleges they are applying to.

- Colleges will only receive the scores that the student sends to them.

- Individual sections of a specific test date cannot be selected—only the entire test of the particular SAT will be sent.

- It does not cost more to send one or multiple copies or all test scores to a college.

- Scores can be sent by paper, CD, or Electronic Score Reports. If the student requests a second report to a college, the report will only include the unique set of scores chosen by the student, which may or may not include previous test scores.

- For more information, check with the College Board. http://professionals.collegeboard.com/testing/sat-reasoning/scores/policy

13 - WHEN SHOULD I SEND MY A.P. TEST SCORES TO COLLEGE?

If you are a high school junior and you will be applying early action to the college of your dreams in the fall, you may wonder if you should send in your AP (advanced placement) exam scores. What if you received scores of a 4 and a 5 on the two exams you took, should you send them in May of your junior year? Are they part of the college application process? Will they help in the decision process?

AP or Advanced Placement courses are college level classes with exams given each May for students who complete the AP coursework. The fact that you took rigorous courses will indicate to a college that you are college ready. You'll improve your writing skills, sharpen your problem-solving abilities, and develop time management skills, discipline, and study habits. These characteristics may be helpful in the admissions process. The scores may or may not be a factor in the admissions decision. If the college asks you to report the scores, it will look at them. The scores should be sent directly from the College Board testing service. The AP course and test results could also be a factor in class placement at college. Each college will decide if credit will be given for courses you completed in high school. Once you have determined where you will enroll, you will need to order score reports for that college if you expect to earn credit for your AP results.

Another tip: As you begin to send materials (e.g., recommendations, test scores, resume) to colleges where you plan to apply, the admission staff will keep these materials in a file until your application comes in. Once your application and fee (or fee waiver) arrives, the admissions staff will open a file for you and connect the materials.

14 - CAN I EARN CREDIT BY TAKING A CLEP EXAM?

Know Your College's CLEP Policy -The College Board shared there 2,900 colleges and universities which will grant credit for CLEP. Each institution sets its own CLEP policy. Each institution determines the exams for which it awards credits, the minimum qualifying score required to get credit, and the amount of credits that will be granted per exam. CLEP exams test mastery of college-level material acquired in a variety of ways — through general academic instructions, significant independent study or extracurricular work. CLEP exam-takers include adults just entering or returning to school, military service members and traditional college students.

http://clep.collegeboard.org/search/colleges

How Much Credit Can I Earn? If you pass a CLEP exam, you may earn up to 12 credits. The amount of credit you can earn on an individual CLEP exam varies with each college. Some colleges place a limit on the total amount of credit you can earn through CLEP. Other colleges may grant you exemption but no credit toward your degree. Some colleges may offer six credit hours versus three credit hours.

Prior Course Work - Some colleges won't grant credit for a CLEP exam if you've already attempted a college-level course closely aligned with that exam. For example, if you successfully completed English 101 or a comparable course at another campus, you'll probably not be permitted to receive CLEP credit in that same subject. Also, some colleges won't permit you to earn CLEP credit for a course that you failed.

Can I Take the Exam More Than Once? Be sure to wait at least six months before repeating a CLEP exam of the same title. Scores of exams repeated earlier than six months will not be accepted (and test fees will be forfeited).

Colleges usually award CLEP credit only to their enrolled students. Here are some additional questions to consider:

- Does the college require that you "validate" your CLEP score by successfully completing a more advanced course in the subject?

- Does the college require the optional free-response (essay) section for the examinations in Composition and Literature as well as the multiple-choice portion of the CLEP exam you're considering?

- Will you be required to pass a departmental test such as an essay, laboratory, or oral exam in addition to the CLEP multiple-choice exam?

Learn the answers to these questions. *Source: Collegeboard.com*

15 - WHAT ARE THE BENEFITS OF SUMMER READING?

Summer is a great time to catch up on reading about some of your favorite topics. It's time to let your imagination take you on a journey. Reading for pleasure can help turn you into a lifelong learner. For some, reading also can be a lot of fun! It can be a time to get cozy in an environment that is conducive to your reading. So grab your favorite snack, choose your spot, sit back, and enjoy the story.

What are the benefits of reading:

- It is a skill that develops over time with practice.

- Builds comprehension skills and vocabulary.

- Lets you have discussions with friends and family about the book, the characters, new words learned, and the themes.

- It is important to do as a daily routine.

- Lets you choose books according to interest and comfort level.

- Allows you to expand your interests; magazines can also be a great alternative if tailored to a particular interest.

- Exposes you to great literature; reading stories by great writers can help you become a better writer yourself.

- Develops problem solving skills.

- Improves scores on standardized tests.

- Is practical; there are plenty of books that inform and educate,

Success breeds success, so don't let the summer slide catch you by surprise. Start your own book club with a group of your friends. Meet at your house, the pool, or the coffee shop. Embrace the experience and read, read, read!

16 - IT'S TIME TO THINK ABOUT SUMMER – WHAT IS THERE TO DO?

Younger students may enjoy heading off to camp, including theme-based camps. Campers are encouraged to learn about topics such as art, music, leadership, or special topics such the environment. They will engage in the learning experience through songs, skits, day trips, games, and other camp-wide activities.

High school students may be looking for a more fulfilling summer experience. Some may choose to attend a pre-college program that allows them to test the waters in an area of interest such as writing, technology, the arts, film, sports, science, travel, business, debate, and community service or activism. Volunteering at charitable organizations is a great way to match talents and interests. Others may choose a study abroad program that immerses the participant in hands-on learning experience. Engaging in an internship can offer students the opportunity to gain more knowledge about possible college majors.

Students might find summer work at local establishments including restaurants, recreation centers, retail stores, amusement parks, resorts, or camps. Look for support staff positions found at the library, in businesses, and medical offices. A caregiver might enjoy babysitting, being a home companion, working at a YMCA, life guarding, or being a swim instructor. Love animals? Check with local veterinarians to see if they are hiring.

Remember, if the student is under eighteen, he or she may need to obtain working papers or Employment/Age Certificates at the local high school. A student should create a resume and practice filling out job applications. A template for resume writing can be found in the Microsoft Works program under templates. Before a student says "yes" to a job offer, he or she should make sure the company is legitimate. Check with the Better Business Bureau to see if there have been complaints. Use the work experience as a way to learn what you enjoy doing and what you don't.

Are you creative, organized, or ambitious? A student can try his or her entrepreneurial skills by offering services to friends and families. Create a business: Mow lawns, pet-sit, tutor, program computers, create crafts or jewelry to sell, Photoshop family photos, run a car wash, landscape yards, web development, paint, cook, household cleaning, or run an errand service.

Time goes fast, so get on board for summer fun and a chance to learn!

17 -STANDARDIZED TEST PREPARATION AND INFORMATION WEBSITES

Source: Website descriptions are quoted from the individual website.

- **4Tests.com** - This site is a world-wide provider of free, online practice exams. We exist to serve the education and testing markets and we're proud to help you pass your upcoming exams. http://www.4tests.com/exams/exams.asp

- **ACT and Registration** - FAQs about ACT; strategies & sample questions. Like the SAT, the ACT is accepted by almost all colleges and universities. But instead of measuring how you think, the ACT measures what you have learned in school. http://www.act.org/aap

- **ACT** - A chart that converts SAT and ACT scores. http://www.act.org/aap/concordance/

- **AP® Tests** - Short for Advanced Placement, AP tests give you the chance to earn college credit while still in high school. Many students take them after completing AP classes. http://www.collegeboard.com/student/testing/ap/about.html

- **Classic Hangman** - Test your vocabulary with SuperKids. http://www.superkids.com/aweb/tools/words/hangman/sat1.shtml

- **CLEP® Tests** - Short for College Level Examination Programs, these tests can help you earn college credit in many different subjects. They are often taken by homeschooled students, or people who are returning to college after being in the workforce. http://www.collegeboard.com/student/testing/clep/about.html

- **College Board Home Page** - Register for the SAT test online. This test measures your ability to think and solve problems. Almost all colleges and universities accept the SAT as part of the admissions process. You can take the test in your junior and senior years. http://www.collegeboard.com/

- **College Board SAT Prep** - Information and preparation for the SAT. http://www.collegeboard.com/student/testing/sat/prep_one/prep _one.html

- **College Board SAT** - These tests measure your knowledge and skills in a variety of subjects. Some colleges use them for admissions and to help students choose the right courses. Some schools require

them. In other schools, they are optional.
http://www.collegeboard.com/student/testing/sat/about/SATII.html

- **CollegeBoard** - The Official SAT - Six free online courses—PSAT code needed.
  https://satonlinecourse.collegeboard.com/loginAction.do?loginType=schoolStudent

- **FairTest** - Test Optional Schools - Schools that do not use SAT or ACT scores for admitting substantial numbers of students to Bachelor Degree Programs. http://www.fairtest.org/university/option

- **Free Rice** - Test your vocabulary for free - http://www.freerice.com

- **GED** Testing Service - The General Development Education Testing Service-find a testing center.
  http://www.acenet.edu/AM/Template.cfm?Section=GED_TS

- **International Baccalaureate Diploma Program** - This is a two-year program designed for college-bound high school students. It is accepted by hundreds of colleges and universities in the U.S. The course can help you earn college credit. Ask your guidance counselor if your school offers it. http://www.ibo.org/

- **Khan Academy** - With a library of over 2,400 videos covering everything from arithmetic to physics, finance, and history and 150 practice exercises - http://www.khanacademy.org/

- **MajorTest.com** - Free SAT practice. http://www.majortests.com/

- **Number2.com** - Free test prep for SAT, ACT, and GRE. http://www.number2.com/

- **SAT** - The SSD guidelines for students can be explored by using these links:
  http://www.collegeboard.com/disable/students/html/indx000.html

  - Eligibility
    http://www.collegeboard.com/ssd/student/eligible.html

  - Documentation
    http://www.collegeboard.com/ssd/student/document.html

  - Diagnosis & Functional Limitations
    http://www.collegeboard.com/ssd/student/limitations.html

- Accommodations
  http://www.collegeboard.com/ssd/student/accom.html
- After Approval
  http://www.collegeboard.com/ssd/student/after.html
- Important Dates
  http://www.collegeboard.com/ssd/student/time.html
- Scores http://www.collegeboard.com/ssd/student/scores.html
- SAT
  http://www.collegeboard.com/ssd/student/sat.html
- AP
  http://www.collegeboard.com/ssd/student/ap.html
- Disabled
  http://www.collegeboard.com/disable/students/html/indx000.html

- **Sparknotes.com** - More free test prep.
  http://www.sparknotes.com/testprep/

- **TOEFL (Test of English as a Foreign Language)** - International students have additional requirements when applying to US colleges. http://www.toefl.org/

18 - THE IMPORTANCE OF AN ACTIVITIES RESUME

Involvement in extracurricular activities can make you stand out in the college application process. Are you a leader? Have you achieved a noteworthy level of achievement? How does the activity make you distinctly different from others with similar interests?

This same resume will also be helpful for teachers and counselors whom you may ask to write your letter of recommendation. So gather the following information: name, address, professional email address, cell phone/home phone number, objective or summary, education, extracurricular activities, volunteer service, awards and certificates, skills/academic achievement, music /artistic achievements, references, and other information.

Think about your qualities:

☐ Time Management

☐ Teamwork

☐ Goal-Oriented

☐ Competitiveness

☐ Confidence

☐ Persistence/Endurance

☐ Loyalty

☐ Discipline

☐ Taking Criticism

☐ Dealing with Setbacks

☐ Leadership

☐ Flexibility/Adaptability

Complete the following statements:

☐ My most significant activities I am involved in are ... because...

☐ I hold a leadership position in ... as a ...

☐ I am responsible for...

☐ My proudest accomplishment is ... because ...

☐ The most significant accomplishment I achieved in the academic arena...

☐ My favorite subject to study is ... because ...

☐ I think my grades reflect my ability to ...

☐ In college I hope to study ...

☐ I have pursued my interest in subjects outside of school by ...

☐ I have received awards/honors for my accomplishments in ... (academic courses)

☐ I have earned certificates for my achievement in... (music, art, and/or athletics)

☐ I have participated in...(activity) for .... (number of) years—list leadership first

☐ My most significant contribution to my community is ...

☐ I volunteer my time by ...

☐ I spent my summer ...

☐ In my leisure time I like to ...

☐ My favorite book is ... because ...

☐ My favorite movie is... because ...

☐ I have a job where I am responsible for...

Check out Microsoft's free resume templates to build stunning traditional resumes and modern web resumes, update and email your resume with a click of the mouse, and energize your career with a great resume! http://office.microsoft.com/enus/templates/results.aspx?ctags=CT010144894

- Career One Stop Resume Samples - View excellent sample resumes here. A few samples are on the next pages.

  http://www.careerinfonet.org/resume/resume_type.asp?nodeid=2

- WetFeet -Advice about careers, resumes, job interviews, internships and much more.

  http://www.wetfeet.com

NOTES

19 - SAMPLE RESUMES

SUE SMITH
smiths@gmail.com

2222 Mill Plain Rd, Fairfield, CT 06614 / Cell 203-555-1111

PROFILE

High school senior skilled in athletics and working with children in sports-related activities. Dependable and mature; seeking admission to a college where I can study Sports Medicine.

EDUCATION

HS Diploma: Graduation Date - June 2011 from NC High School, Fairfield, CT

GPA: 3.6 **SAT:** Critical Reasoning - 620 Math - 540 Writing – 560

AP Courses Completed: English, Biology, U.S. History

HONORS AND AWARDS

- High School Honor Roll (2006-Present)
- High School Coaches Association Award (2008)
- Varsity Indoor Track (2008- 2009)
- Varsity Lacrosse (2007-2009)
- All Conference Lacrosse (2008)
- All Conference Academic (all sports 2006-Present)

EXTRACURRICULAR ACTIVITIES

- Varsity Swim Team (2005-2008, Captain 2009); YMCA Swim Team (2005-2007)
- Varsity Indoor Track - Sprinter (2008- Present)
- Lacrosse Varsity (2007-09); Captain (2008-Present)
- Key Club Participant (2007-Present)

COMMUNITY SERVICE

- Teacher's Assistant - Physics/Science teacher (2008-2009)
- Relay for Life - Organized events for three years (2007-Present)
- Big Brother/Big Sister - Coordinated after-school activities- JR Middle School (2008-Present)
- Brookfield Youth Lacrosse Clinic – trained techniques to 8-10 year olds (2008)

EMPLOYMENT

- Lifeguard/Instructor - Lake Town Park, Stamford, CT (2007-Present)
- Lifeguard/Swim Instructor, Green View, YMCA, Fairfield, CT (2007-Present)
- Cashier, TJ Maxx, Fairfield, CT (2006-2008)
- Soccer Referee, YMCA, Fairfield CT (2004-2007)

ADDITIONAL TRAINING

Red Cross CPR/AED Certification, Waterfront Lifeguard, Certified Soccer Referee

JOHN THOMAS

170 East Street, New York, NY 20202

Jthomas@gmail.com

Cell (212) 555-7000

EDUCATION John's High School, New York 2006-2010
Current Cumulative GPA 4.07
Junior Year Term III GPA 4.14
SAT: Critical Reading 760, Math 780, Writing 790
SAT Subject Tests: Biology E 720, Mathematics Level 1 740,   US History 730
AP European History Exam Score: 5; AP US History Exam Score: 5; AP Biology
Exam Score: 5

HONORS AND AWARDS

- National Honor Society, Latin Honor Society, Full Year Dean's List
- University of Notre Dame Book Award 2009
- President Latin Honor Society 2009-10
- Treasurer Junior Classical League 2008-09
- Governor's Honors John High School nominee for Latin 2009
- Excellence in Modern and Classical Languages award for Latin, 2006-07, 2007-08, 2008-09
- National Latin Exam Award for top John's HS Score on level National Latin Exam, 2006-07, 2007-08, 2008-09
- Varsity Track and Field, discus and shot put, 2006-10
- John's HS Academic Team 2008-10
- Peer 2 Peer Latin Tutor 2008 - 09, 2009-10
- Model Arab League John's HS delegate 2009-10
- Peer Leader for new students 2008-09, 2009-10

WORK AND SERVICE EXPERIENCE

Reach for Excellence Summer Program Intern, Summer 2009
A tuition free program of the John High School that prepares talented middle school students from under-served schools to succeed in challenging high schools and college preparatory programs; led book group discussions, activity periods; tutored; assisted teachers.

The Greenhouse, Maintenance Assistant, Summer 2007–2008
Performed summer maintenance tasks for store and greenhouse including cleaning, painting, moving

Cathedral of Christ the King, Year-round, 2006–2008
Parish Council Teen Nominee; *Teen Apostle* Leadership Team; Eucharistic Minister; *Life Teen* Member; Middle School *Edge* Assistant Leader; *Cardboard Campout* (for New York City Homeless); participant and Assistant Coordinator

Project FIAT International Missionary, Summer 2009
Worked to engage the Cathedral community in the mission trip to El Salvador; planned and participated in numerous activities to raise funds to support trips and contribute to needs in the community served; mission work includes labor/construction and education/recreation for village children.

JUDY SCHOOL

9292 School Drive, Miami, Florida   22222   414-555-1111
jschool@gmail.com
The Academy, Miami, Florida
May 2011 Graduation
GPA: 3.98 / 4.0   SAT: 2390 (M: 800, CR: 790, W: 790)   **ACT: 34**
AP Courses: Chemistry, English, Calculus, Government, Physics, Spanish, Art History

LEADERSHIP AND AWARDS

Academic Team Captain - 2008-2010
Mosaic, Program Coordinator - 2009
Mu Alpha Theta President - 2009-2010
Peer 2 Peer Program Tutor - 2009
National Honor Society Member - 2008, 2009
Eucharistic Minister - 2007-2010
Spanish Honor Society Member - 2007-2010
Student Ambassador - 2007-2010

INTERNSHIPS

Florida School of Medicine – Research Lab, Miami, FL   **Summer 2009-10**
Lab Assistant – Intern (20 hrs/wk)
Performed immuno-histochemistry research; focus on the presence of viral antigens in tissues of patients with Crohn's Disease
Publication of research procedures, methodology, and finding published June 2009, Journal Medicine
Cartoon Network – Miami, FL   **Summer 2009**
Assistant Writer – Intern (part-time)
Selected to write copy for design programming
Research, brainstorming sessions regarding new scripts and ideas for new story line
Special Skills: *Computer Programming: Java, Python, C, and Visual Basic*
City Search Magazine – Miami, FL   **Summer 2008**
Assistant Editor – Highlights (part-time)
Research event stories for City Search weekly magazine.
Edited copy, ran print, promoted column and ad space for buyers

VOLUNTEER SERVICES

Habitat for Humanity Build – *Board Member* **– Miami, FL**   **2006-Present**
Promoted five "builds" for school community; organized fund raising earning $10,000
Collected from over 5,000 donors; all proceeds were donated to "High School Builds"
Volunteer – St. Francis Table – 100 hours completed   **2007-2009**
Volunteer – Ashton Woods Nursing Care – 25 hours completed **2007-2008**
Volunteer – Café 211 – 25 hours completed   **2006-2007**
Volunteer – Tutoring – Sheltering Arms – 25 hours completed **2005-2006**

20 - HOW TO REQUEST A LETTER OF RECOMMENDATION

Colleges may require a letter of recommendation, or they may not. You will need to review what each school requires as part of the application. There are several people who may need to write on your behalf including your counselor and/or a teacher. Sometimes colleges will specify what they are looking for more specifically, like a letter from a teacher who taught you your junior year or the one who taught you in a core course like English, math, science, history or foreign language. Review the following tips to help you get an effective letter of recommendation:

- The letter should be from someone who knows you well. He or she will need to be able to produce a well-written piece that will help the admissions office learn something new about you.

- Set a time to speak with the individual you would like to write your letter. Share a resume of activities and academic achievements that will help him or her develop an initial letter. Anecdotes and illustrations will help him or her get their image of you across on the page.

- Be sure to give the deadline when the letter is due to the college as well as a stamped, addressed envelope to the admissions office.

- Give the person at least four weeks in advance of the deadline. Ask in person – not by email.

- Additional recommendations may be appropriate, but consult with your college counselor for sure. One additional recommendation from an employer or supervisor, a mentor, or a leader in the community, that provides additional information that may not be found in the teacher or counselor evaluation is acceptable, but more than one is generally discouraged.

- Send a thank-you note in a few weeks to show your appreciation for submitting this information on your behalf.

- Once you hear of your acceptances, let the person know the outcome since he or she had a hand in the process with you.

If you are drawing a blank on what to share with your teachers, counselors, moderators or employers, answer the following questions on a separate piece of paper and turn them in with a copy of the resume when making your request:

1. I consider my best work in your class to be (e.g., paper, project, presentation, lab) ...

2. In your class, my greatest strengths were ...

3. My biggest improvements during your class were ...

4. Looking back, my effort level in our class was (above potential, satisfactory, why?) ...

5. My style of participation was revealed by (my leadership in discussions, in groups, assisting other students) ...

6. My most valuable extracurricular experience has been ...

7. I am most proud of ...

8. The most significant accomplishment I achieved in the academic arena is ...

9. I spent my summers during high school ...

10. My responsibilities at home include ...

11. I spend my leisure time ...

12. My favorite author is ... my favorite character in the book... is... because...

13. One of my favorite movies is ... because ...

14. My best friend would describe me as...

15. My favorite subject to study is ... because ...

16. I think my grades reflect my ability to ...

17. In college I hope to study ...

18. The person with the most impact on my life is ... because ...

19. My role in the family is to ...

20. I have grown in my attitude about ...

21. I was able to overcome an obstacle (name one) by ...

22. The following people ... could be a reference for me because ...

23. In five years I will ...

24. In 10 years I will ...

If you are at a loss for what to present to your teacher or counselor, use the college recommendation and/or counselor form in the next section.

College Recommendation Form

Create a form like the following one, making as many copies as you need, and give them to the person writing your letter of recommendation. Include a stamped envelope addressed to the Undergraduate Admissions Office. Online college applications may ask you for your counselor and teacher email addresses so the college can send the writer an electronic recommendation form.

Name (Last / First / Middle)

I.D.#

E-mail Address

Cell Phone Number

I. FAMILY

Write the college attended and the highest degree earned by each:

Mother _____Associate's - Bachelor's - Master's - Doctorate

Father _____Associate's - Bachelor's - Master's - Doctorate

Brother(s) _____Associate's - Bachelor's - Master's - Doctorate

Sister(s) _____Associate's - Bachelor's - Master's - Doctorate

II. ACTIVITIES (check years participated)

Activity   9   10   11   12   Level of involvement

III. COMMUNITY/NON-HIGH SCHOOL - ACTIVITIES

Religious organizations, summer programs, volunteer (years participated), work, etc.

                  9   10   11   12   Levels of involvement

IV. WORK EXPERIENCE

Employer Position / Title/ Hours/ Week Length of Employment

V. COLLEGE/CAREER GOALS AND ACADEMIC INTEREST

List all colleges to which you are applying and deadline date for recommendations.

What major/area of study are you considering for college? "Undecided is ok."

What career(s) are you considering pursuing?

Do you feel that your transcript accurately reflects your academic ability?

If no, explain what factors/circumstances have interfered with your academic performance?

What do you think are your academic strengths? Give examples.

List 3 academic faculty members (preferably junior year) who could give you a positive appraisal and why.

VI. PERSONAL

Who are your personal heroes, men and women you admire, and why?

What special interests or hobbies do you pursue outside of school?

What personal experience, summer experience, school/work experience, or travel has been of significant importance to you, and why?

Is there any information you would like for me to emphasize in my recommendation to help the colleges make a more accurate appraisal of your application? Let me know what else you would like me to include or emphasize.

Self Evaluation

RATINGS	Below Average	Average	Good	Excellent	Outstanding
Ability to organize/use time					
Self-confidence					
Desire to learn new information					
Willingness to take risks					
Ability to get along with others					
Willingness to work hard					
Imagination/Creativity					
Ability to express self					
Sense of humor					
Concern for others					
Emotional maturity					
Reaction to setbacks					
Understanding new concepts					
Self-discipline					
Growth potential					
Leadership					
Energy					
Motivation					
Warmth of personality					
Personal initiative					
Respect accorded to faculty					

Pick five descriptive words and provide an example how each word applies to you. Example: *I am very creative. I work on the Win-Win magazines and had some of my photos featured in the publication...*

accountable	dependable	intuitive	reflective
active	determined	knowledgeable	reliable
adaptable	diplomatic	leader	resourceful
adept	discerning	loyal	respected
aggressive	disciplined	mature	responsible
alert	discreet	methodical	responsive
ambitious	economical	mobile	self-directed
analytical	efficient	motivated	self-reliant
articulate	empathetic	objective	sense-of-humor
assertive	energetic	observant	sensitive
attentive	enterprising	open-minded	serious
broad-minded	enthusiastic	optimistic	sincere
capable	experienced	organized	skilled
charismatic	expert	outgoing	sophisticated
clever	expressive	patient	spontaneous
collaborative	extroverted	perceptive	stimulating
committed	fair	persevering	strong
communicative	forceful	personable	sympathetic
competent	goal-oriented	persuasive	systematic
concise	helpful	pleasant	tactful
confident	honest	poised	talented
conscientious	humorous	positive	team-oriented
consistent	imaginative	practical	tenacious
constructive	implements	precise	tolerant
conversant	improvises	solves problems	understanding
cooperative	independent	productive	versatile
creative	industrious	professional	vigorous
critical	innovative	proficient	warm
curious	instinctive	proven	well-read
decisive	intelligent	realistic	well-rounded

College List / Student Questionnaire for Counselor Recommendation

DIRECTIONS: Create a form similar to the one below and answer the questions as completely as possible. This information is extremely important and will be used by your counselor in composing your letter of recommendation. Give your counselor notice of a minimum of four (4) weeks. Include a stamped envelope addressed to the office of undergraduate admissions with the return address of your school or let them know if they will be receiving an electronic form from the college.

Name

Phone

Address

I give my counselor permission to send a letter of recommendation, transcript, and school profile to my colleges.____ Initials

College Information

Please list the colleges you will be applying to this year. Make sure you list at least two Foundation schools where you are assured of admission.

Name of College

EA/ED/REGD/ROLLING (Early Action/Early Decision/ Regular Decision/ Rolling Admission)

Deadline Date

Letter and/or Forms Requested

1.

2.

3.

4.

5.

6.

Foundation Schools — Two "likely-to-be admitted" schools; one should be a "financial safety"(you can pay for it)

1.

2.

Recommendations

Write the names of the teacher(s) you will ask to write your letter(s) of recommendation:

First:

Second:

Personal Information

Apart from your resume, your counselor would like to know more about you in order to distinguish you as a student. Although you do not need to answer every question, please complete as many of the statements below as thoroughly as possible. The more depth you provide, the more your counselor has to work with in presenting your contributions, accomplishments, and special attributes.

1. Please write your senior quote below or record a special quote or saying which you feel is significant. Indicate why you selected this quote and what important meaning it has for you.

2. The activity I have contributed the most to and/or the activity that has meant the most to me is …

3. My greatest moment at my school was when …

4. If they could see into my future, they would see me at college actively involved in …

5. My dreams for the future include a job where I could …

6. Something you would be surprised to know about me is …

7. I would like my counselor to make special mention of this aspect about me or my life circumstances in my letter of recommendation OR what qualities would you like mentioned that really distinguish you as a college applicant?

8. I would also like to mention … (Have you had to work? Why? What summer programs/study have you participated in? Do you speak more than one language?

Character/Anecdotal Statement - Optional

Name of Student:

Name of Writer:

Relationship to Student:

Directions to the Student: Have this form filled out by someone who knows you well. This could be a parent, grandparent, older brother or sister, or community member. This statement will not be considered confidential, so do read and approve it before giving it to your counselor.

Directions to the Writer: The job of the counselor is to write a comprehensive letter distinguishing this student's academic accomplishments and unique character qualities.

Please choose one of the following ideas and write a short statement on behalf of this student. This information will be considered by this student's counselor in writing a letter of recommendation. This information will not be considered confidential.

Is there a story or event which would exemplify the positive character traits of this student? Describe.

What do you most admire about this student? Are there any incidents that how these qualities?

What would you want this counselor to include in a letter of recommendation for this student?

Please write below, or type on a separate sheet.

21 - THE COLLEGE ESSAY

Recently I read an article by an admissions representative from St. Mary's College of Maryland regarding the college essay. The advice seemed worthy of repeating so here it goes. When asked about the length of the essay, the representative explained that "the ones that got read at our college, the ones that really showed the admissions committee the real person, and the ones that jumped out at us and caught our attention were the ones that: 1) were from the 'heart', 2) were 'student-written' (you would be surprised how many have 'adult hands' on them...and you can tell the difference when you read them), and 3) told us why they are special; not necessarily if they were special. If students can do that and it happens to be a little over 500 words, don't sweat it."

So, remember it is important to start early, be familiar with your topic, be yourself, be original, include information that may set you apart from other applicants, check to be sure you answered the question asked and follow the directions for each essay (some online applications count the number of characters allowed), and proofread for grammar and punctuation. It can't hurt to have another set of eyes review your work.

Tips:

- Start early. Give yourself enough time to think about your essay and revise it as needed.

- Write about something with which you're familiar. The admissions office has your data including your GPA, test scores, and course curriculum. What else do they need to know about you?

- Be yourself. The admissions team is interested in who you are –- not someone you think they want you to be.

- Be original. Though many college applications will have standardized essay questions, try to be original and creative on your response. Make the essay your own.

- Write an essay that shows how you're unique. For example, one student wrote about his rather large ears, and he was accepted to one of the highly selective universities.

- Include any experiences or jobs that might set you apart from other applicants.

- Be authentic. There is no need to embellish your experiences. Colleges often limit the number of words from 250 to 500. Double spacing will make it easy for the admissions representatives to read your essay.

- Use a relaxed, comfortable tone of voice but avoid being too familiar, sarcastic, or comic. You never know what mood the reader is in or how he or she will perceive your tone since he or she cannot see your eyes, hear your voice, or read your body language.

- Check to make sure your essay answers the questions asked. Avoid wandering too far from your subject matter.

- Review, review, review. Proofread your essay for spelling, punctuation, and grammar. Many individuals at your school are willing to offer feedback. Ask for assistance from your English teacher or counselor.

- Mail your application early to avoid any postal mishap or Internet complications.

- BLOOPERS or mistakes you will want to avoid...

  - The admissions departments at Bates and Vassar Colleges have compiled a list of bloopers from their admissions essays, including the following:

  - "If there is one word to describe me, it would be profectionist"

  - "I was abducted into the National Honor Society"

  - "I have never been to New England, but I hear it is a beautiful country"

  - "I want a small liberal in the northeast part of the country."

  - "I'm very excited about watching football games in the fall at Emory."

  - "I function well as an individual and as a group."

  - "I can speak, read, and write fluently in Greek. My other two sports are volleyball and tennis."

  - "I have taken many curses in literature and writing."

Websites that may be helpful in the essay writing process:

- Application Essays - Tips for writing application essays from Carleton University.
  http://apps.carleton.edu/admissions/apply/essay_tips/

- Bloopers for College Essays - Counselor Newsletter, an update on essay ideas
  http://www.collegeview.com/admit/?p=419

- Essay2Review - A free website designed for all your essay needs.
  http://www.essay2review.com/work-up-your-common-application-essay.html

- Purdue Owl - Writing a Personal Statement.
  http://owl.english.purdue.edu/owl/resource/642/01/

22 - TIPS FOR THE COLLEGE INTERVIEW

There are different types of interviews in which students may participate. Meetings with the admissions officer can be formal and kept as part of the student's application file, or informal and held for the purpose of gathering data about the college or university. Students may attend an alumni reception held by a college for the purpose of learning more about the school. This type of session is informal and usually held in a student's hometown. Many schools have eliminated personal interviews altogether, and they have chosen to use group information session on campus to share data with prospective students. Lastly, some colleges create alumni networks for interviewing individuals who cannot visit a campus and would like to talk to someone about their interest in a college. Interviews may also be held for students competing for scholarships related to academic, athletic, or extracurricular activities.

If the college allows you to have an interview, take it up on that opportunity. It will show your demonstrated interest in its' program. I know you may be nervous, so practice your responses with family members, counselors, or friends before you meet. Remember to turn off your cell phone before the interview starts. Wear what you would wear to dinner at a good restaurant. Do not wear jeans or baseball caps. Avoid lots of jewelry, makeup, and perfume. Don't chew gum! Don't swear!

Arrive on time; greet the admissions representative with a solid handshake and a smile. Remember to maintain eye contact throughout your time together. Take a moment to think before you answer your questions, highlight your academic and extracurricular accomplishments, and place a positive focus on your past. Do your research about the university, share information about your visit to their institution, and prepare some questions for your interviewer to answer.

Ask about their admissions process. What makes their program different from other institutions? Do you accept advanced placement or international baccalaureate credit? Ask about their approach to technology in the classroom. Is a personal laptop required, or when did you school become a laptop school?

Ask about their academic programs. Does your college use teaching assistants to teach the classes? Is faculty available for students? Do you have any off-campus or study abroad opportunities? Ask about housing. Is housing guaranteed? Are the residence halls coed? Can I get a single room as a first-year student? What percent of students live in dorms? Is housing guaranteed for four years? Are there off-campus apartments? Can I bring a car on campus?

Ask about standardized testing. What tests are required for admission? If test option, why did your college make the SAT/ACT optional for admission? How will your college evaluate each applicant? Never tell the school it is your "safety."

The interview or may ask you questions as well. Make it a conversation. Be prepared to answer questions like these: Tell me about your experiences at your high school. Is there a particular experience you had there that stands out? What would you change about your school if you had the power to do so? What might your teachers say is your greatest strength as a person and as a student, and what are your weaknesses in each area? What has been the most important person or event in your self-development? What magazines and newspapers do you like to read? What sort of things do you like to do outside of school? What books or articles you read in the last year had special meaning for you? What do you want to do in the future? If you had a time machine and could go back anytime and change history, what time period would you go to and what would you do? Keep up on current events.

Remember, this is your interview and you need show the individual you can think on your own – you need to leave your parents behind. Never refuse an interview; your refusal will usually be noted. Always follow up with a thank-you note to the interviewer. After you leave the interview, jot down something that you discussed so you can mention it later in the thank-you letter.

23 - SAMPLE COLLEGE INTERVIEW QUESTIONS

Questions to Ask During the Interview

Admissions Information
- What makes your college different from other independent, liberal arts colleges?
- Do you consider whether a student has taken advanced, honors, or AP courses?
- My high school does not rank students. Will this hurt my candidacy?
- Do you accept Advanced Placement (AP) or International Baccalaureate (IB) credit?
- Do you accept credit for courses taken in high school?

- If admitted under the Early Decision (ED) program, must I enroll? What if I have applied for financial assistance? What are the benefits of applying ED?

- What type of student are you looking for? To what other schools do your applicants typically apply?

- Are there any recent or upcoming changes happening at your school?

- What is the biggest challenge facing this university or college?

Computer Technology

- Will a personal computer be required?

- When did your college become a "laptop school?"

- How do students use their laptops in class?

- Are there restrictions on how the laptops are used out of class?

- What is the technology infrastructure like on campus?

- Do you provide training?

- Are there non-academic benefits to your college's approach to technology?

- Can students get involved in the technology department?

Academic Program

- Does your college use teaching assistants to teach classes?

- How large are the classes? Do you have helpful faculty advisors and do students meet with them regularly?

- Are faculty members accessible to students? Who teaches lecture classes? What is the student-faculty ratio? Who teaches lab sections? Can I get individual help?

- Where do students study? What hours do students have access to libraries, computers, labs, etc.? How many hours a week do students typically study?

- Is this an openly competitive environment? How are tests and exams administered? Who grades exams?

- Do you have any off-campus/study abroad programs?

- Do you offer internships?

- Can I be considered for both the Seven-Year Dual Degree (B.A./M.D.) Program and the regular B.A. program?

- What is your acceptance rate for students who apply to medical school? Law school? Graduate school?

- Do you have any literature on the career placement of your graduates?

Student Life

- Is housing guaranteed? Are the residence halls coed? Can I get a single room as a first-year student? What percent of students live in dorms? Is housing guaranteed for four years? Are there off-campus apartments?

- Is the campus safe? Are there regular patrols, escort vans, emergency phones, etc.?

- Can students have a car on campus? Do many students go home during the weekends?

- Do you have fraternities/sororities?

- Will I be able to pursue my extracurricular activities here? Ask about specific interests.

- Is your campus "liberal" or "conservative"?

- What is the student's relationship with the surrounding community?

- Could I have an email address of a current student with whom I could ask questions about student life?

- Are campus jobs readily available?

- What is the ratio of male to females?

- How tolerant is the school community of diversity?

- What leadership positions in this community do women hold? Men?

- What would students say they like best and/or least about being a student here?

What do students complain about the most?

SAT/ACT Optional Admissions Consideration

- What tests are required for admission?

- If test option, why did your college make the SAT/ACT optional for admission? How will your college evaluate each applicant?

24 - A SUMMARY – TOP 10 STEPS FOR SENIORS

Seniors – you head back to school, many important events are about to take place. You will reconnect with friends, meet your teachers, start your classes and activities, and begin the college application process. With all that, what are the top 10 items that need to be on your "to-do" list?

ONE: Review your list of colleges. The schools should be those you're interested in, have programs with majors you are considering, and fit your needs, values, interests and learning/instructional style. Are you interested in a Four or Two-Year program? How about a technical, vocational or trade school option? Have you considered the military? The average number of applications most seniors submit is 5 to 7 schools. Consider two schools that might be a reach or stretch, those you dreamed about attending all your life. Next, consider 2-3 that are possible, your testing, grades, and coursework meet the middle 50% of those admitted in the past. Then, 2-3 schools where you are likely to be admitted (your statistics are in the top 25% of the previous admitted class). Check the range of test scores and grade point averages of previously admitted students to determine this set on the college's website.

TWO: When are the deadlines? Are you applying early decision or early action? Check out what this means for you. Those applying early will hear by December. You should be competitive in this pool of applicants. Remember, they will probably not see your term one grades of senior year, test scores of standardized tests taken after the October sitting, or recommendations. Each college will have their specific expectations. Early Decision is for the serious student who will commit to that one school. You can only apply to one school Early Decision, and if you gain entrance you will attend. Early Action does not mean you will commit to attend a school if you are accepted; it is an early notification format. In recent years, colleges have been taking an increasing number of students in the early action and early decision rounds—sometimes as high as 40 to 50 percent of the entering freshman class. This means that there are far fewer seats available during the regular admission round and many more applicants. Here are some things you can do now to be ready for those strategic fall application deadlines. You don't want to miss the deadline – many are set for October 1 or 15, or as late as November 1 to December 1. Regular Decision allows you to know by March 30 at the latest while Rolling Decisions are made as each applicant's file is complete. Review the directions on the application for specific requirements and application methods.

THREE: Register for the SAT and/or the ACT. October is generally the last test date that will be scored in time for early action or early decision deadlines. Register for the ACT at www.act.org and the SAT at www.collegeboard.com. If your colleges require SAT Subject Tests and you have not taken them, you will also need to allow test dates for those. To see which colleges do not require standardized testing, go to http://www.fairtest.org. If English is your second language, talk with your counselor about taking the TOEFL test - http://www.toeflgoanywhere.org/   Remember, practice makes perfect so spend some times preparing for the test. Try http://www.number2.com for starters!

FOUR: Schedule visits to colleges. Can you see yourself living there? Do they have the programs you are interested in? Are you within the admissions statistics range? Talk these over with your parents.

FIVE: Visit with college admissions representatives. They may be reading your application for admissions. Attend a session at your school, a local information session, a college fair, or take a tour of the college in person or online.

SIX: Focus in on completing your application essays. Before you know it, you will be involved in your classes and activities and the essay task could slip to the back of your priorities. Because the essays can be the "tipping factor" in the admissions process, take your time to write an essay that tells the school more about you beyond the numbers and grades. Answer the question, revise, proof and double check your essay. Watch your grammar and syntax. Your English teacher and guidance counselor would be happy to review it and share their opinion. The essay may be one of the most important documents you submit!

SEVEN: Ask your teachers and counselors to write letter of recommendations. Check the application directions to see what is required and follow this lead. If they do require two, the college is usually looking for two teachers who taught you during your junior or senior year in a core subject area such as math, English, science, history, or modern and classical languages. The teachers may want additional information from you such as your activities and leadership experience. Teachers and counselors will need a few weeks to write your letter. Your counselor will need time to coordinate additional pieces beyond your recommendation including your transcript and other supporting documents.

EIGHT: Will you be applying for financial aid and scholarships? Many scholarships have early deadlines. Some colleges may ask you to prepare the institution's financial aid form, or if you are applying to a private college, you may need to prepare the CSS Profile for an aid package. The CSS Profile is due when you file applications (or shortly after), unlike the FAFSA form (http://www.fafsa.gov) which isn't due until February or March at most schools. For a list of colleges that require the CSS Profile, go to: https://profileonline.collegeboard.com/prf/index.jsp.

NINE: Focus on your school work! Prepare for classes, improve your note-taking skills, build your reading comprehension abilities, and give yourself lead time when preparing for quizzes and tests. You will want to show the institutions to which you are applying that you are a great catch. Set up a schedule for studying, organize your notebooks, find a "great place" to study where you can stay focused, and limit your "texting" to friends. I've heard many seniors lament, "If I only spent more time on my school work rather than on my iPhone or computer, I would've had great grades."

TEN: Last tip, keep challenging yourself, stay involved, set goals for the future, strive for balance, and avoid the senior slump! Good luck seniors – you are on your way!

25 - SOCIAL NETWORKS – MORE ON FACEBOOK

The Intended College Use of Facebook is Not the High School Reality.

Social networking is a great way to find a job, network, and stay in touch with those who matter most. But how do you protect yourself while on the Internet?

Facebook was the first large scale networking site made specifically for college students. Though it still requires a valid email address to sign-up, anyone can now join and network. http://www.facebook.com/

Yahoo! Kickstart is a new social networking site for college students that allow you to stay in contact with friends and help in the job search. It was just launched, so it may take time to start up.

http://mashable.com/2007/08/30/yahoo-kickstart/

MySpace was the first major social networking website. It contains people of all ages and is known to allow users to customize their own profile.

http://www.myspace.com/

Social Networking Tips for College Student

- It is a college student's responsibility to protect his or her online accounts

- Companies and colleges may research potential candidates

- Be sure to change your privacy settings often

- Remove all inappropriate pictures

- Watch what you provide in your profile

- You may want to think twice about having a "Facebook" or "MySpace" account

- Be aware that pages on the Internet get cached (saved) and can be brought up even after the page no longer exists, so it is very important you remove inappropriate material from your profile as soon as possible!

26 - ADMISSIONS DECISIONS ARE IN! ACCEPTED, WAITLISTED, DENIED...WHAT'S NEXT?

You run to the mailbox every day only to find a letter that is not one of acceptance, and not one of denial either – instead it is a waitlist letter. Colleges use waitlists when they have accepted the maximum number of applicants but still view some applicants as well qualified. Fastweb.com describes the waitlist as, "a safety net colleges use to fill their classes if not enough accepted students enroll."

Most schools send out a letter asking you if you will accept a position on the waitlist. You can choose to accept or refuse this offer. How long you wait depends on the school's enrollment statistics. Though most students receive a decision in May or June from colleges using their waitlist, others have been known to receive acceptances a week before classes start.

The best strategy is to work with your counselor to:

- Choose and make a deposit at a good second choice.

- Get as much information from the "waitlist" college as you can.

- Let the admission office know that the college is your first choice.

- Strengthen your application, if possible:

  - Offer achievements that you may not have mentioned in your application and send new supplemental information.

  - Emphasize your strong desire to attend the college and make a case for why you're a good match. You can indicate that if accepted you'll enroll, but such a promise should be made only if you're absolutely certain.

  - You can also enlist the help of an alumnus and request another (or first) interview.

  - Study hard and send your final grade transcript.

- Stay involved in extracurricular activities.

NACAC Information for Waitlisted Students

NACAC's "Statement of Students' Rights and Responsibilities in the College Admission Process" offers the following information for waitlisted students:

If you are placed on a waitlist or alternate list:

The letter that notifies you of that placement should provide a history that describes the number of students on the wait list, the number offered admission, and the availability of financial aid and housing.

- Colleges may require neither a deposit nor a written commitment as a condition of remaining on a waitlist.

- Colleges are expected to notify you of the resolution of your waitlist status by Aug. 1 at the latest.

Source: The National Association for College Admission Counseling

http://www.nacacnet.org/

27 - YOU ARE ACCEPTED TO COLLEGE...HOW DO YOU DECIDE WHERE TO GO?

Congratulations, you have been accepted into your colleges, now how do you decide where to send your deposit? You are at a crossroad and choosing a college can be a difficult task. It is time to make your well-researched and well-matched decision.

Here are common mistakes that are made when choosing a college:

- Choosing a college because your high school sweetheart or best friend is going there.

- Your parents are alumni and you want to please them, but will it be the right choice for you?

- The website or brochure looks great and you have not visited. Don't just rely on online matching. When possible, check it out first hand.

- Choosing a school solely on prestige and reputation. Look at "fit," major, and opportunities while defining your criteria.

- Picking a college because you love their sports team and you have been wearing their logo on your clothing since you were seven years old.

- Tuition is low. Don't forget to compare packages and talk to the financial aid office you have further questions about your award letter. Consider all factors when making your decision.

- It's a school known for partying. While school should be fun, it is also a place for you to learn new ideas and earn your degree.

- Choosing a college because someone told you to. Opinions vary from person to person, so form your own opinion.

- Deciding on a school to spite or to impress someone.

- Do not be scared to move away from home. Though location is important, take advantage of this growing experience and this time to expand your horizons.

Good reasons for choosing a college may include: it feels like where you belong; it reflects your values and interests; it challenges you and provides you the opportunity to learn more about yourself; and lastly, the college will prepare you with skills that ready you for life.

28 - HOW TO HANDLE COLLEGE REJECTION

Handling rejection is never easy. As a matter of fact, it can be pretty devastating unless you prepare yourself ahead of time. Many students apply to a variety of schools. Some "shoot for the stars" while also applying to realistic colleges they would also be happy at; ones that are in-line with their abilities.

This month, the majority of college decisions will arrive home. While there might be a jubilant celebration for admittance to an institution, there also might be disappointment. The college application process is a time of transition and growth, and rejection may be part of the process.

If you receive a rejection letter there are several ways to work through the disappointment.

- Read the rejection letter carefully to make sure you have actually been completely rejected.

- React however you feel. Talk to someone you trust who will listen to your feelings. Everyone has dealt with rejection some time in his or her life.

- Do not take it personally. Colleges may have had many similar applicants with a limited number of seats to fill.

- Reappraise the situation and decide how to solve this issue by seeking feedback on your application from the guidance counselors or college admissions office itself. Understand how you can improve on your application should you apply in the future.

- If you contact the admissions office, ask if they have an appeal process. If so, follow through on their suggestions and to see if they will reconsider your admissions status. If the appeal process doesn't work, that's okay too.

- Check out if you can be admitted on a summer probationary basis.

- Rejection isn't fatal— you can appeal, postpone, reapply, or transfer.

- Remind yourself you are a worthy candidate for many colleges and you do have excellent qualifications for college.

- Avoid the temptation to stew in anger or wallow in sadness. Visit the colleges where you have been accepted; develop a new plan, and put a positive spin on the experience.

- Remember, it is not the end of the world. Students rebound and often console each other in these situations. Sometimes it is a blessing in disguise, and there are many paths down the road to success.

- Look six months down the road ... in September you will be moving into a dorm, meeting your roommate, wearing new school gear, and promising your parents you will have contact with them at least once a week.

Tip for parents—young adults are relatively new to this and will follow your lead on how to handle disappointments. Be excited about the schools who said "Yes!"

29 - CAN I APPEAL THE ADMISSIONS DECISION?

You may be asking yourself if you can appeal a decision of denial from a college. There may be a chance you can. Some colleges have very strict policies stating if you were denied acceptance to their institution, the decision stands and there is no appeal process. Other colleges will allow for an appeal. My suggestion would be to contact the college directly to see if this is an option. Check their website or speak directly to the admissions office.

If you have a legitimate reason to appeal, you may want to discuss this with your admissions representative. Some of the circumstances that might warrant a review could include:

- Significant new information that was not presented at admission time such as new test scores, major awards, clerical errors, inaccurate information on your transcript, and reasons outside your control.

The following scenarios are often grounds for an appeal not to be offered:

- You want the admissions office to review your application again.

- A friend got in with a similar application as you.

- Your scores and grades fall into the range listed in their information (but grades and test scores are not the only thing college's review).

- You received acceptances in what you feel are more competitive schools.

- The decision was unfair.

If you can write for an appeal, what should you do next?

- Write a letter addressing new information. Include a reason for the appeal, new semester grades, an additional teacher, counselor, coach or moderator recommendation.

- Correct any errors and update information from your original application including any personal circumstances the admissions office may need to know about.

- Act quickly and send all documentation in one envelope registered mail and meet the appeal deadlines which may be around April 15.

- Be realistic – the reason to appeal must be exceptional!

Only spend your time on this process unless you feel your position is truly unique.

30 - WHAT IS "DOUBLE DEPOSITING?" IS IT ETHICAL?

The clock is ticking down and the April 1st has arrived. High school seniors across the country are checking their email and mailboxes for the admissions decisions from the college they applied to. Many students may receive more than one acceptance. The stress and the cost of college is a major decision, so for students who cannot make up their mind where to go, they may consider double depositing.

What is the definition of double depositing? Double depositing means putting down a deposit, and thus accepting admission, at more than one college.

I often hear, "This decision is not easy!" Or "I love all my schools for different reasons." Student should re-visit their colleges and look to teachers and friends (and even parents) for guidance. So what do they do? Sending a non-refundable enrollment deposit check can cost as little as $100, while at others it can be as much as $500 or $1,000 can be costly, but the student just can't decide.

The main reasons are:

- Students may do this to guarantee themselves a space at their favorite school.

- Buying time. The usual decision deadline is May 1; by double depositing, a student can delay deciding until fall.

- To continue negotiating for financial aid past the deadline.

- Because the student is on a waiting list at one college and wants to ensure that he or she is enrolled somewhere in case he or she is turned down by the waiting-list school. This scenario is the only one in which NACAC considers double depositing acceptable.

What many of these students and their parents don't know is that double depositing is a violation of their responsibilities as established by the National Association for College Admission Counseling (NACAC).

So, why is double depositing unethical?

- It is deceitful according to NACAC guidelines.

- It is unfair to the college. Colleges don't know how to estimate the size of the incoming class.

- It is unfair to other applicants. The double depositor is taking up a spot that could go to another student, who will instead be wait-listed or turned down.

- Playing a dangerous game. If a college discovers a student double deposited, it is within its rights to withdraw that individual's offer of admission.

31 - TRANSFER PLANNING

Are you thinking about transferring from one college to another? Answering the following questions will help you decide your next move:

- Did you take enough time to adjust to the academics and social life at your present college? Do you understand why you are making the change – homesickness, monetary needs, family issues?

- Do you understand the transfer process to the college you would like to attend?

- Have you gotten advice from your present school? They may be able to address credit transfer issues that will be important in the admission to the next school.

- Do you have transfer plans? Does the next school have your major? What credits will transfer? Talk to your advisor.

- Have you done your research? Have you found a better "fit" for you?

- Have you taken the core curriculum needed to make the change? Check into your field of study.

- Do you meet the universities' requirements to switch from one school environment to the next? Talk to the admissions representative at the school you're applying to. Send transcripts and test scores if applicable.

Transferring from a Community College – A Checklist

If a student is planning to transfer from a community college to a four year program, he or she should check with his or her advisor to see what credits will transfer. Here is a list of things to do:

☐ Request transcripts

☐ Complete school application

☐ Search for scholarships

☐ Complete departmental application if needed

☐ File the FAFSA online – request PIN

☐ Complete other financial aid forms

☐ Review and return financial aid award letter

☐ Apply and endorse loans if needed (Stafford, PLUS, private)

☐ Develop a budget and stick to it.

College Transfer Information - Information on transferring from one college to another.

http://search.collegeboard.com/servlet/sitesearch?mss=cb&kl=XX&i=CBI&searchType=site&q=transfer

32 - ENRICHMENT OPPORTUNITIES AND SUMMER PROGRAMS

There are many opportunities in the summer for students to explore educational, artistic, or cultural interests. Through these programs students can develop a talent, pursue a hobby, or experience a different culture. Students can also demonstrate to colleges that they have an interest in development outside the classroom. The cost and dates for summer programs vary greatly. Below is just a sampling of what is available.

Pre-College Programs

Universities and Colleges are always creating summer programs. Be sure to check the colleges you may be interested in to see if they have a program for you. Here are a few suggestions:

Adelphi University
http://academics.adelphi.edu/hsp/precollege/

Alfred University
http://www.alfred.edu/summer/hs.cfm

American University
http://www.american.edu/sis/precollege/index.htm

American School TASIS, Switzerland
http://www.tasis.com/

Art Institute of Boston
http://www.lesley.edu/aib/curriculum/precollege.html

ASA
http://www.asaprograms.com/

Barnard College
http://www.barnard.edu/

Baylor University
http://www.baylor.edu/summerscience/

Blueprint Admissions
http://www.bpadmissions.com/

Boston College
http://www.bc.edu/schools/summer/bce/

Boston University
http://www.bu.edu/summer/program_high_school_students/

Brandeis University
http://www.brandeis.edu/

Brown University

http://www.brown.edu/scs/pre-college/

California College of the Arts

http://www.cca.edu/academics/precollege

Cal Tech

http://www.capsi.caltech.edu/

Calvin College

http://www.calvin.edu/admin/precoll/academy/

Cambridge College, England

http://www.cambridgecollegeprogramme.org/

Carleton College

http://apps.carleton.edu/summer/clae/

Carnegie Mellon

http://www.cmu.edu/enrollment/pre-college/

Clemson University

http://www.clemson.edu/summer/

Columbia College Chicago

http://www.colum.edu/

Columbia University

http://www.ce.columbia.edu/hs

Converse College

http://www.converse.edu/summerworkshops

Cornell University

http://www.sce.cornell.edu/sc/

Davidson

http://www3.davidson.edu/cms/x3808.xml

Duke

http://www.learnmore.duke.edu/youth/

Earlham

http://www.earlham.edu/~eac/

Emerson College Professional Studies

http://www.emerson.edu/academics/professional-studies

Emory University

http://www.college.emory.edu/program/precollege/

Fashion Institute of Technology

http://www.fitnyc.edu/5915.asp

Ferrum College
http://www2.ferrum.edu/fcsec/

Fordham University
http://www.fordham.edu/academics/summer_session/

Furman University
http://www.furman.edu/campsandconferences/camps.htm

Georgetown
http://www12.georgetown.edu/scs/sphs/index.cfm

Governor's School
http://ncogs.org/web/index.php/View-users-list/All-Governor-s-School-
Programs

Hampton University
http://www.hamptonu.edu/academics/summer/precollege/

Hofstra University
http://www.hofstra.edu/Academics/CCEPA/SC/Index.html

Hollins University
http://www.hollins.edu/summerprograms/hollinsummer/

Indiana University
http://summer.indiana.edu/index.php?nodeID=precollege&programsID=36

Ithaca College
http://www.ithaca.edu/gps/summer_college/

Johns Hopkins
http://cty.jhu.edu/summer/summer-programs.html

Julliard
http://www.juilliard.edu/precollege/precollege.html

Kettering University
http://www.kettering.edu/futurestudents/precollege/

Lake Forest University
http://www.lakeforest.edu/academics/summer/wtw/

Lewis University
http://www.lewisu.edu/admissions/visits/undergraduate/summerpreview/

Loyola University
http://www.luc.edu/summer/

Marist College
http://www.marist.edu/summerinstitutes/

Marymount Manhattan
http://summer.mmm.edu/summer-college-nyc.html

Middlebury Language Programs
http://www.middlebury.edu/academics/ls/mmla.htm

Missouri University of Science and Technology
http://precollege.mst.edu/mets/index.html

NC State University
http://www.ncsu.edu/summer/

NJ Science Institute of Technology
http://www.njit.edu/precollege/about/index.php

Northland College
http://www.northland.edu/academics-specialty-program-upward-bound.htm

Northwestern
http://www.ctd.northwestern.edu/

Notre Dame
http://precollege.nd.edu/

NYU
http://specialprograms.tisch.nyu.edu/page/hsStudents.html

Pace University
http://pace.edu/page.cfm?doc_id=9934

Oxbridge, England
http://www.oxbridgeprograms.com/index.php

Parsons
http://www.parsons.edu/pre_enrollment/summer_precollege.aspx

Penn State University
http://www.ems.psu.edu/educational_equity/programs

Pratt
http://www.pratt.edu/ccps-precollege

Princeton
http://www.princeton.edu/sjp/

Ramapo College
http://www.ramapo.edu/summer/

Rensselaer Polytechnic Institute
http://summer.rpi.edu/update.do

Rhode Island School of Design
http://www.risd.edu/precollege.cfm

Ringling College of Art and Design
http://www.ringling.edu/PreCollege.77.0.html

San Diego State

http://www-rohan.sdsu.edu/dept/sdsutrio/index.html

Savannah College of Art and Design

http://www.scad.edu/savannah/summerprograms/index.cfm

School of Visual Arts

http://www.schoolofvisualarts.edu/adm/index.jsp?sid0=4&sid1=63

Sea Education Association

http://www.sea.edu/academics/program_highschoolprograms.asp

Skidmore College

http://cms.skidmore.edu/odsp/programs/precollegiate/index.cfm

Smith College

http://www.smith.edu/summerprograms/ssep/index.php

Southern Methodist University

http://smu.edu/education/youth/summeryouth/

Southern Oregon University

http://www.sou.edu/youth/high_school.html

Sterling College

http://www.sterlingcollege.edu/AD.summerfarm.html

Stevens Institute of Technology

http://www.stevens.edu/undergrad/summer

Syracuse University

http://www.summercollege.syr.edu/

The Catholic University of America

http://summer.cua.edu/precollege/

The College of Saint Rose

http://www.strose.edu/Future_Students/Adult_Continuing_Education/Summer_Academy/default.asp

The College of William and Mary

http://www.wm.edu/academics/precollege/index.php

Thomas More College

http://www.thomasmorecollege.edu/index.php?/content/view/37/41/

Tisch School, NYU

http://clivedavisdept.tisch.nyu.edu/object/recmusicsum.html

Transylvania University

http://www.transy.edu/about/camps.htm

Tufts

http://ase.tufts.edu/summer/

Tuskegee
http://www.tuskegee.edu/Global/story.asp?S=1172479

Tyler School of Art
http://www.temple.edu/tyler/spi/

United States Naval Academy
http://www.usna.edu/admissions/stem.html

University of Arkansas
http://precollege.uark.edu/menu.html

University of California, Davis
http://ysp.ucdavis.edu/

University of California System (Math & Science)
http://www.ucop.edu/cosmos/

University of California, Santa Barbara
http://www.summer.ucsb.edu/precollegeprograms.html

University of Chicago
http://summer.uchicago.edu/

University of Iowa
http://www.continuetolearn.uiowa.edu/ccp/summer/summer_youth_programs.htm

University of Maryland
http://www.precollege.umd.edu/

University of Miami
http://www6.miami.edu/summerscholar/

University of Michigan
http://www.umich.edu/summer_prog.php

University of Pennsylvania
http://www.sas.upenn.edu/lps/highschool/summer

University of Richmond
http://summer.richmond.edu/scholars/

University of Southern California
http://cesp.usc.edu/

University of the Arts
http://cesp.usc.edu/

University of Vermont
http://www.uvm.edu/~summer/

University of Virginia
http://fusion.web.virginia.edu/yww/index.cfm

Upward Bound

http://www.ed.gov/programs/trioupbound/index.html

Washington University

http://ucollege.wustl.edu/programs/highschool

William and Mary

http://www.wm.edu/

Wright State

http://www.wright.edu/academics/precollege/ricc/riclasses.html

Yale

http://www.yale.edu/summer/programs/

Other Summer Opportunities or Study Abroad Programs

Academic Treks

http://www.academictreks.com/

American Colleges Overseas

http://www.aco.eu.com/

American Institute of Foreign Study

http://www.studyoverseas.com/

AmeriCorps

http://www.americorps.org/

Architecture Programs

http://www.aia.org/ed_k12programs

Australian Universities

http://www.study-australia.com/?id=515

Community Service for Latino Americans

http://www.amigoslink.org/

Cybercamps

http://www.cybercamps.com/

Dynamy

http://www.dynamy.org/

Earthwatch

http://www.earthwatch.org/

Education Unlimited

http://www.educationunlimited.com/

Experiment International

http://www.experimentinternational.org/

Explo

http://www.explo.org/

Gap Year Experience-Global Awareness with Carpe Diem Education
http://carpediemeducation.org/about.php

Gap Year Programs
http://www.gapyearprograms.net/

Glimpse of China
http://www.foundationprograms.com/

Global Service Corps
http://www.globalservicecorps.org/

ID Tech
http://www.internaldrive.com/index.php

Interim Programs
http://www.interimprograms.com/

International Student
http://www.internationalstudent.com/

Julian Krinsky Pre-College Summer Camps
http://www.jkcp.com/camps/highschool-pre-college.php

Leap Now
http://www.leapnow.org/

Map the Gap International
https://www.mapthegapinternational.com/index.html

National Outdoor Leadership School
http://www.nols.edu/

Outward Bound
http://www.outwardbound.org/

Peterson's Guide to Summer Programs
http://www.petersons.com/summerop/code/ssector.asp?spons

Planet Gap Year
http://www.planetgapyear.com/

Teen Ink
http://www.teenink.com/Summer/

Thinking Beyond Borders
http://www.thinkingbeyondborders.org/

Semester at Sea
http://www.semesteratsea.org/

Study Abroad
http://www.studyabroad.com/

Study Overseas

http://www.studyoverseas.com/

Study in Canada

http://www.studyincanada.com/english/index.asp

Summer Institute for the Gifted

http://www.giftedstudy.org/

Traveling Abroad

http://www.edupass.org/

TRIO Federal Talent Search Program

http://www2.ed.gov/programs/triotalent/index.html

Volunteer Organizations – Servenet

http://www.servenet.org/

Check out local associations like **Hands on Atlanta Volunteer Corp** for volunteer opportunities. http://www.handsonatlanta.org/

NOTES

NOTES

CHAPTER 5

Special Admission Topics

1. Visual and Performing Arts

2. A General Guide to Types of Degrees in the Arts

3. Recruited Athletes

4. Military Options

5. How to Apply to the Military Service Academies

6. Cooperative Education Programs or "Co-ops"

7. The College Search for Students with Disabilities

8. Gay and Lesbian College Students

9. Homeschooled – Navigating the Next Step

10. The Value of Community Service

11. "Gap Year," Volunteerism, and Study Abroad

12. Study Abroad Checklist

13. Distance Learning: Earning a Degree Online

14. Advantages of a Women's College and Other Special Programs

15. Understanding Pre-Professional Programs

16. Combined Degree (3:2) Programs

17. Social Networking Tips for Students – More on Facebook

18. Handling "Senioritis"

19. Reporting Disciplinary Incidents to Colleges

Whether you are interested in the arts, athletics, the military, or taking a "gap year," there are several parts of the college application process that need to be completed. This chapter will address aspects of the fine arts (dramatic arts, dance, studio art, or music), athletic recruiting, and the military application process. Issues such as disabilities and the college search, the transition from home school to the college, and studying abroad or online will be discussed. Students must make many choices. Sometimes that entails the type of college they may want to attend such as a women's college or choosing a college that has special programs like pre-professional or dual degree programs. Whatever choice a student makes, he or she will need to know how to combat "senioritis," a situation that can creep up on students unknowingly in their senior year of high school. Lastly, the topic will be how to address discipline issues with colleges.

1 - VISUAL AND PERFORMING ARTS

Like athletes, students thinking about attending art school or a conservatory in one of the performing arts have many additional details to pay attention to in the application process. Below are some things to consider, and some helpful hints as you explore options for your education after high school. Most high school students interested in the fine arts will attend liberal arts colleges with strong art and/or performing arts departments. Other students will prefer conservatories or art schools. Our recommendation is always to include several liberal arts colleges on your list even if you are primarily interested in a conservatory. This will provide you with flexibility should you change your mind about your educational plans before the end of your senior year; it also helps ensure that you will have college options, since conservatory and art school admissions are extremely difficult to predict.

2 - A GENERAL GUIDE TO TYPES OF DEGREES IN THE ARTS

Even schools offering the same degrees may have very different structures and programs. For example, many art schools offering BFAs have highly structured foundation years, while other schools offering BFAs have no such prescribed program.

In general, if you want to continue studying subjects other than those in the arts (e.g., French literature, or economics, or the sciences), then a liberal arts college is definitely the right choice. Only students ready for pre-professional training should consider a conservatory approach.

- How can you know whether a conservatory or art school is right for you? We recommend that, if you have not yet done so, you strongly consider enrolling in an intensive summer program in your area of interest. You need to experience what it is like to "do art" (or music or theater or dance) all day (and often all evening) long; this is what your life will be like at a conservatory. If you love the experience, that's good to know; if you don't, that's just as important to realize. Talent is not enough; energy, confidence, courage, and endurance are just as important.

- Once you have decided that, you would like to include some conservatories on your list, use the Internet, guidebooks, and of course teachers and other knowledgeable people to find the programs that suit you best.

- Make visits to those schools that interest you before the date is set for an audition or portfolio review, so that you can see the place without having to worry about anything else. Facilities are very important for artists, as are advising and career counseling. Ask many questions. For example, did you know that many of the most competitive theater programs eliminate students at the end of the first or second year, keeping through until graduation only a select few? Can you live with that level of risk?

- Ask your current teachers about your level of talent and what they think your prospects may be. More importantly, you need to do a frank assessment of yourself. Many an accomplished professional had to persevere despite negative feedback, little support, and poor reviews.

- Finally, remember that there are many fine graduate programs in the visual and the performing arts. A foundation in the liberal arts can do wonders to deepen your craft as an artist, actor, or even a singer. The exceptions to this include dance and instrumental music, which are more highly dependent on intensive training at a younger age.

Artists/Musicians/Actors

Supplementary materials may be needed for the application process if you are interested in applying to the arts in college. Each section below will offer suggestions about each particular area of interest.

Artists

- Create a portfolio of art work; check college requirements for submission of size, type, and format of work.

- Refine your skills in art classes.

- Sign up for art history. If your school doesn't offer it, look into classes at the local community college or university.

- Visit museums and galleries at home and on vacation.

- Pay attention in English: you'll use writing skills to craft everything from artist's statements to grant applications.

- Take business and accounting courses to build skills you'll use in managing your career.

- Join the stage crew to get experience building and painting on a large scale.

- Work on the yearbook and newspaper staff to learn about the role of art in publishing.

- If your state has a Governor's School for the arts, compete for a place in it.

- Click here for list of Art Colleges and University Programs in the US. http://www.uscollegesearch.org/art-colleges.html

Musicians

- Create and send a CD or cassette with name and address, instrument (or voice), work's title and composer to department at college.

- Create a resume indicating how long you have trained, any ensemble or solo experience, and future plans for involvement in college.

- Listen to lots of music – and not just the kind you're already familiar with. Add new sounds – from Argentine tango to Appalachian fiddling – to your musical toolkit.

- Read the biographies of composers.

- Sign up for music theory and history classes.

- Visit a website such as Young Composers where you can listen to recordings by peers, join a chat session, and submit your own compositions. http://www.youngcomposers.com/

- Take voice or instrument lessons.

- Join a band. You can understand a great deal about composing by seeing how a group of musicians learns the score of an accomplished composer.

- Click for List of Music Colleges, Universities and Conservatories in the US. http://en.wikipedia.org/wiki/List_of_colleges_and_university_schools_of_music_in_the_United_States

Theatre and Dance Students

Send a videocassette of a performance; think about including contrasting monologues. Create a resume of titles of works performed, your training, and experience.

Theatre

- Act, dance, and sing in high school productions of such stage classics as Evita and Death of a Salesman.

- Take drama and theater classes at your high school. If these classes are not offered, look into taking acting classes at a community center.

- Make the most of English; learn how to read and analyze a wide range of plays.

- Work for your high school radio station.

- Perform with local theater groups.

- Attend acting-camp or summer acting workshops.

- Click here for Drama and Theater Arts Programs in Colleges and Universities in the US. http://www.uscollegesearch.org/drama-/-theater-arts-general-colleges.html

Dance

- Take dance and drama classes at your high school. If these classes are not offered, look into classes at local community centers or private dance studios.

- Practice at least two different types of dance, such as ballet and modern.

- Dance and act in high school productions.

- Train and perform with community dance groups.

- Enroll in a summer dance camp or workshop.

- Attend as many professional dance performances as possible.

- Learn about good nutrition, cross-training, and other ways of taking care of your body.

- Click here for Dance Programs in Colleges and Universities across the US. http://www.uscollegesearch.org/dance-colleges-6.html

3 - RECRUITED ATHLETES

The Recruited Athlete

Athletic talent can provide opportunities for student athletes in the college search process. While it can present unique advantages for students, it also can bring unique challenges. The following guidelines should help to answer some basic questions about the recruiting process.

- If you are an athlete who desires the opportunity to play at the collegiate level, you must speak to your high school and/or outside coach regarding your ability level. Ask your coach for an honest and realistic assessment of your prospects in collegiate athletics. At which level does he or she believe you can compete? You should use the information as a guideline for targeting schools at which you can realistically compete.

- After speaking to your coach, you should begin to create a balanced preliminary list of schools based on your athletic ability. For example, if your coach's assessment places you at the Division III level, you should begin to think about most Division I schools as "reach" schools and some Division III schools as "probable" and "possible" schools in terms of your athletic ability. Five of each is a good place to start.

- Athletic recruiting is not a science, so you should continue to pursue all options until the official recruiting process begins during your senior year. Once you have identified a preliminary list of schools, you should visit each athletic website of those schools to complete the prospective-athlete questionnaire online and begin contacts with the coaches.

- All schools do not have a questionnaire online; some will have a paper form, but you should complete the necessary data for each school. This data will be placed in the individual school database and will supply each school's coaching staff with your contact data.

- This is a preliminary step in the recruiting process that only places your name in a database and does not mean that you are going to be recruited by the school. Thousands of students fill out these forms, but it is necessary to get the information to the schools in which you have interest. Be sure to include involvement with club teams or other teams outside of school.

- Once you have visited some college campuses and have identified some of your favorite schools, you should contact the coaching staff at those schools to learn about the possibility of attending a camp in the summer of your sophomore or junior year.

- Athletic camps give the individual coaching staffs the opportunity to evaluate you as a potential player at that particular school. Although coaches do evaluate students who attend their summer camps, they do not limit their recruiting to those students. Be careful. They can "hurt" or "help" depending on your camp. Camp is not like a game situation.

- If you do attend a camp, you should take the opportunity to speak to the college coaches about your ability as a player. They will be able to provide you with feedback regarding your potential as an athlete at the collegiate level.

- You must be proactive in the recruiting process and market yourself. While your coach will be helpful in the process, you must take the lead and contact coaches at the schools for whom you wish to play.

- Please use the assessment your high school and/or outside coach provided you as a guiding factor in your decision regarding which colleges may be a good match athletically as well as academically.

- Please be advised that the only other time before the application process that you will be able to be seen by college coaches will be in the summer. Thus, you must notify coaches when you have contests so they can have the opportunity to evaluate your ability.

- You should request a copy of your best game film to send to coaches upon their request. Your coach should be able to help you with this process.

- Develop a sports resume including your statistics, SAT /ACT scores, grade point average, and coursework.

- During your junior year, email is the best way to remain in contact with coaches. For most sports, July 1 of the summer before your senior year is the earliest that coaches are able to call you on the phone or speak with you in person when they are traveling on the road.

- If you intend on competing in athletics at the Division I or II level, you must register with the NCAA Eligibility Center. Preferably, register by the end of the summer prior to the senior year. Request a transcript be sent to NCAA through your Athletic Office. http://eligibilitycenter.org/ECWR2/NCAA_EMS/NCAA.html

Senior Year Guidelines for Athletes

- You may begin to feel as though you are being recruited when college coaches contact you over the telephone or by email. Understand that coaches will contact a large number of athletes. If you are offered an official visit to a Division I level school, it may be an indication of strong interest on the part of the coach; however, this does not automatically result in an offer. You are restricted to taking only five official visits at the Division I and II levels combined.

- An official visit is one that is paid in part or in full by the college. An unofficial visit is one in which the student incurs the cost of travel, food and lodging and does not count against your five official visit opportunities.

- There are no restrictions to the number of overnight visits you can take at the Division III level. Thus, the level of commitment from coaches at the Division III level is not as strong as at the Division I and II levels in terms of the visit.

- In some cases, coaches will push you toward deciding to apply to their school Early Action or Early Decision. You must understand that they are also encouraging other athletes they are recruiting to do the same, and therefore admission is not guaranteed. If you elect not to apply early, know that if a coach only has "x" spaces and if "x" players are admitted, he or she has completed the recruiting for the year.

- This is by no means a reason to apply early, but it is a reality of the recruiting process. You should not apply Early Decision to a college unless you are 100% sure it is the right school for you. If you are offered a visit and elect to take it, you need to ask direct questions of the coaches.

More for Athletes

- Will I receive a likely letter of admission? (Division 1 only) A likely letter states that you are "likely" to be admitted to the institution unless your performance drops in or out of the classroom. (These are offered mostly at Ivy League and Patriot League institutions.)

- Has the admission office deemed me as an "admissible student" through an early read process?

- Has an admission officer reviewed my application and made a decision?

- Where am I on your recruitment board?

- Many coaches rank order their players in terms of their needs, positions, etc. How many athletes are you supporting and what does your support mean in the admission process?

- Choose the school that is the right place for you; coaching is a unique profession, and coaches tend to switch college positions often. Choose the college for the community and the program, not for the coach you most admire.

- Do you get slots? Are there academic bands?

- The athletic recruiting system is not designed to protect you as a student athlete; instead, it is designed to protect the schools and the coaches. No matter how supportive a coach may seem, only the admission office can make the final decision.

- The recruiting process is not over until you receive an official letter of acceptance from the admission office. For example, even if a coach brought your application to the admission office for a pre-read, even if admissions deemed you acceptable, and even if the coach guarantees his or her full support of your application, there is still a chance you may not be accepted to the school. It is imperative that you continue to work with all parties involved in your college process to craft a balanced list of schools that you believe will offer you a successful and enjoyable experience.

- A Division I level recruit may be asked to sign a National Letter of Intent. Because restrictions exist upon signing an N.L.I., it is critical that the student read the letter carefully and share it with his or her parents, coaches, and college counselor.

- Throughout a recruitment cycle, a college coach's recruiting list can change dramatically. Needs of the team, academic credentials of the recruits, and interest—or lack thereof—of the recruits can all play a major role in the shifting of a recruitment list. Communicate with coaches to gain a sense of where you stand on their list. It may become clear—if the communication is not reciprocated—that you may not fit in the recruiting scheme of a particular coach or program.

- First, remember that there are many talented athletes out there who are competing for the same scholarships the student is hoping to receive. The student may need to walk on at a college to get the opportunity he or she desires. Secondly, the student should not overlook some of the benefits that walk-on athletes enjoy that are similar to full-scholarship athletes: first choice of classes, preferred housing, and more. Finally, being a walk-on athlete doesn't mean that the student can't be the star. If he or she is committed to his or her athletic and academic career at the college level and the student can get the chance to show a coach his or her talent-- anything can happen.

- The student should contact coaches at the colleges his or her they might be interested in pursuing and find out what opportunities exist. Ask about the college's walk-on policy, and find out how the college awards scholarships. Doing this will answer many questions and will allow the student to approach the final months of his or her high school career with an eye toward college athletic opportunities.

Websites for Athletes

Source: Website descriptions are taken directly from the individual websites.

- **Be Recruited** - Join the largest and most successful online network connecting high school athletes and college coaches. Register for FREE today to: Create a profile to market your ability to college coaches, research athletic scholarships and college academic standards, and Find the college program that is right for you. http://www.berecruited.com/

- **College-Athletic Scholarships** - Search for athletic scholarships in all sports on all levels. http://www.college-athletic-scholarships.com/

- **Home School Legal Defense Association** - If you want to play college athletics and you have been homeschooled, this site is for you. http://www.hslda.org/docs/news/hslda/200112120.asp

- **National Association of Intercollegiate Athletics (NAIA)** - The NAIA promotes the education and development of students through intercollegiate athletic participation. Member institutions, although varied and diverse, share a common commitment to high standards and to the principle that participation in athletics serves as an integral part of the total educational process. http://naia.cstv.com/

- **National Junior College Athletic Association** - The NJCAA is the governing body of intercollegiate athletics for two-year colleges. Its programs are designed to meet the unique needs of a diverse group of student-athletes who come from both traditional and non-traditional backgrounds. http://www.njcaa.org/

- **National Letter of Intent** - Explanation of what the letter means to the student-athlete. http://www.ncaa.org/wps/wcm/connect/nli/nli

- **NCAA Eligibility Center** - A prospective student-athlete is someone who is looking to participate in intercollegiate athletics at an NCAA Division I or Division II institution in the future. https://web1.ncaa.org/eligibilitycenter/common/

- **NCAA Online Student Guide** - An excellent online guide for students. http://www.ncaastudent.org/

- **NCAA** –Div I, II, III - Sports/College List - The website for finding schools in Divisions I, II, and III according to sports category. http://web1.ncaa.org/onlineDir/exec/sponsorship

- **NCAA's Quick Reference Sheet for Student Athletes** - http://fs.ncaa.org/Docs/eligibility_center/Quick_Reference_Sheet.pdf

- **Sports Resumes** - Review sample sports resumes. http://www.sportsresumes.org/

- **Women's Sports Foundation** - A leading authority on the participation of women and girls in sports—advocates for equality, educates the public, conducts research and offers grants to promote sports and physical activity for girls and women. http://www.womenssportsfoundation.org/Issues-And-Research/Title-IX/What-is-Title-IX.aspx

Glossary, Terms, and Definitions

Contact – Any face-to-face encounter, which is more than a greeting, between a prospect or his or her parents, relatives or legal guardian(s) and a university staff member or an athletic office representative. A meeting that is prearranged or takes place at the prospect's school, competition site or practice site is considered a contact regardless of the conversation that occurs.

Evaluation – Any off-campus activity that assesses the academic qualifications or the athletic ability of a prospect. It includes any visit to a prospect's school (during which no contact with prospect occurs) or watching a practice or competition at any site where the prospect participates.

Contact Period – Period of time when it is permissible for authorized athletics department staff to make in-person, off-campus recruiting contacts and evaluations of a prospect.

Evaluation Period – Period of time when authorized athletics department staff may be involved in off-campus activities designed to assess the academic qualifications and athletic ability of prospects. No in-person, off-campus recruiting contacts shall be made with the prospect during an evaluation period.

Quiet Period – Period of time when it is permissible to make in-person recruiting contacts only on the institution's campus. No in-person, off-campus recruiting contacts or evaluations may be made during the quiet period.

Dead Period – The period of time when it is not permissible to make in-person recruiting contacts or evaluations on or off campus. In addition, there can be no official or unofficial visits to the campus by a prospect. However, it is permissible for a staff member to write or phone a prospect during this period.

Extra Benefit – Any special arrangement by either the university or its representatives to provide student-athletes, their friends, or their relatives with any benefits not expressly authorized by the NCAA. A benefit is not considered a violation if it is one that is generally available to the students determined on a basis unrelated to athletic ability.

Full-Time Program – A student-athlete must be enrolled in no fewer than 12 semester hours during the time of competition. This rule has limited exceptions.

Official Visit – A visit financed in whole or in part by the university.

Unofficial Visit – A visit made at the prospect's own expense. The university may provide only limited benefits to the prospect during his visit. These benefits include complimentary admissions to an on-campus athletics event in which the institution's team competes and transportation to view off-campus practice or competition sites within a 30-mile radius of the institution's campus when accompanied by a staff member. The provision of any other expenses or entertainment shall require the visit to become an official visit.

4 - MILITARY OPTIONS

Every year thousands of young men and women make the choice to serve their country. They enjoy a military career by enlisting in one of the following branches: Air Force, Army, Coast Guard, Marines, Navy, US Merchant Marine Academy, and National Guard. Some individuals will apply directly to a four year service academy such as U.S. Military Academy-West Point, New York; U.S. Naval Academy in Annapolis, Maryland; the Air Force Academy in Denver, Colorado; and the Coast Guard Academy in Groton, Connecticut. Completing your education at one of these programs will earn you a bachelor's degree, commissioned reserve officer status, and a commitment to the military for a number of years. Another option is applying to a Reserve Officers' Training Corps (ROTC) scholarship program at a college.

http://www.airforce.com/

http://www.goarmy.com/#/?channel=careers&marquee=strongStories
http://www.uscg.mil/default.asp
http://www.marines.mil/Pages/Default.aspx
http://www.navy.mil/
http://www.usmma.edu/
http://www.arng.army.mil/

These are two-, three-, and four-year scholarship programs that help you decide which direction you would like to pursue (ROTC College Profiles). http://www.collegeprofiles.com/rotc.html

The Reserve Officer Training Corp - ROTC

Scholarships and stipends in Navy, Air Force, and Army ROTC help you focus on what is important. Namely, getting that college degree — not how you will pay for it. You graduate with a degree and serve in the U.S. Military as a commissioned Officer.

ROTC Scholarships

Whether you are a college-bound high school student or already attending a college or university, ROTC has scholarships available. Scholarships are awarded based on a student's merit and grades, not financial need.

ROTC scholarships consist of:

- Two-year, three-year, and four-year scholarship options based on the time remaining to complete your degree

- Full-tuition scholarships

- The option for room and board in place of tuition, if you should qualify

- Additional allowances for books and fees

Upon graduation and completion of the ROTC program, you will be a commissioned officer in your selected service. Your commitment for service will range from 2-5 years depending on the time your scholarship was in effect during your college education.

Thinking about Enlisting?

Questions a student needs to ask himself or herself include, "Is the military right for me?" and "In which branch do I have the most interest?" Are you interested in travel, job security, technical training, or money for college, or a good paying job? Finding out the facts about each of your options is the next step.

Contact your local recruiter and ask about:

- The length of enlistment

- Advanced pay grade

- Length and type of training

- Enlistment bonuses

- Other pay and allowance; ability to pursue higher education

- Taking the ASVAB - a battery of tests that will help you identify a vocation - http://www.military.com/ASVAB

There are several ways to pay for your education if you choose this career path. See the following websites:

Source: Website descriptions are taken directly from the individual websites.

- **Access to Military Service and Pension Records** - Information about how to get copies of military service records from the National Archives and Records Administration (NARA), the official repository for those records. http://www.archives.gov/research/order/order-vets-records.html

- **Center for Women Veterans (US Dept. of Veterans Affairs)** - The Center for Women Veterans, within the Department of Veterans Affairs (VA), is the primary advisor all programs, issues, and initiatives for and affecting women veterans. Good links and resources for women veterans. http://www.va.gov/womenvet/

- Chapter 33 GI Bill Education Benefits - Individuals who are eligible for the new Post - 9/11 GI education benefits may begin using the benefits August 1, 2009 for training that begins on or after that date. GI Bill http://gibill.va.gov/resources/benefits_resources/benefit_comparison_tools.html

- **DUSA Scholarships** - The Society of Daughters of the U.S. Army (DUSA) offers $1,000 scholarships to the daughters and granddaughters of active duty or retired Army officers. Find out if you're eligible and how to apply.

http://www.studentscholarships.org/foundation/24415/dusa_schol
arships.php

- **Education Center (US Army National Guard)** - Learn about the
continuing education opportunities available to you and your family
through the Army National Guard, including college benefits, tuition
assistance, scholarships, and a variety of other programs.
http://www.pec.ngb.army.mil/

- **GI Bill Benefits Forms (US Dept. of Veterans Affairs)** - The easy way
to get the GI bill education benefits forms you need from the VA.
Download them from this website! Or to make it even easier to
apply, link from this page to VA's Electronic Application Form.
http://www.gibill.va.gov/apply-for-benefits/

- **LifeLines Education Services (US Navy)** - Learn about the many
educational benefits and programs offered to family members of
the Navy and Marine Corps on the Education Services pages of
LifeLines, the Navy's award-winning quality-of-life portal for service
families. http://www.cnic.navy.mil/CNIC_HQ_Site/index.htm

- **Military Scholarships** - http://aid.military.com/scholarship/search-
for-scholarships.do?ESRC=ggl_edu_sch.kw

- **Money for School (US Air Force Reserve)** - Air Force reservists
interested in a college or trade school education may qualify for
financial assistance under the Montgomery GI Bill. Find out here if
you qualify.

- **Money for College (US Navy)** - Continue your education with
money for college from the U.S. Navy. Read about all the options
available to you, including the Baccalaureate Degree Completion
Program, which can pay future officers a salary while they're in
college. http://www.navy.com/joining/benefits.html

- **Montgomery GI Bill–Active Duty** -
http://www.gibill.va.gov/pamphlets/ch1607/ch1607_pamphlet.pdf

- **Montgomery GI Bill–Selected Reserve** -
http://www.gibill.va.gov/pamphlets/ch1606/ch1606_pamphlet.pdf

- **MyMilitaryEducation.org** - Created by MN Dept. of VA and MN
Online to serve the unique higher educational needs of veterans,
military members, and their families. Read information about

education benefits, state schools and related issues from a team of experienced advisors and counselors. https://mymilitaryeducation.org/

- **Navy-Marine Corps Relief Society** - NMCRS offers education programs to help eligible Navy and Marine Corps families pursue their academic goals by providing a source of education financing. Awards are provided solely on the basis of the applicant's financial need. http://www.nmcrs.org/

- **Naval Postgraduate School (US Navy)** - The NPS's mission is to enhance U.S. security through graduate & professional education programs. Students are U.S. military officers and government employees and its allies. Graduate fellowships are available. http://www.nps.edu/

- **Navy College Program (US Navy)** - Earn a degree while serving in the Navy. The Navy College Program is a one-stop educational resource for college prep, financial aid, academic advice, and all Navy college, training, and officer programs. http://www.military.com/education/content/money-for-school/navy-education-programs.html

- **Post-911 GI Bill** - http://www.gibill.va.gov/pamphlets/ch1607/ch1607_pamphlet.pdf

- **Reserve Educational Assistance Program (REAP)** - http://www.gibill.va.gov/pamphlets/ch1607/ch1607_pamphlet.pdf

- **ROTC - US Air Force Scholarships** - http://www.afrotc.com/

- **ROTC - US Army Scholarships** - http://www.goarmy.com/rotc/scholarships.html

- **ROTC - Navy Scholarships** - http://www.navy.com/benefits/education/nrotc/

- **ROTC Navy and Marine Scholarships** - http://www.navy.com/careers/nrotc/life/

- **Turbo Tap** - Connects individuals to money, benefits and jobs related to the military – the department of defense's transition assistance program http://www.turbotap.org/register.tpp

- **US Air Force Enlisted Education** - The US Air Force offers enlisted officer healthcare and educational opportunities. Follow the links to the officer and healthcare education pages to see what's available. http://airforce.com/benefits/enlisted-education/

- **US Army Education Benefits** - Be a full-time soldier and earn credits towards a degree. Find information about earning money for your education, ROTC scholarships, and repaying college loans. http://www.goarmy.com/benefits/education-benefits.html

- **US Coast Guard Institute** - Further your education while serving in the US Coast Guard! The Coast Guard Institute is your education center for college programs, examinations, financial assistance, and getting credit for your Coast Guard experience. http://www.uscg.mil/hr/cgi/

- **US Naval Education and Training Command** - The U.S. Naval Education and Training Command offers both enlisted and officer programs. Some highlights include Command Leadership School, Summer Cruise Program and Navy Military Training. http://www.navy.mil/local/cnet/

- **Veterans Educational Assistance Program (VEAP)** - http://www.gibill.va.gov/pamphlets/ch32/ch32_pamphlet.pdf

5 - HOW TO APPLY TO THE MILITARY SERVICE ACADEMIES

The mission of the U.S. service academies and private military institutions is to provide instruction and experience to all cadets so that they graduate with the knowledge and character essential to leadership and the motivation to become career officers in the U.S. military.

Application Process for the Military Service Academies
Check Eligibility

An individual must be:

- A citizen of the United States

- Of good moral character

- Unmarried with no dependents

- At least 17, but less than 23 years of age by July 1 of the year you would enter.

How Selections Are Decided

Factors that are important include a well-rounded program of leadership, academic, and athletic preparation. A candidate must consider the characteristics of dedication; desire to serve others, ability to accept discipline, sense of duty and morality, and the enjoyment of challenge in deciding if an individual wants to pursue an Academy education.

Choices of Military Academies

Choices include the Air Force, Army, Coast Guard, Marines, Navy, and the US Merchant Marine Academy. Visit to get a feel for each institution and gather data by talking to cadets or midshipmen about their experiences.

Academic Preparation Includes

A young person who has the desire to attend one of the service academies must take a college preparatory curriculum in high school that stresses English and Math. Also, he or she should plan on taking the ACT and SAT test including the Writing section as early as possible and more than once.

Be Physically Prepared

During the admissions process, prospective cadets will be given the Candidate Fitness Assessment. All three academies have the same physical fitness events: the basketball throw; pull-ups (men & women) or flexed-arm hang (women); shuttle run; modified sit-ups; push-ups; and the one-mile run. The purpose of these tests is to evaluate a candidate's upper body strength and endurance. Check with each academy on its specific requirements for the Candidate Fitness Assessment. Complete a medical examination. The medical exam is given by the Department of Defense Medical Examination Review Board (DODMERB).

General Information

The minimum SAT scores for the academies are 500 verbal and 500 math. The average SAT scores at the academies are 540-620 verbal and 630-710 math. The minimum ACT scores for the academies are 21 English, 19 Social Studies, 24 Mathematics, and 24 Natural Science. The average ACT scores are 23-27 English; 24-29 Social Studies; 27-32 Mathematics; 28-32 Natural Science (minimum and average scores are slightly higher for the Naval Academy). Virtually all cadets are from the top 25% of their high school class.

How to Apply

- Download the application or ask for one to be mailed to your home address during the spring of the junior year in high school.

- Apply by obtaining an official nomination to qualify for admission to an academy. Those qualified to nominate candidates include the U.S. Vice President, U.S. Representatives, and U.S. Senators (a Congressional nomination is not needed for the Coast Guard Academy). Nominations are based on merit, not political connections. It is possible to receive a nomination from more than one Academy, but you may be asked for preference by your Congressperson.

- The interview with a Congressman will focus on goals and qualifications.

- Be aware of deadlines.

The Application Process for Private Military Academies

- Complete an online or paper application and submit the required fee along with your application.

- Remember to have transcripts for the last four years of academic work submitted. Request teachers and/or counselor to submit recommendation forms. Check to see if particular teachers such as math and English teachers need to send evaluations.

- Send standardized test scores to the institutions.

- Be sure to send other documentation such as immunization records and birth certificate.

List of Private Military Academies

- The Citadel and The Military College of South Carolina (Charleston, South Carolina; four-year public college)

- Mary Baldwin College (Staunton, Virginia: four-year private college)

- North Georgia College and State University (Dahlonega, Georgia; four-year public university)

- Norwich University (Northfield, Vermont; four-year private university)

- Texas A&M University (College Station, Texas; four-year public university)

- Virginia Military Institute (Lexington, Virginia; four-year public college)

- Virginia Tech (Blacksburg, Virginia; four-year public college)

Military Websites

Source: Website descriptions are taken directly from the individual websites.

- Air Force - Information on the Air Force. http://www.airforce.com/

- Army - Information on the Army. http://www.goarmy.com/

- ASVAB - The Armed Services Vocational Aptitude Battery (ASVAB) is a timed multi-aptitude test, given at over 14,000 schools and Military Entrance Processing Stations (MEPS) nationwide and is developed and maintained by the Department of Defense. http://www.military.com/ASVAB

- Coast Guard - Information on the Coast Guard. http://www.uscg.mil/default.asp

- Dantes - In accordance with the Department of Defense Instruction 1322.5, February 1997, Enclosure 7, DANTES' mission is to support the off-duty voluntary education programs of the Department of Defense and conduct special projects and development activities in support of education-related functions of the Department. http://www.dantes.doded.mil/Dantes_web/DANTESHOME.asp

- Marines - Information on the Marines. http://www.usmc.mil/Pages/Default.aspx

- US Merchant Marine Academy - Information on the Merchant Marines. http://www.usmma.edu/

- National Guard - Information on the National Guard. http://www.arng.army.mil/Pages/Default.aspx

- Navy - Information on the Navy. http://www.arng.army.mil/Pages/Default.aspx

- ROTC College Profiles - Colleges that have ROTC programs. http://www.collegeprofiles.com/rotc.html

- Student Veterans - Student Veterans of America (SVA) is a coalition of student veterans groups from college campuses across the United States. http://www.studentveterans.org/

- United States Military Schools and Academics - List of all military and academics.
  http://en.wikipedia.org/wiki/List_of_United_States_military_school
  s_and_academies

6 - COOPERATIVE EDUCATION PROGRAMS OR "CO-OPS"

One definition of a cooperative education program is a structured experience which combines practical work and the classroom-based education. Such programs provide academic credit for job experience to help a student from school-to-work and encourage service or volunteer learning.

- Provide an opportunity to learn from some experienced and supportive colleagues in the workplace.

- Gain practical experience while earning a degree and getting a head start in career.

- Students gain a level of maturity, are more experienced, and already respected for accomplishments in Co-op work assignments.

- Gain hands-on work experiences in specialized fields like engineering and business, etc.

- Co-op at certain companies could mean excellent wages, stipends for travel, and assistance with locating housing during their co-op term.

- Faculty and staff at these institutions also have years of industry experience as well as lasting relationships companies.

- Co-ops enhance the learning experience.

- Test drive a career to see which professional or occupational field is preferred.

- Chance to develop solid skills in resume writing.

- Learn how to negotiate corporate structures.

- Manage professional assignments.

- Develop network skills that will serve them for their entire career.

- Co-op students obtain employment immediately upon graduation.

- Some students graduate with up to two or three years of professional experience, an attribute that employers seek.

- Possibly a path to a debt-free college education.

- Co-ops could last a semester or up to four years.

- Those involved are typically paid by the employer and approved by the colleges.

- Co-ops may not earn class credit but a notation could be made on at a transcript.

- Explore the Co-op options at colleges with noted programs.

- Colleges with Cooperative Education Programs

7 - THE COLLEGE SEARCH FOR STUDENTS WITH DISABILITIES

All colleges and universities, public and private, are required by the American with Disabilities Act (ADA) to provide support and access to programs, services, and facilities. Most schools have disability offices to answer questions prospective and attending students may have.

A student with a documented learning difference may choose to disclose his or her LD to colleges. In cases where disclosing an LD may help a college more accurately interpret the student's transcript, it might be beneficial. A student should discuss his or her specific circumstances with his or her counselors. Colleges are required by law to accommodate students with disabilities, but it is helpful to know what types of accommodations the college offers.

Here are several tips for students with disabilities:

- Documentation of your disabilities with letters from your physician(s), counselors, therapists, case managers, school psychologist, and other service providers such as teachers, may be needed.

- Letters of recommendation from teachers, coaches, mentors, family, and friends can be helpful.

- Read and understand the federal laws that apply to students with disabilities.

- Do your research for support groups and advocacy approaches.

- Visit campuses —review living conditions, support services, classroom support, and campus lifestyle.

- Ask about an orientation program especially for students with disabilities—check to see if you need to register early for classes.

- Ask about an individualized education program (IEP).

- Check out what the school offers in the way of technology – voice synthesizers, voice recognition, and /or visual learning instruments.

- Does the school offer adapted programs such as intramural activities/social activities?

- Learn the entire layout of the campus – are all buildings easily accessible?

- Be realistic about your desires, a hilly campus may not be your best choice no matter what accommodations they have.

Questions might include the following:

- What type of support is available for students with learning disabilities?

- Is the program monitored by a full-time professional staff?

- Has the program been evaluated, and if so, by whom?

- Are there any concerns for the program's future?

- Who counsels students with learning disabilities during registration, orientation, and course selection?

- How does the school propose to help with the specific disability?

- Which courses provide tutoring?

- What kind of tutoring is available, and who does it—peers or staff?

- Is tutoring automatic, or must the student request assistance?

- How well do faculty members accept students with learning disabilities?

- May students with learning disabilities take a lighter load?

- Are courses in study skills or writing skills offered?

- Have counselors who work with students with learning disabilities received special training? Whom can you contact if you have concerns during the academic year?

- How do students on campus spend their free time?

- May students with learning disabilities take more time to graduate?

Learning Differences and the College Search - Websites

Source: Website descriptions are taken directly from the individual websites.

- **AHEAD** - A professional membership organization for individuals involved in the development of policy and in the provision of quality services to meet the needs of persons with disabilities involved in all areas of higher education. http://www.ahead.org/

- **Asperger Foundation International** - For students with Aspergers http://www.aspfi.org/college/

- **Asperger's Syndrome College Guide** - Browse through this directory of two-year colleges; four-year colleges and universities; and non-degree programs designed to give transition-age individuals experience living independently in preparation for (or in conjunction with) college or working. http://www.aspfi.org/college/

- **Books Without Barriers** - Bookshare® is free for all U.S. students with qualifying disabilities. http://www.bookshare.org/

- **College for Students with LD/AD/HD** - A great piece of information for students with these disabilities. http://www.dys-add.com/CollegeInfo.pdf

- **College Living Experience** - College Living Experience helps special needs students attend universities, community colleges and technical and vocational schools near one of the five CLE locations across the country. http://www.cleinc.net/home.aspx

- **College Planning for Students with Learning Disabilities** - Because there are many more colleges seeking, or at least admitting, students with learning disabilities than actually have well-developed programs, it is imperative that professionals help these students act cautiously during the selection and application process. http://www.kidsource.com/kidsource/content3/college.planning.LD.html

- **Dyslexia and College** - Information for dyslexic students at college or university. http://www.dyslexia-college.com/

- **Education Quest** - As a student with disabilities, you face unique considerations as you plan for college. To help you address these issues, the University of Nebraska-Lincoln Project NETS and Education Quest Foundation have developed a handbook titled, College Planning for Student with Disabilities – a supplement to the College Prep Handbook. View a condensed online version. http://www.educationquest.org/

- **Going to College with a Disability** - http://www.going-to-college.org/overview/index.html

- **Great School's** - College resources for students with LD or AD/HD - Whether your teen with LD or AD/HD is college-bound or already on campus, he or she will find this resource list invaluable. http://www.greatschools.org/special-education/health/college-resources-for-students.gs?content=798

- **The HEATH Resource Center** of The George Washington University, Graduate School of Education and Human Development, is an online clearinghouse on postsecondary education for individuals with disabilities. http://www.heath.gwu.edu./

- **Hello Friend** - For people with dyslexia. http://www.hellofriend.org/

- **LD Friendly Colleges** - PDF list of colleges that support students with Learning Differences. http://www.marist.com/ftpimages/216/misc/misc_58939.pdf

- **LD.org Comparison Chart for IDEA and Section 504** - Comparison chart IDEA and Section 504. http://www.ncld.org/students-disabilities/iep-504-plan

- **National Center for Children with Learning Disabilities** - Transition planning is a process that should help ensure your child's happiness, success, and satisfaction after high school and in further work, future education, and adulthood. http://www.ncld.org/adults-learning-disabilities/post-high-school

- **Preparing Students with Autism and /or Asperger's for College** - These ideas have been compiled from our work with students with high functioning autism/Asperger's Syndrome who are thinking about or attending college. Each student has a unique profile of strengths and needs, so each recommendation should be considered with the specific student in mind. http://www.ncld.org/adults-learning-disabilities

- **Recording for the Blind and Dyslexic** - With titles available in every subject area and grade level, RFB&D's digitally recorded audio textbooks on CD and downloadable audio textbooks help students challenged by the printed page. http://www.rfbd.org/

- **The SALT Center**, at the University of Arizona, has maintained an ongoing commitment to providing comprehensive services designed to promote academic success to students who learn differently. Over the last two decades, interest in the SALT Center's services has broadened to include not only students defined as LD or ADHD, but also those with any number of challenges impacting their potential for academic success. http://www.salt.arizona.edu/

- **Students with Disabilities Transition to College** - The College Living Experience (CLE) is a post-secondary program for students who require additional support with academic, social and independent living skills. http://www.cleinc.net/about_cle.aspx

- **Students with LD or AD/HD: Considering College** - With titles available in every subject area and grade level, RFB&D's digitally recorded audio textbooks on CD and downloadable audio textbooks help students challenged by the printed page. http://www.greatschools.org/special-education/health/college-planning.gs?content=913

- **Succeeding in College with AD/HD** - http://www.additudemag.com/adhd/article/1873.html

- **Think College** - Information with students with disability who plan to attend college. http://www.thinkcollege.net/for-students/getting-started

- **Transition Coalition** -This site provides online information, support and professional development on topics related to transition from school to adult life for youth with disabilities. There are online modules for job training, college and everyday life. http://transitioncoalition.org/transition/index.php

Additional Websites for Students with Disabilities

- Alliance for Technology Access - http://www.ataccess.org/

- Family Center on Technology and Disability - http://www.fctd.info/

- Rehabilitation Engineering and Assistive Technology Society of North America - http://www.resna.org/

AUTISM

- Autism Society of America - http://www.autism-society.org/

- Center for the Study of Autism - http://www.autism.org/

- Families of Adults Afflicted with Asperger Syndrome (FAAAS) - http://www.faaas.org/

- Online Asperger Syndrome Information and Support (O.A.S.I.S.) - http://www.udel.edu/bkirby/asperger

- Talk About Curing Autism – College funding resources. http://www.talkaboutcuringautism.org/resources/college-programs-and-funding.htm

CAREER AND TECHNICAL EDUCATION

- Association for Career and Technical Education - http://www.acteonline.org/

- National Career Development Association - http://www.ncda.org/

- National Centers for Career and Technical Education - http://www.nccte.org/

- National Collaborative on Workforce and Disability for Youth - http://www.ncwd-youth.info

- National Institute for Work and Learning - http://www.niwl.org/

COLLEGE READINESS

- Back to College - http://www.back2college.com/

- The College Board - http://www.collegeboard.com/

- Degrees & Colleges-Search Online - http://www.colleges-degrees-searches-online.org/

- Educational Testing Service - http://www.ets.org/

- Go College: the Collegiate Web Source - http://www.gocollege.com/

- Guidance Resources - http://www.wisemantech.com/guidance/

- How to Help Your Child Prepare for Education Beyond High School - http://studentaid.ed.gov/PORTALSWebApp/students/english/parents.jsp

- National Association for College Admissions Counseling - http://www.nacacnet.org/

- National Center for Homeless Education at the Serve Center - Supporting the education of children and youths experiencing homelessness. http://center.serve.org/nche/index.php

DEAF-BLIND

- American Association of the Deaf-Blind - http://www.aadb.org/

- DB-Link, National Information Clearinghouse on Children Who Are Deaf-Blind - http://www.tr.wou.edu/dblink

- Deaf Blind International - http://www.deafblindinternational.org/

- Helen Keller National Center for Deaf-Blind Youth and Adults - http://www.helenkeller.org/

- National Family Association for Deaf-Blind - http://www.nfadb.org/

EMOTIONAL DISTURBANCE

- American Psychiatric Association - http://www.psych.org/

- Bazelon Center for Mental Health - http://www.bazelon.org/

- Center for Mental Health Services - http://www.mentalhealth.org/

- Depression and Bipolar Support Alliance - http://www.dbsalliance.org/

- Family First Aid: Help for Troubled Teens - http://www.familyfirstaid.org/

- Kolob Canyon Residential Treatment Center for Girls with Special Needs - http://www.kolobcanyonrtc.com/

- Moonridge Academy for Boys with Special Needs - http://www.moonridgeacademy.com/

- National Alliance for the Mentally Ill - http://www.nami.org/

- National Mental Health Association - http://www.nmha.org/

EMPLOYMENT

- Able to Work Consortium/ Business & Disability Council - http://www.ncds.org/

- ADA Technical Assistance Program - http://www.adata.org/

- America's Job Bank - http://www.ajb.dni.us/

- Career Opportunities for Students with Disabilities (COSD) - http://www.cosdonline.org/

- Careers in Vocational Rehabilitation - http://www.rehabjobs.org/

- Developmental Disabilities Resource Center (DDRC) - http://www.ddrcco.com/

- Disabled Businesspersons Association Employer Assistance Referral Network - http://www.earnworks.com/

- Employment Support Institute (ESI) - http://www.workworld.org/

- Equal Opportunity Publications, Inc. - http://www.eop.com/

- GLADNET - http://www.gladnet.org/

- Goodwill Industries International, Inc. - http://www.goodwill.org/

- Institute for Work and Health - http://www.iwh.on.ca/

- Job Accommodation Network (JAN) - http://askjan.org/

- Job Access - http://www.jobaccess.org/

- Just One Break, Inc. - http://www.justonebreak.com/

- National Business & Disability Council - http://www.business-disability.com/

- Project HIRED - http://www.projecthired.org/

- Project SEARCH - http://www.cincinnatichildrens.org/ps

- Rehabilitation Research and Training Center on Workplace Supports - http://www.worksupport.com/

FEDERAL GOVERNMENT RESOURCES

- Access Board - http://www.access-board.gov/

- ERIC Clearinghouse - http://www.eric.ed.gov/

- High School/High Tech Programs - http://www.dol.gov/odep/programs/high.htm

- National Council on Disability - http://www.ncd.gov/

- National Institute on Disability and Rehabilitation Research (NIDRR) http://www.ed.gov/about/offices/list/osers/nidrr/index.html?src=mr

- Office of Disability Employment Policy, Department of Labor - http://www.dol.gov/odep

- USAJOBS   http://www.usajobs.opm.gov/

- U.S. Department of Education - http://www.ed.gov/

- U.S. Department of Justice ADA - http://www.ada.gov/

- U.S. General Services Administration Section 508 - http://www.section508.gov/index.cfm?fuseAction=Laws

HEARING IMPAIRMENTS/DEAFNESS

- Auditory-Verbal International - http://www.auditory-verbal.org/

- Alexander Graham Bell Association for the Deaf and Hard of Hearing - http://www.agbell.org/

- American Speech-Language-Hearing Association - http://www.asha.org/

- Deaf-REACH - http://www.deaf-reach.org/

- Gallaudet Research Institute - http://aaweb.gallaudet.edu/Gallaudet_Research_Institute.html

- Laurent Clerc National Deaf Education Center - http://clerccenter.gallaudet.edu/

- National Association of the Deaf - http://www.nad.org/

- National Association of the Deaf, Captioned Media Program - http://www.cfv.org/

- National Institute on Deafness and Other Communication Disorders - http://www.nidcd.nih.gov/

- National Technical Institute for the Deaf - http://www.ntid.rit.edu/

- Registry of Interpreters of the Deaf - http://www.rid.org/

- Self Help for Hard of Hearing People - http://www.shhh.org/

INDIVIDUALS WITH DISABILITIES EDUCATION ACT

- Council for Exceptional Children - http://www.cec.sped.org/

- Family & Advocates Partnership for Education - http://www.fape.org/

- Federal Resource Center for Special Education - http://www.dssc.org/frc

- IDEA Partnership - http://www.ideapartnership.org/

- IDEA 2004 Resources - http://www.ed.gov/policy/speced/guid/idea/idea2004.html

- Least Restrictive Environment Coalition - http://www.lrecoalition.org/

- National Center on Secondary Education and Transition - http://www.ncset.org/

- Office of Special Education Programs' IDEA 2004 Fact Sheets - http://www.pacer.org/

- Parent Information Centers - http://www.taalliance.org/ptidirectory/

INTELLECTUAL DISABILITIES AND DEVELOPMENTAL DELAY

- American Association on Mental Retardation (AAMR) - http://www.aamr.org/

- Association for Children with Down Syndrome - http://www.acds.org/

- Association of University Centers on Disabilities - http://www.aucd.org/

- Institute for Community Inclusion - http://www.communityinclusion.org/

- National Association for Down Syndrome - http://www.nads.org/

- National Association of Councils of Developmental Disabilities (NACDD) - http://www.nacdd.org/

- National Down Syndrome Society: Education, Research, Advocacy - http://www.ndss.org/

- Rehabilitation Research and Training Center on Aging with Developmental Disabilities - http://www.uic.edu/index.html/learning.shtml

- Research and Training Center on Community Living - http://rtc.umn.edu/main/index.asp

- TASH (formerly Association for Persons with Severe Handicaps) - http://www.tash.org/

- The Arc - http://www.thearc.org/

LEARNING DISABILITIES

- Coordinated Campaign for Learning Disabilities - http://www.aboutld.org/

- Council for Learning Disabilities - http://www.cldinternational.org/

- International Dyslexia Association - http://www.interdys.org/

- LD Online - http://www.ldonline.org/

- Learning Disabilities Association - http://www.ldaamerica.org/

- Literacy & Learning Disabilities - http://ldlink.coe.utk.edu/

- National Center for Learning Disabilities (NCLD) - http://www.ncld.org/

- National Association for Adults with Learning Difficulties (NAALD) - http://www.naasln.org/

- Roads to Learning - http://www.difflearn.com/

- Schwab Learning - http://www.schwablearning.org/

ORTHOPEDIC IMPAIRMENTS

- American Academy of Orthopedic Surgeons - http://www.aaos.org/

- Amputee Coalition of America - http://www.amputee-coalition.org/

- March of Dimes - http://www.marchofdimes.com/

- Muscular Dystrophy Association, Inc. - http://www.mdausa.org/

- National Multiple Sclerosis Society - http://www.nationalmssociety.org/

- National Spinal Cord Injury Association - http://www.spinalcord.org/

- Spina Bifida Association of America - http://www.sbaa.org/

- Spinal Cord Injury Network International - http://www.spinalcordinjury.org/

- United Cerebral Palsy Association, Inc. - http://www.ucp.org/

- United States Cerebral Palsy Athletic Association - http://www.uscpaa.org/

OTHER HEALTH IMPAIRMENTS

- American Cancer Society - http://www.cancer.org/

- American Diabetes Association - http://www.diabetes.org/

- American Institute for Cancer Research - http://www.aicr.org/

- American Sickle Cell Anemia Association - http://www.ascaa.org/

- Arthritis Foundation - http://www.arthritis.org/chapters/western-pennsylvania/

- Attention Deficit Information Network (AD-IN) - http://www.addinfonetwork.com/

- Attention Deficit Disorder Association - http://www.add.org/

- Bone Marrow Foundation - http://www.bonemarrow.org/

- Children and Adults with Attention Deficit Hyperactivity Disorder (CHADD) - http://www.chadd.org/

- Corporate Angel Network for Cancer Patients - http://www.corpangelnetwork.org/

- Cystic Fibrosis Foundation - http://www.cff.org/

- Easter Seals - http://www.easter-seals.org/

- Epilepsy Foundation of America - http://www.epilepsyfoundation.org/

- Hemophilia Galaxy - http://www.hemophiliagalaxy.com/

- Hereditary Nephritis Foundation (HNF) - http://www.cc.utah.edu/~cla6202/HNF.htm

- Immune Deficiency Foundation (IDF) - http://www.primaryimmune.org/

- Joint Center for Sickle Cell and Thalassemic Disorders - http://sickle.bwh.harvard.edu/

- Little People of America, Inc. - http://www.lpaonline.org/

- Lupus Foundation of America - http://www.lupus.org/

- National Association for Rare Disorders (NORD) - http://www.rarediseases.org/

- National Cancer Institute - http://www.cancer.gov/

- National Hemophilia Foundation - http://www.hemophilia.org/

Disability-Related Scholarships and Awards

General

- Lime Scholarship - Google & Lime - http://googleblog.blogspot.com/2009/04/introducing-google-lime-scholarship.html

- Paul G. Hearne Leadership Award - http://www.aapd-dc.org/DMD/PaulHearneAward.html

- Proyecto Vision - http://www.proyectovision.net/english/opportunities/scholarships.html

- Undergraduate Scholarship Program Central Intelligence Agency - https://www.cia.gov/offices-of-cia/equal-employment-opportunity/no-fear-act/nofear-act-notice.html

Hearing Loss/Deafness

- AG Bell Financial Aid and Scholarship Program Alexander Graham Bell Association for the Deaf and Hard of Hearing - http://nc.agbell.org/NetCommunity/Page.aspx?pid=493

- Graduate Fellowship Fund Gallaudet University Alumni Association - http://financialaid.gallaudet.edu/Financial_Aid/Scholarships.html

- Hard of Hearing and Deaf Scholarship Sertoma International - http://www.sertoma.org/NETCOMMUNITY/Page.aspx?pid=344&srcid=190

- Minnie Pearl Scholarship Program The EAR Foundation - http://www.earfoundation.org/

- William C. Stokoe Scholarship National Association of the Deaf: Stokoe - http://www.nad.org/

Visual Impairments

- ACB Scholarship American Council of the Blind - http://www.acb.org/

- AFB Scholarships American Foundation for the Blind - http://www.afb.org/scholarships.asp

- CCLVI Scholarships Council of Citizens with Low Vision International - http://www.cclvi.org/

- CRS Scholarship Christian Record Services for the Blind - http://services.christianrecord.org/scholarships/index.php

- Ferrell Scholarship Association for Education and Rehabilitation of the Blind and Visually Impaired - http://www.aerbvi.org/modules.php?name=Content&pa=showpage&pid=77

- Guild Scholar Award Jewish Guild for the Blind - http://www.jgb.org/guildscholar.asp

- Lighthouse Scholarships - Lighthouse International - http://www.lighthouse.org/services-and-assistance/scholarship-award-programs

- Mary P. Oenslager Scholastic Achievement Award Recording for the Blind and Dyslexic - http://www.rfbd.org/applications_awards.htm

- NFB Scholarships National Federation of the Blind - http://www.nfb.org/scholarship-program

Physical/Mobility Impairments

- 1800Wheelchair.com - http://www.1800wheelchair.com/Scholarship/

- AmeriGlide Achiever Scholarship AmeriGlide - http://www.ameriglide.com/scholarship/

- ELA Foundation Scholarship Ethel Louise Armstrong Foundation - http://www.ela.org/

- National MS Society Scholarship Program National Multiple Sclerosis Society - http://www.nationalmssociety.org/living-with-multiple-sclerosis/society-programs-and-services/scholarship/index.aspx

- SBA Scholarship Program Spina Bifida Association of America - http://www.spinabifidaassociation.org/

Health Impairments

- HFA Educational Scholarship Hemophilia Federation of America - http://hemophiliafed.org/%20programs-and-services/educational-scholarships/

- IDF Scholarship Program Immune Deficiency Foundation - http://primaryimmune.org/patients-and-families/idf-scholarship-programs

- Kevin Child Scholarship National Hemophilia Foundation - http://www.hemophilia.org/NHFWeb/MainPgs/MainNHF.aspx?menuid=53&contentid=35

- Pfizer Epilepsy Scholarship Award Intra Med Educational Group - http://www.epilepsy-scholarship.com/

- Scholarships for Survivors Program Patient Advocate Foundation - http://www.patientadvocate.org/events.php?p=69

- Solvay Cares Scholarship Solvay Pharmaceuticals - http://www.solvaycaresscholarship.com/

- Ulman Cancer Fund for Young Adults - http://www.ulmanfund.org/Services/Scholarship/20092010ScholarshipProgram/tabid/565/Default.aspx

Learning Disabilities

- Anne & Matt Harbison Scholarship P. Buckley Moss Society - http://www.mosssociety.org/page.php?id=30

- Learning Through Listening Award Recording for the Blind and Dyslexic - http://www.rfbd.org/applications_awards.htm

- Hydrocephalus Association - http://www.hydroassoc.org/education_support/scholarships

Mental Health

- Lilly Reintegration Scholarship - http://www.reintegration.com/

8 - GAY AND LESBIAN COLLEGE STUDENTS

As for many young students, going away to college is a big step. For gay and lesbian students, finding a college that is gay-friendly is especially important. For some gay and lesbian students, college may be the first place they feel free enough to be out and open. So how does one go about gathering such information?

What do you want to study?

Do you have a passion for a certain subject area? Do you like working with people or things? Do like working outdoors or in a lab? Do your research by taking a self-assessment. Find your niche by volunteering, interviewing professionals in the career you are interested in, research using the internet, and talking to your school counselor. Pick a college based on what you wish to study.

Use the Internet for Research

Are you looking for a certain campus environment? After you have narrowed your school choices down to the ones that offer the major you want to study, spend some time on the college web site. Look at the groups on campus, the class offerings, and the university policies that match your desires.

Read Up on the Colleges Nondiscrimination Policies

If you do your research, you will find information on the college's website regarding their nondiscrimination policy. Every school should have one. Does the school you want to attend have a nondiscrimination policy that includes sexual orientation or gender identity? If yes, it may also mean that the school administration has given the issue of gay and lesbian students and employees some consideration and attempts to make the campus a welcoming environment.

What Classes are offered?

Is it important to have courses that offer information on sexuality and gender, such as Women's and Lesbian Studies? Do your homework and review the offerings.

Check out the Directory and Student Organizations

The National Consortium of Directors of Lesbian, Gay, Bisexual and Transgender Resources in Higher Education has a listing of all colleges who have gay and lesbian student organizations with paid staff. Many universities have gay and lesbian centers that are run by student volunteers, so even though your college is not on this list, it may still have a gay and lesbian student group. http://www.lgbtcampus.org/

Visit the School

You can search the Web, but paying a visit to a college campus in person is best. Take an official campus tour. How do you feel there? Do you see other students on campus that you think you could be friends with? Check out flyers and posters on the walls. Are any advertising gay events? Pick up a school newspaper. What does the climate seem like in the school cafeteria?

Check Out the Surrounding Area

Does the city or town the college is located in have an active gay community? These can all be indicators of a gay-friendly environment.

LGBT Websites

Source: Website descriptions are taken directly from the individual websites.

- The Advocate Guide For LGBT Students - http://www.campuspride.org/advocatecollegeguide/

- Applying to School - Founded for the purpose of linking college admissions offices, universities, graduate and law schools across the United States with students through a powerful online communication that provides a more efficient and cost-effective method of student recruitment and gives students maximum exposure. http://www.applyingtoschool.com/

- Campus Climate Index - A LGBT National Assessment Tool. http://www.campusclimateindex.org/?gclid=CMCSvJzEIKQCFRFW2g odtiiuHw

- Campus Pride - Many LGBT and Ally young people are coming out in high school and are looking for college scholarship and other financial assistance. Here ares some places to get started. http://www.campuspride.org/finding_scholarships.asp

- Finaid - Financial Aid for Lesbian, Gay, Bisexual and Transgendered Students. http://www.finaid.org/otheraid/gay.phtml

- The Gay and Lesbian Guide to Colleges - A comprehensive resource for Lesbian, Gay, Bisexual, Transgender Students and Their Allies. http://amzn.to/q9Gv3A

- Human Rights Campaign - The following is a list of scholarships, fellowships and grants for LGBT and allied students at both the undergraduate and graduate-level. http://www.hrc.org/issues/youth_and_campus_activism/8644.htm

- Inside College - Information on Gay Friendly Colleges. http://www.insidecollege.com/reno/GayFriendly-Colleges/451/list.do

- Point Foundation - Point Foundation provides financial support, mentoring, leadership training, and hope to meritorious students who are marginalized due to sexual orientation, gender identity, or gender expression. http://www.pointfoundation.org/

- Scholarships for LGBT Students - A growing number of scholarships are devoted exclusively to students who are lesbian, gay, bisexual, and transgender. http://www.collegescholarships.org/scholarships/lgbt-students.htm

9 - HOMESCHOOLED – NAVIGATING THE NEXT STEP

Is the Application Process Different for Home Schooled Students?

Colleges view applications from homeschooled students differently. Therefore, it is important for students to take more time with their application process.

- Take the college preparatory curriculum and build your transcript portfolio.

- Check deadlines and dates.

- Create a resume of your extracurricular activities.

- Ask for recommendations from those who know you well.

- Speak with the colleges about your situation, and learn what schools are Homeschool friendly— they will want to see a letter of completion and transcript of your grades.

- Take a standardized test such as the SAT or ACT with writing plus the SAT Subject Area tests.

- Go on a college interview.

- Apply for financial aid if needed.

- Placement testing may be required prior to registration.
- Check out this website: Home School Friendly Colleges. http://homeschoolfriendlycolleges.com/
- If you want to play college athletics, review this website.
- Home School Defense Association , http://www.hslda.org/
- If you are interested in the arts, be sure to meet the requirements and deadlines for portfolios and auditions.

10 - THE VALUE OF COMMUNITY SERVICE

Do you have a passion for involvement in community service? Are you interested in the improvement of our society? Participating in community service is one way. Start by thinking about your values and your interests.

Many students are involved in community service every day. Here are some reasons they found the service to be of value:

- Gain an understanding about each other.
- A sense of human compassion.
- Never feels like an obligation or responsibility; can be energizing.
- Provide support to others.
- Affects someone's life.
- Builds a stronger community.
- Utilized strengths to have a beneficial impact on our society.
- Positive impact on someone's life.
- Gain intense awareness of self.
- Gain knowledge outside the classroom.
- Way to experience diversity to enhance mind and spirit.
- Help others with struggles.
- Make a difference.
- Make the most of your life; look at life from different perspectives.
- Learn about accepting help.

- Collaborate with community.

- Builds a bond among those who are working together for a common goal.

- Investment in the future and the well-being of those around us.

- An act of responsibility, not just generosity.

- Take pride in what you do.

- Learn about strength, compassion, and vulnerability.

- Learn lessons in life about people, culture and society around us.

- Crucial part of well-rounded education.

- Development of productive members of society.

- An important part of who you are.

- Learn about current events.

- Teaches about courage, compassion, love, appreciation, teamwork, and humility.

- In order to serve well, you must listen, be patient, and not judge.

- It can start in the community around you and stretch to people across the world.

- Allows you to find out who you really are.

- Can change your life in unexpected ways; learn to be humble and grounded.

- Check out sites online like http://www.Servenet.org.

11 - "GAP YEAR," VOLUNTEERISM, AND STUDY ABROAD

According to the University of Delaware, the definition of "Gap Year" is a "temporary position (1 – 3 years) between college, graduate school or a full-time job." Many students are interested in "taking a year off" before buckling down to a "serious" job or graduate school. These temporary "in-the-meantime" jobs can provide experience, direction, emotional and cognitive growth, and satisfy curiosity about the real world.

Ask yourself these five questions:

1. Do you enjoy traveling?
2. Do you like learning new languages?
3. Are you a hands-on learner?
4. Do you like making new friends?
5. Are you open to new ideas and challenges?

Other questions to consider:

- What is the cost; is it a factor, and how can you supplement the cost?

- What type of health insurance do you need to have to make sure you are covered for emergencies?

- What are the health requirements (vaccinations) needed?

- What are the safety issues you need to be aware of when traveling?

- How will you stay in touch with my family and friends?

- How will you adjust to "culture shock" going and coming home?

- If you answered yes to the questions, think about taking a gap year, volunteering, or studying abroad. Below are lists of websites that might help you find an outlet for your intellectual and academic enthusiasm.

"Gap Year" Resources

Source: Website descriptions are taken directly from the individual websites.

General Resources

- The Gap Year - A complete guide to "taking time out" - http://www.gapyear.com/

- Idealist - http://www.idealist.org/

- One Small Planet - http://www.onesmallplanet.com/geninfo.htm

- Planet Gap Year - Provides FAQ about a GAP Year, stories, GAP options, planning, books, parents concerns, GAP news and news releases. http://www.planetgapyear.com/

- ServeNet - http://www.servenet.org

Service/Volunteer

- **AmeriCorps** - National, State, NCCC, VISTA, network under the Corporation for National and Community Service, all different types of service. http://www.americorps.gov/

- **Avodah** - Jewish Service Corps http://www.avodah.net

- **Catholic Network of Volunteer Services** - https://catholicvolunteernetwork.org/

- **City Year** - 10 months of full time community service to a specific community or area. http://www.cityyear.org/default_ektid13307.aspx

- **Jesuit Volunteer Corps** - http://www.jesuitvolunteers.org/

- **Lutheran Volunteer Corps** http://www.lutheranvolunteercorps.org/template/index.cfm

- **Peace Corps** - Advocates friendship and world peace in developing countries. http://www.peacecorps.gov/

- **Public Allies** - Full time paid apprenticeships in nonprofit organizations to lead positive community change. http://www.publicallies.org/site/c.liKUL3PNLvF/b.5106423/k.BD7E/Home.htm

- **The Red Cross** - Humanitarian organization to protect human life and health, many different types of opportunities. http://www.redcross.org/

- **Teach for America** - A non-profit organization designed to diminish the academic achievement gap between students of different economic backgrounds; teaching term is typically two years. http://www.teachforamerica.org/

- **United Nations Volunteers** - Volunteers directly support UN partners in the field. http://www.unv.org/

- **VolunteerMatch** - An organization that matches volunteers with experiences. http://www.volunteermatch.org/

Fellowships and Internships

- **College Internship Programs** - A GAP program for individualized Post- Secondary Programs - http://www.collegeinternshipprogram.com/

- **The College of the University of Chicago** - Fellowships, Research Opportunities, Grants, etc. a list of a wide range of opportunities. https://frogs.uchicago.edu/

- **Fulbright Scholarships** - The largest U.S. international exchange program offering opportunities for students, scholars, and professionals to undertake international graduate study, advanced research, university teaching, and teaching in elementary and secondary schools worldwide. http://fulbright.state.gov/

- **Nationally Coveted College Scholarships, Graduate Fellowships & Postdoctoral Awards** - List of fellowship opportunities in various fields organized by minimum educational qualifications. http://scholarships.fatomei.com/

- **Rising Star Internships** - A database of internships spanning a broad range of categories. http://www.rsinternships.com/

International

- **Academic Treks** - Academic and Service Adventures – a summer without borders. http://www.academictreks.com/

- **African Leadership Academy** - Students engage in building relationships with Africa's future leaders along with community service opportunities. http://www.alagapyear.org/

- **AFS Intercultural Programs** - AFS offers Community Service programs in more than 20 countries across the globe. http://www.afs.org/afs_or/home

- **Alliances Abroad** - A variety of programs providing high-quality placement and support before, during and after the experience. http://www.allianceabroad.com/

- **American Institute of Foreign Study** - The American Institute for Foreign Study (AIFS) has more than 40 years of experience in organizing study abroad programs – summer advantage, college semester and/or year programs for high school graduates. http://www.aifs.com/

- **AmeriCorps NCCC** - Spend 3 to 24 months living and working abroad! A variety of volunteer positions are available, on and off the construction site. http://www.americorps.gov/about/programs/nccc.asp

- **Amerispan** - Amerispan's academic semester abroad programs are available to college students who wish to study abroad for a semester, summer or quarter and earn transferable academic credit. http://www.amerispan.com

- **AustraLearn** - AustraLearn and Queenstown Resort College have created a unique 18 week GAP experience that allows students to develop the leadership characteristics, real world skills, and experience that employers and universities seek. http://www.australearn.org/Login/

- **BridgeYear** - The BridgeYear offers six different GAP Year Spanish study abroad programs in Santiago, Chile and Buenos Aires, Argentina. http://www.bridgeyear.com

- **Bridgton Academy** - The program offers a transitional experience between high school and college, rather than another year of high school. http://www.bridgtonacademy.org/

- **Brown Ledge** - Gives students life and work skills, as well as training them in documentary production to help them investigate and respond to the world around them. http://www.brownledge.org/

- **Building Bridges for Coalition** - A project of the Brookings Institute on International Volunteering and Service working collaboratively to double the number of international volunteers serving abroad. http://buildingbridgescoalition.ning.com/

- **Center for Cultural Interchange** - A non-profit international education exchange organization dedicated to the promotion of cultural understanding, academic development and world peace. http://www.cci-exchange.com/

- **CITY Term** - CITYTerm challenges students to think, question, speak up and grow. http://www.cityterm.org/

- **College Internship Program** - The College Internship Program provides comprehensive individualized academic, internship and independent living experiences for young adults, ages 18-25, with learning differences, Asperger's Syndrome, High Functioning Autism, Nonverbal Learning Differences, ADHD, Dyslexia, and PDD-NOS. http://www.collegeinternshipprogram.com/

- **Council on International Educational Exchange (CIEE)** - A year or a semester living with a family abroad, studying and improving fluency in a modern language, and volunteering in the community. http://www.ciee.org/

- **Cultural Experiences Abroad** - A college study abroad programs to U.S. and Canadian students in 15 countries and 28 cities across the globe. http://www.gowithcea.com/

- **Disney CareerStart Program** - The Disney Career Start Program is a 7 month structured living, learning and earning program for high school graduates who are unsure of their future path. http://disney.go.com/disneycareers/careerstart/index.html

- **Dynamy** - Internships in over 240 organizations with urban and back country leadership experiences, personal and college/career advising, city apartment living, and the company of a remarkable group of peers. http://www.dynamy.org

- **Earthwatch** - Supports scientific field research by offering volunteers the opportunity to join research teams around the world. http://www.earthwatch.org

- **El Casal** - El Casal is a multi-faceted program combining seminars in Spanish language and other subjects, travel, outdoor activities, internships and community service. http://elcasalbarcelona.com/

- **Flying Fish** - Students become an experienced yacht skipper or action sports instructor, and you can spend your holidays being paid to enjoy your favorite activity. http://www.flyingfishonline.com/

- **The French Culinary Institute** - Located in New York City, the pros teach most of the 250 essential skills used in their famous full-time Culinary Arts course. http://www.frenchculinary.com/

- **Experiment International** - Dynamic summer programs for high school students in 27 countries around the world. http://www.experimentinternational.org/

- **First in the Family** - http://www.firstinthefamily.org/

- **G.A.P. Adventures** - Create your own trip from over 1000 choices in 100 countries. http://www.gapadventures.com/

- **GAP Consultant** - Center for Interim Programs Princeton Office - They have built relationships with organizations worldwide and offer a database of over 5,200 programs opportunities worldwide - http://www.interimprograms.com/

- **Gap Year Experience**-Global Awareness with Carpe Diem Education - Carpe Diem International Education runs international academic programs that work with youth in an educational capacity to get them both out of the country and out of their comfort zones. http://www.carpediemeducation.org/about.php

- **Global College** – Long Island University - Students engage with a variety of cultures and people through various learning methods including coursework and fieldwork, through service learning projects and internships, and through independent studies built upon their own interests developed in consultation with a faculty advisor. http://www2.brooklyn.liu.edu/globalcollege/

- **Global Crossroad** - Offers many volunteers abroad and internship abroad experiences, mini-escapes and summer escapes, paid teaching programs, rural community insights and cultural immersion programs to international volunteers in twenty countries across Asia, Africa, and Latin America. http://www.globalcrossroad.com/

- **GlobalQuest** - An experiential study abroad program offering summer and semester programs in Thailand and Ecuador/Galapagos Islands. http://www.gquest.org

- **Global Volunteer Network** - The program offers academic year, short-term home-stay, internship, work and travel, language study, environmental and volunteer programs in over thirty countries worldwide. http://www.backdoorjobs.com/adventureabroad.html

- **Going Global** - login to Blue Hen Jobs for access; Going Global career and employment resources include world-wide job openings, internship listings, industry profiles and country-specific career information. http://www.goinglobal.com/

- **Habitat for Humanity** - This is a 10-month residential national service program for young men and women between 18 and 24 years of age. http://www.habitat.org/ivp/

- **Independent Secondary Schools** - Is the only U.S.-based non-profit educational association exclusively serving American and international boarding schools and students. http://www.schools.com/

- **InterExchange** - Numerous working abroad opportunities are provided through this organization. http://www.interexchange.org/

- **IIE Passport** - A list of study abroad programs. http://www.iiepassport.org/

- **International Jobs Center** - Paid subscription for job and internship opportunity updates. http://www.internationaljobs.org/

- **International Student -** Your international student and study abroad online portal for those who are looking to further their education overseas. http://www.internationalstudent.com/

- **Jewish United Fund** - Israel and Overseas Programs are available in Israel that offers a number of unique opportunities for personal growth and development in a variety of settings. http://www.juf.org/israel_experience/default.aspx

- **LEAPNOW: Transforming Education** - During the LEAPNOW program, students venture out for 3-months in Asia or Latin America, followed by an intensive "Rite of Passage" and a 3-month individual internship anywhere in the world. http://www.leapnow.org/

- **LEAPYear Experiential College Alternative** - The program is meant to replace the first year of college or function as a year "on" between high school and college. The year contains formal and informal rites of passage – a vital necessity in a society that does not give its youth markers for the journey into adulthood. http://www.leapnow.org/

- **Magic Carpet Rides** - A non-profit educational program offering high school graduates a "GAP Year" for international service and travel in Central America. http://www.magiccarpetrides.org/

- **Map the Gap International** - Offers structured "service-learning programs" that combine language and cultural immersion, community service, and socio-political insights from experts to

create a meaningful and impacting adventure for students.
https://www.mapthegapinternational.com/index.html

- **MASA Israel Journey** - MASA enables young Jews (ages 18-30) from around the world to build a lasting relationship with Israel, strengthen their Jewish identity, and gain meaningful and beneficial experiences by participating in a long-term program in Israel. http://www.masaisrael.org/masa/english/

- **Mine the Gap, Inc.** - These encompass internships and learning opportunities that fall into three major categories: service, academic and career-oriented. http://www.minethegap.us.com/

- **National Civilian Community Corps (NCCC)** - Cross with hurricane relief efforts, to building low-income housing with Habitat for Humanity, to helping combat soil erosion with the U. S. Forest Service.
http://www.searchnut.com/?domain=freegovernmentscholarships.com

- **National Outdoor Leadership School** - Takes people of all ages on real wilderness expeditions, teaching outdoor skills, leadership and environmental ethics in some of the world's wildest and most awe-inspiring classrooms - http://www.nols.edu/

- **Outward Bound** - Outward Bound USA provides challenging adventure education for youth and adults. http://www.outwardbound.org/

- **One Small Planet** - Resources for travel, volunteer work, internships, and work abroad. http://www.onesmallplanet.com/geninfo.htm

- **Overseas jobs** - Databases that allow job seekers to search jobs, view employers, and access a career information center. http://www.overseasjobs.com/

- **Pacific Challenge** - Offers unique and extensively researched study abroad and experiential programs including Australia, New Zealand, South America, and Nepal. http://www.pacificchallenge.org/

- **Pacific Discovery** - A program that combines study abroad, adventure travel, cultural immersion and volunteering. http://www.pacificdiscovery.org/

- **Projects Abroad** - Volunteers will learn from their placements and the people they meet while gaining experience in a chosen field. http://www.projects-abroad.org/gap-year-abroad/

- **The Riley Guide** - Up-to-date, comprehensive compilation of international career resources and job websites organized by country. http://www.rileyguide.com/internat.html

- **Rotary Youth Exchange International** - Spend up to a year living with a few host families and attending school in a different country. http://www.rotary.org/en/StudentsAndYouth/Pages/ridefault.aspx

- **Rothberg International School** - Includes an ULpan in Hebrew and/or Arabic language instruction, and a wide variety of courses taught in English, which can count towards your degree. http://overseas.huji.ac.il/

- **Rustic Pathways** - Offer gap year experiences in every country where we operate, encompassing most of Asia, Africa, the South Pacific, Central, and South America. http://www.rusticpathways.com/

- **School for Field Studies** - Enable students to come away from their experience with an understanding of the complexity and inter-relatedness of environmental issues, as well as an increased commitment and new skills to help improve the environment and the lives of people dependent on that environment. http://www.fieldstudies.org/

- **SeaMester** - Delivers unique educational journeys at sea where students spend a semester sailing between islands, countries, even continents throughout global locations. http://www.seamester.com

- **Sojourns Abroad** - The twelve-week programs in Siena, Italy, Barcelona, Spain and Paris, France, include social service internships, language study, home-stay, excursions, outdoor adventures and cultural enrichment. http://www.sojournsabroad.org/

- **Southern France Youth Institute** - A GAP Year study abroad program for young adults interested in other cultures, the arts, adventure, travel, and language immersion. http://www.sfyi.org/

- **Student Conservation Association** - A 3-to-12 month, expense-paid internship opportunities in all 50 states, in more than 50 professional fields with the National Park Service, the U.S. Forest Service, the Bureau of Indian Affairs, the U.S. Fish and Wildlife Service, the U.S. Geological Survey, and state and local agencies, among others. http://www.thesca.org/

- **Study Overseas** - Provides free advice for students worldwide that are considering studying abroad for an international education. http://www.studyoverseas.com/

- **Taking Off** - Taking Off invests the time and effort to help students identify interests, evaluate priorities, and secure opportunities. http://takingoff.net/

- **Thames Academy at Mitchell College** - It is a year of academic preparation that students take between the end of high school and the start of their college studies. http://community.mitchell.edu/page.aspx?pid=347

- **Up With People** - Student ambassadors experience an intense, hands-on, education in which they form a global network of lifelong friendships. http://www.upwithpeople.org/

- **Volunteer for Peace** - A program that offers placement in over 3,000 volunteer projects in more than 100 countries. http://www.vfp.org/

- **Transitions Abroad** - Information and database for short term jobs, internships, and full time employment. http://www.transitionsabroad.com/

- **Where There Be Dragons** - It is an encounter that puts students close to the lived experiences of people in Asia. http://www.wheretherebedragons.com/

- **Where You Headed** - Is designed to serve students and their families who are looking for information and advice about the passage through high school and college. http://www.whereyouheaded.com/

- **Woolman Semester** - Is a high school semester studies program for juniors and seniors, and first year post-graduates with a focus on the issues of peace, justice and sustainability. http://woolman.org/

- **WWOOF (Worldwide Opportunities On Organic Farms)** - An international movement that is helping people share more sustainable ways of living. http://www.wwoof.org/

- **Youth for Understanding** - An international exchange program has many opportunities for year, semester, and summer students in 35 countries.http://www.youthforunderstanding.org/

- **Youth International** - Focuses upon inter-cultural exchange, volunteer work, home stays, and outdoor adventure. http://www.youthinternational.org/

- **Youth Outreach Volunteer** - South America is an amazing location for a GAP Year – an inexpensive continent but rich in culture and adventure. http://www.gicarg.org/

- **Young Judaea** - A dynamic year of study and volunteering in Israel for recent high school graduates. http://www.youngjudaea.org/site/c.nuIYKfMWIvF/b.5349257/k.BEEA/Home.htm

Odd and Adventure Jobs

- **Adventure, Outdoor & Fun Jobs** - Listings of a wide range of non-traditional jobs. http://www.funjobs.com/

- **Backdoorjobs.com** - Listings of all types of non-traditional short term jobs. http://www.backdoorjobs.com/

- **Check out Gap Year** - Created by travelers to assist people traveling on a budget by providing extensive information about accommodations, travel, short time employment, and activities. http://www.gapyear.com/

- **Looking for Adventure.com** - A warehouse of information about adventure travel, recreation, sports, jobs, school, and more. http://www.lookingforadventure.com/

Source: University of Delaware's Career Center – 5/5/12

Recommended Reading

The Gap Year Advantage by Karl Haigler and Rae Nelson.

They have a combined forty years of experience in the fields of education policy and practice. They have written a comprehensive guide to planning time off before or during college. Taking a "Gap Year" between high school and college or structuring time off during college offers the opportunity for students to gain focus and discipline, learn to set realistic goals, get real world experience, and build a stand-out-resume. Ready or Not, Here Life Comes by Mel Levine, M. D. "Instead of making a smooth transition into adulthood, many students find themselves trapped in their teenage years, traveling down the wrong career road, unable to function in the world of work...These young people have failed...to properly assess their strengths and weaknesses and have never learned the basics of choosing and advancing through stages of a career."

Time Out or Burn-Out for the Next Generation by William Fitzsimmons, Dean of Admission and Financial Aid, Harvard College; Marlyn McGrath Lewis, Director of Admissions, Harvard College; Charles Ducey, Adjunct Lecturer in Psychology, Harvard Graduate School of Education.

"The pressures placed on many children probably have the unintended effect of delaying a child's finding themselves and succeeding on their own terms. Burn-out is an inevitable result of trying to live up to alien goals. Time out can promote discovery of one's own passions."

12 - STUDY ABROAD CHECKLIST

Study abroad can be an exciting and life changing experience; begin by planning ahead. The following checklist will help you remember some important things that need to be done before you depart.

- Apply early enough for a new passport or to renew an old one, and do the same for your student visa.

- Get a complete physical, including immunizations. It's a good idea to have a copy of your medical records sent ahead of time to your study abroad program.

- Fill prescriptions.

- Meet with your academic counselor for a review before your trip.

- Be sure necessary financial aid documents are complete including scholarship applications, loan applications, and FAFSA renewal.

- If you will be away from the first of the year through April 15, complete and file your tax return ahead of time.

- Make multiple copies of important documents – one for yourself, one for your parents, and one for your study abroad program administrators. Include credit cards, passport, insurance information, etc.

- Make a list of important phone numbers, addresses, and other contact information. Put a copy in with your important documents package (see above).

- Check out international phone cards and cell phones.

- Bring enough converted currency for the first few days in your new country.

13 - DISTANCE LEARNING: EARNING A DEGREE ONLINE

Of the many options open to students after high school, one of them includes earning online a traditional college degree, professional certificate or continuing education (CEU's). Making the decision to complete coursework in this format has many benefits.

- You can take credits that apply towards a degree.

- If you take non-credit courses, they may help you acquire a specialization in a certain concentration.

- Instead of traveling a long distance to a university, the resources are brought to you.

- You have control of the hours you spend on the course work, and by emailing your professor, you may have answers to your questions sooner than the next day.

- Many employers support furthering the education of their employees since they do not need to miss work to take classes.

- You still need to apply to a degree program as you would at any other college

Choosing an Online College can be tricky. Here are some tips for making the right choice for you:

- Investigate and request information from several online college programs – take good notes.

- Be open to a college or university program even if you do not recognize the name.

- Do research on what you would like to major in, and see if the college has what you want to study. A program in general business or a major in something more specific like accounting.

- Ask questions by talking to an admissions representative

- Speak with a financial aid representative before you rule out a college due to the cost.

- Talk with family, friends, and counselors about this method of earning a degree.

- Assess your own abilities, be organized, motivated, and develop time management skills. Chances are you will need good written communication, computer skills, the time to commit to this format, and the flexibility to be successful online.

- Ask yourself if you are willing to reflect and collaborate with other virtual students and virtual faculty members online versus in the traditional classroom—and understand your own learning style.

Hot Tip: *Read How To Impress Your Online Instructor: Quick Tips to Success for the Virtual Student by Dr. Harold T. Gonzales, Jr., Ed. D.* *http://amzn.to/Pqt667*

14 - ADVANTAGES OF A WOMEN'S COLLEGE AND OTHER SPECIAL PROGRAMS

Although women's college graduates account for a mere 4 percent of college-educated women, they have made impressive contributions to all facets of society. So, what would a woman gain by attending a women's college?

- Women are more likely to perceive their colleges as caring about them and their learning.

- Promotes a woman's intellectual and social self-confidence, academic ability, and cultural awareness.

- Women participate more fully in and out of class and engage in higher order thinking activities.

- Students are likely to trust institution's mission statements and exhibit leadership traits such as public speaking skills and promote racial understanding.

- Overall satisfaction academically, developmentally, and personally.

- Students often have higher academic and professional aspirations.

- These institutions employ many women faculty members who are high quality teaching-oriented individuals.

- Students score higher on standardized achievement tests.

- Women tend to receive more doctoral degrees and enter medical school.

- An increase in salaries along with opportunities for women alumnae to develop leadership and management skills, and lifelong career advancement.

- Higher percentage of majors in economics, math, life science, and engineering.

- There are strong benefits gained from mentoring, small classes, and personal interaction with professors.

- Resources are set aside for sophisticated research equipment to preeminent athletics facilities to internship and fellowship funding, all focused on and available to women students.

- Women's colleges underscore the need for critical thinking, global knowledge, intercultural competence, and real-world abilities; women's colleges surpass all public and private colleges in helping students learn to think analytically, bring social and historical perspective to issues, work as part of a team, write and speak effectively, make sound decisions, gain entry to a career, prepare for career change or advancement, and be politically and socially aware.

- Indicate greater gains in understanding themselves and others, general education, ability to analyze quantitative problems, and desire to contribute to the welfare of their community.

- Tend to be more involved in philanthropic activities after college.

Some statistics about women who graduated from women's colleges:

- In the 2008 election, a record number of women won seats in the U.S. Senate and House of Representatives of the 111th Congress. Of the 100 seats, 17 are held by women and two of those were graduates of women's colleges.

- Four women on President Barrack Obama's new administration were women's college graduates - Nancy Pelosi, Hillary Rodham Clinton, Desiree Rogers, and Mona Sutphen.

- Of *Business Week's* list of the 50 women who are rising stars in corporate America, 15 - or 30% - received their baccalaureate degree from a women's college.

- Of the 4,012 highest paid officers and directors of 1990 Fortune 1000 companies, 19 - or less than one-half of 1% - were women. Of these women, 36% are women's college graduates.

- In a 1997 magazine survey, 20% of the 100 most powerful women in Washington, D.C., attended women's colleges.

- Graduates of women's colleges are more than twice as likely as graduates of coeducational colleges to receive doctorate degrees, and to enter medical school and receive doctorates in the natural sciences.

- 20% of women identified by *Black Enterprise Magazine*, as the 20 most powerful African-American women in corporate America, graduated from women's colleges.

- Almost half of women's college graduates in the work force hold traditionally male-dominated jobs at the higher end of the pay scale such as lawyer, physician or manager.

- 9 out of 10 women's college alumnae have participated in at least one civic or professional organization since college.

- Review the list of Women's Colleges and Scholarships for Women. http://www.usnews.com/education/articles/2009/03/11/list-of-womens-colleges - http://www.collegescholarships.org/women.htm

Other Special Programs
- **The American Indian College Fund** - Links to 31 Tribal Colleges, plus information about students and scholarships. http://www.collegefund.org/

- **The National Catholic College Admission Association** - A searchable list of Catholic institutions. http://www.catholiccollegesonline.org/

- **College and Character: The Templeton Guide** - "Colleges that Encourage Character Development" profiles 405 exemplary college programs in ten categories that inspire students to lead ethical and civic-minded lives. http://www.collegeandcharacter.org/

- **Colleges That Change Lives** is a college educational guide by Loren Pope. It was originally published in 1996, with a second edition in 2000, and a third edition in 2006. http://ctcl.org/

- **Hillel Foundation** - Contains a "Guide for Jewish Life on Campus" that describes Jewish activities at U.S. colleges. http://www.hillel.org/index

- **Historically Black Colleges and Universities** - Click on "Members Institutions" for a complete list of all the 118 institutions of the HBCU, "providers of equal educational opportunity with attainment and productivity for thousands of students." http://colleges.usnews.rankingsandreviews.com/best-colleges/rankings/hbcu

- **KOACH** - Choosing a college from the Jewish perspective. http://www.uscj.org/koach/choosing.htm

- **Migrant Students** - Serves the tens of thousands of existing migrant farm worker families within the U.S. today. http://www.migrantstudents.org/

- **Sea Grant Colleges** - The sea grant colleges are a group of 30 U.S. universities that are involved in the National Sea Grant College Program. Members of the program are involved in scientific research, education, training, and extension projects geared toward the conservation and practical use of U.S. coasts, the Great Lakes and other marine areas. http://www.seagrant.noaa.gov/

- **Space Grant Colleges** - The space-grant colleges compose a network of 52 consortia, based at universities across the U.S for space-related research. http://www.nasa.gov/offices/education/programs/national/spacegrant/home/index.html

- **Tribal Colleges and Universities -** A list of all tribal colleges and universities by state. http://www2.ed.gov/about/inits/list/whtc/edlite-tclist.html

- **Women's College Coalition** - The coalition represents 70 member colleges in the U.S. and Canada. The site presents the benefits of attending an all-women's college, and gives links to member web pages. http://womenscolleges.org/

- **Work Colleges** - A work college is a type of institution of higher learning where student work is an integral and mandatory part of the educational process, as opposed to being an appended requirement. http://www.workcolleges.org/

15 - UNDERSTANDING PRE-PROFESSIONAL PROGRAMS

Most professional schools and universities throughout the United States require a baccalaureate degree for admission to programs such as medicine, dentistry, and law. Or students may also choose to complete two years of coursework before transferring into a professional school for a baccalaureate degree. Students who plan to transfer to a professional school should plan their programs using the professional school catalog from the college or university to which the transfer is planned.

Certain programs offered at various colleges and universities prepare students for professional study at the graduate level or by transferring to an undergraduate professional program at another school after 1-3 years. Programs may include:

- Pre-Architecture
- Pre-Chiropractic
- Pre-Dentistry
- Pre-Engineering
- Pre-Law
- Pre-Medicine
- Pre-Nursing

- Pre-Occupational Therapy
- Pre-Optometry
- Pre-Physical Therapy
- Pre-Podiatry
- Pre-Seminary
- Pre-Veterinary

In some programs a student can earn two degrees (or 3-2 program) resulting in more than one Bachelor of Arts and/or Science degree.

Students interested in Dentistry, Medicine, Optometry, Physical Therapy, and Veterinary Medicine can be accepted to these professional schools with majors in a variety of fields. Regardless of major, however, a strong science and math background and a high score on the appropriate admissions test increase the probability of acceptance into the professional school of choice.

Students interested in law should follow closely the recommendations made by the Association of American Law Schools. For assistance in preparing for law school, see the Dean of Arts and Sciences. The LSAT, which is usually taken during the senior year, may be taken on campus. Although no particular undergraduate specialization is required, the Association of American Law Schools advises that the pre-law curriculum include the development of basic skills (including comprehension and expression in language), a critical understanding of human institutions and values and creative power in thinking.

Students should seek pre-professional advisors in their interest area early in their academic careers to ensure development of sound, comprehensive study programs which fulfill the admission requirements of the professional program to which they wish to apply.

Pre-professional programs are not degree programs; therefore, for financial aid purposes, students should declare a major from among the degree programs offered by the University in addition to their pre-professional program.

16 - COMBINED DEGREE (3:2) PROGRAMS

What is a Dual Degree Program?

With a 3:2 plan a college has "standing agreements" with several other universities for students to combine their undergraduate studies at one school with graduate studies in another subject at a different university.

Types of 3:2 Programs called Dual or Joint Degree

- The degree levels which can be obtained jointly include Associates, Bachelor, Master's and Doctoral Degree level.

- Double Degrees (conjoint or simultaneous degree) involve a student working towards two degrees. A student might obtain two degrees from different institutions. The two degrees might be in the same subject or in different areas of concentrations.

- A student might spend three years at one school and two years in the graduate program in another school and receives a bachelor's degree from the first as well as a bachelor's or master's degree from the affiliated program.

- Dual or double degree programs are widespread.

Benefits of a Dual or Double-Degree Program

- Reduces the amount of time required to be spent on each program.

- Common undergraduate programs might be found in Engineering, Business, and Computer Science.

- Postgraduate double degrees include J.D. /M.B.A degrees, and master degrees in politics, economics, urban planning, and international relations. Many medical schools also offer joint M.D. degrees with J.D. and M.B.A., as well as other Master level programs.

- A student studies for three years at one school followed by two years at the other school. The student is awarded two bachelor's degrees at the end of the five-year period, one from each school, and generally of different types (e.g., a B.A. and a B.S.). For example, the first school is a liberal arts college and the second is a university offering an engineering program.

Note: Earning two degrees from separate colleges of the same university could require a student to spend five years or more at one institution.

Double Degree or Double Major

It is important to understand the difference between a double degree and a double major. Double majors or dual majors consist of two majors attached to a single degree, as opposed to two separate degrees each with its own field of study.

17 - SOCIAL NETWORKING TIPS – MORE ON FACEBOOK!

The Intended College Use is Not the High School Reality

Keeping in contact with friends and family across the world is comforting. Social networking is a great way to find a job, network, and stay in touch with those who matter most. But how do you protect yourself while on the Internet?

Facebook was the first large scale networking site made specifically for college students. Though it still requires a valid email address to sign-up, anyone can now join and network in regions such as a major city, workplaces, colleges, and high schools. http://www.facebook.com

Social Networking Tips for Students

- It is a student's responsibility to protect his or her online accounts.

- On one hand, companies and colleges may research potential candidates. On the other hand, Facebook is an excellent way to learn more about colleges and receive quick communication from the school or current students. Many colleges have pages or groups that you can join or that you can use to learn more about clubs, majors or athletics. By using the Facebook search function, you can find out if a school you are interested in has an active presence on the network. Just be sure that if you choose to communicate with colleges that you've updated your privacy settings.

- Remove all inappropriate pictures and think about setting your album privacy setting of photos to be viewed only by friends.

- Probably more important than albums that you upload, are the photos that other people upload. In your original profile privacy settings, there is an option to limit who can see tagged photos of you. Be sure to change this if you don't want any picture added by others to be viewed by your Facebook friends.

- Watch what you provide in your profile.

- You may want to think twice about having a "Facebook" account.

- Be aware that pages on the Internet get cached (saved) and can be brought up even after the page no longer exists, so it is very important to remove inappropriate material from your profile as soon as possible!

- So remember, be sure to change your privacy settings often.

18 - HANDLING "SENIORITIS"

Is "senioritis" a myth? Every year students across the country struggle with a change in attitude. High school seniors try to balance responsibilities including academics, extracurricular activities, a social life, college admission, and perhaps a part-time job. Somewhere along the way, homework begins to seem less important. Then they get accepted to college, and after that, high school seems even less important. The students' grades begin to slide—and so does their motivation.

What are the danger signs and symptoms?

- A significant drop in grades in one or more courses.

- A downward trend in GPA will concern a college admissions office.

- Deciding to drop academic courses.

- Quitting extracurricular activities that were once important such as a sports team or music lessons.

- Disciplinary action for conduct such as skipping class.

- Academic misconduct, including cheating or plagiarism.

- An increase in absences or tardiness.

- Suspension for drug or alcohol use.

There are ways to combat it:

- Plan ahead – recognize your sliding away from responsibilities

- A realization that grades do matter through the end of the year.

- Don't obsess about it – work on changing your patterns.

- Talk about it with your parents and the admissions office if you think you need to in order to secure your admissions.

19 - REPORTING DISCIPLINARY INCIDENTS TO COLLEGES

It is your high school's policy to respond to inquiries from colleges about discipline infractions. The counselor will disclose disciplinary violations of the Honor Code that result in probation, suspension, or dismissal. When asked on an application about disciplinary actions received, students are expected to reply honestly.

If, after a student has submitted his or her college applications, a loss of a leadership position occurs as a result of discipline, the student's counselor will send a letter to the colleges to which the student has applied explaining the violation and the subsequent circumstances. If a student is separated from the school and that separation results in a change to the student's transcript, your high school will notify the colleges in a timely manner. In some cases, your high school reserves the right to withdraw its recommendations for a student from a college. For more specifics, please refer to your high school's Student Handbook.

CHAPTER

Financial Aid/Scholarships

1. Get the Basics — Financial Aid 101

2. Glossary of Financial Aid Terms

3. Apply for Federal Student Aid – Fast Track to FAFSA

4. Learn what is Available — Scholarships, Grants, Loans

5. Scholarships, Fellowships…Tell Me More!

6. How Do I Avoid Scholarship Scams?

7. How Can I Save for My Child's College Education?

8. Need-based Versus Merit-based Aid

9. Keep Track of College Costs

10. Sample Award Letter

11. How Do I Appeal My Financial Award?

12. Be Money Smart – Get the Most "Bang for Your Buck!"

13. The Ultimate Budget Worksheet for College Students

14. Financial Aid and Scholarships – Live Links

15. Top Twenty-One Financial Aid Tweeters

With the total costs of many private colleges now exceeding $25,000 to $30,000 per year, financial aid is a topic on the minds of an increasing number of people. You will not know whether or not you qualify for assistance, and you will not receive aid if you do not apply. It is not uncommon for more than a half of the students at some very well-known schools to be receiving some type of financial assistance. It is important not to rule out any college on the basis of cost alone. Often, schools which have higher tuition costs, are better able to provide aid than schools which have a lower cost, according to the US Department of Education.

Undergraduate scholarships and graduate fellowships are forms of aid that help students pay for their education. Unlike student loans, scholarships and fellowships do not have to be repaid. Searching for scholarship money takes as much time as taking a course, so set time aside for the search and the application process.

This chapter will move from the very basics about financial aid and scholarships to details about other types of aid programs such as grants, work study, loans, and so forth. There are many search firms that charge a hefty fee to match students with scholarships and help parents complete financial aid forms. There is no sense in paying someone else to help you save money on college tuition. Chances are you will do as well on your own. Counselors at the high school level and financial aid representatives at each college can help you with forms and information that may be required too. So, let's get started!

1 - GET THE BASICS—FINANCIAL AID 101

What It Costs: See the Big Picture

Many students worry that tuition and the other costs of continuing their education will be out of reach, but don't let the price tag stop you. It's only part of the picture. Keep in mind the major benefits of investing in your education.

Most students receive some kind of financial aid to help pay for the cost of their education. A few students even get a "free ride," where all their costs are paid for. With your determination and assistance from financial aid, you can make the education you dream about a reality. Use this section of the site to learn how.

Use the Net Price Calculator to get started. Each institution will have a Net Price Calculator on their website. The estimate provided by the calculator does not represent a final determination, or actual award of financial assistance, or a final net price; it is an estimate based on price of attendance and financial aid provided to students in a previous year. Price of attendance and financial aid availability often change year to year. The estimates shall not be binding on the Secretary of Education, the institution of higher education, or the State. Students must complete the Free Application for

Federal Student Aid (FAFSA) in order to be eligible for, and receive, an actual financial aid award that includes Federal grant, loan, or work-study assistance. For more information on applying for Federal student aid, go to http://www.fafsa.ed.gov/.

Who Gives Aid: Find the Figures

The U.S. Department of Education should be your first source to access financial aid. They award about $96 billion a year in grants, work-study assistance, and low-interest loans. Aid also comes from scholarships from state governments, schools, employers, individuals, private companies, nonprofits, religious groups, and professional organizations. So, there's money out there. You can find it.

Applying for Federal Aid: Meet the FAFSA

At some point, you need to fill out the Free Application for Federal Student Aid (FAFSA). To help you prepare, read more about the FAFSA. You can also get information from your school counselor. Most colleges also have a financial aid office you can contact for info. http://1.usa.gov/o8tP26

And for even more help, read the U.S. Department of Education's "Steps to Federal Student Aid fact sheet" fact sheet, or use "Completing the FAFSA," a detailed online tutorial. You can also call the Federal Student Aid Information Center at 1-800-4-FED-AID, or click the "Live Help" link on the Contact Us page of the FAFSA Web site; then click the "CUSTOMER SERVICE LIVE" button. http://www.fafsa.ed.gov/ - https://fafsa.ed.gov/contact.htm

What You Pay: Understand the EFC

The aid you qualify for depends on your Expected Family Contribution, or EFC. The EFC is a number that schools use to determine how much federal aid you would receive if you attended that school.

When you apply for federal student aid, you will be asked to provide information about your or your family's finances, such as income, assets, and family size. After you submit the application, you will receive an EFC based on this information.

Your contribution may come from a combination of savings, income, and loans.

What Aid Covers: Add It Up

There are five basic costs associated with going to college. Financial aid may be used for:

1. Tuition and fees
2. Room and board (cafeteria plan)
3. Books and supplies
4. Personal expenses
5. Travel

2 - GLOSSARY OF FINANCIAL AID TERMS

Financial aid has its own vocabulary. To help you speak the language, here are the most commonly used terms and acronyms.

Award Letter

Issued by a college's financial aid office, this is the official notification of the financial aid a student is eligible to receive.

Alternative loans

Loans are available to any student and generally a co-signer is needed. Credit score and debt-to-income ratio are factors in determining the approval of an alternative loan. There are many alternative loan programs available.

Bursar

This college office handles both the distribution of financial aid and the payment of fees and tuition. The Bursar may also be called financial officer, or something similar.

Cost of Attendance (COA)

This is the total amount it will cost a student to attend a particular college. It includes tuition, housing and meals, fees, books, supplies, transportation costs, and personal expenses.

CSS Profile

The CSS Profile is a secondary financial aid form provided by the College Board that the colleges use to help them determine if the student is eligible for the college's money. The CSS Profile should be filed early in October while the FAFSA should be completed on or after January 1 in order to receive early information regarding your status for financial aid. https://profileonline.collegeboard.com/prf/index.jsp

Equal Opportunity

Colleges are committed to assuring equal opportunity with respect to both education and employment and do not discriminate on the basis of race, color, religion, age, national origin, gender, or disability. This complies with Title IV of the Civil Rights Act of 1964, Title IX of the Educational Amendments of 1973, and other applicable statutes.

Expected Family Contribution (EFC)

This is the amount that the federal government estimates that a family should be able to pay toward the cost of a child's education. This information is compiled from the FAFSA by the federal government. In many instances, the EFC is calculated without taking into consideration any unexpected changes in income (not shown by the results from taxes) or other emergencies.

FAFSA

FAFSA is the standard form from the Department of Education that determines eligibility for all state and federal grants. Generally, you must fill this out before a college can begin processing your request for financial aid. Apply as early as possible beginning January 1st of each year. Schools and states have their own deadlines. Contact them for exact deadline dates. Current tax information will be needed to complete the form fully. http://www.fafsa.ed.gov/

Federal Academic Competitive Grant (ACG)

The Federal ACG is available to students who are U.S. citizens, Pell Grant eligible, registered full-time (either freshman or sophomore) and completed a "rigorous" high school program.

http://studentaid.ed.gov/PORTALSWebApp/students/english/NewPrograms.jsp

Federal Community Service Work-Study Program

This program is a partnership between the federal government and the college. It's based on financial need according to a student's completed FAFSA. This program is meant to place eligible students in the community as volunteers. Although students may volunteer for an organization, they're paid. The positions are primarily off campus. U.S. citizenship or eligible non-citizenship status is required.

Federal Pell Grant

The Federal Pell Grant is available to students who qualify by completing the FAFSA. The award can be as much as $4,731 per year and is determined by the Expected Family Contribution (EFC). These government grants are awarded to students who need a great deal of financial aid. They do not need to be repaid. http://www.ed.gov/programs/fpg/index.html

Federal PLUS Loan

Parents may borrow under the Federal Direct Plus Loan Program on behalf of the student. Parents are eligible to borrow the cost of education minus aid based on credit worthiness. Government-subsidized loans are limited to the cost of education. Parents do not need to demonstrate need. Interest rates can vary.

http://studentaid.ed.gov/PORTALSWebApp/students/english/parentloans.jsp

Federal Stafford Loan

Stafford Loans are available to all students who complete the FAFSA. There are two categories of a Federal Stafford Loan: subsidized and unsubsidized. With a subsidized loan, the government pays the interest while the student is in college. With an unsubsidized loan, the student is responsible for interest while in college. Payments for Federal Stafford Loans usually begin six months after the student drops below six credit hours or after graduation. http://www.staffordloan.com/

Federal Direct Stafford Loan limits

First Years $3,500

Sophomores $4,500

Juniors/Seniors $5,500

Please note: An additional $2,000 in unsubsidized loans is available for all students. Independent First Year students and sophomores may qualify for an additional $4,000 in unsubsidized loans. Juniors and seniors may qualify for an additional $5,000 in unsubsidized loans.

Federal Supplemental Education Opportunity Grant (SEOG)

The Federal SEOG is available to students who qualify by being eligible for the Federal Pell Grant. These awards can be as much as $600 per year. http://studentaid.ed.gov/PORTALSWebApp/students/english/FSEOG.jsp

Federal Work-Study Program

Funds for the Federal Work-Study Program come from the federal government. Students are awarded federal work-study money based on their financial need as determined by the completed FAFSA. Students must be U.S. citizens or eligible non-citizens to receive these funds. http://www.ed.gov/programs/fws/index.html

Financial Aid Package

An offer of money for a student from a college. It usually consists of several kinds of aid, including loans, grants, campus jobs, and may or may not include scholarships. This package fills the gap between parents' contribution and the total cost of college.

Free Application for Federal Student Aid (FAFSA)

This is the form a student completes to determine the EFC and the financial aid that will be available.

Grants and Scholarships

Grants and scholarships constitute free money available for education through a college or university, the state, the federal government, and outside agencies.

Grants and scholarships may be awarded based on need, GPA, merit, or all three.

Interest

Interest is the amount charged by a bank for the use of its money through the life of the loan.

Independent Status Student

Independent students can file their FAFSA independently of their parents. To qualify, you must meet one of the requirements below:

- You have reached your 24th birthday before January 1st of the beginning of the academic year for which you are applying for financial aid.

- You are married.

- You have children who received more than half of their support from you.

- You have dependents (other than your children or spouse) that live with you and who will receive more than half of their support from you, now through June 30th of the end of the academic year for which you are applying for financial aid.

- You are an orphan or ward of the court (or were a ward of the court until age of 18 or certified as being homeless.

- You are a veteran of the U.S. Armed Forces.

Merit Scholarships

Merit money given to students based on demonstrated ability—academic, performance, service, athletics, etc. It is not based on need, and does not need to be repaid. Most scholarships come from colleges themselves and vary widely from institution to institution. There are also some scholarships available from businesses, alumni organizations, and programs like the National Merit Scholarship. http://www.meritaid.com/

Student Employment Program (SEP)

This is work—either on or off campus—for students to help them pay for their education.

Work Study

A campus job may be offered as part of a financial aid package. These usually require 15-20 hours a week on campus and usually allow the student to do some studying while working. Examples might include monitoring a welcome desk in university office or working at a library desk.

3 - APPLY FOR FEDERAL STUDENT AID — FAST TRACK TO FAFSA

Introducing the FAFSA: Let the Funds Begin

Getting financial aid starts with the Free Application for Federal Student Aid or FAFSA. http://www.fafsa.ed.gov/index.htm

By filling it out, you apply for the U.S. Department of Education's federal student aid programs, the largest source of student aid in America. In many cases, you are automatically applying for funds from your state and your school as well.

Whom It is for: See If You Are Eligible

You might be eligible if all of these apply to you:

- You are a U.S. citizen or eligible noncitizen

- You are a high school graduate or GED holder

- You are working toward a degree or certificate in an eligible program

- You are not in default on a federal student loan and do not owe money to the government related to other grants or loans

Get complete eligibility information.

http://studentaid.ed.gov/PORTALSWebApp/students/english/aideligibility.jsp?tab=funding

Completing the FAFSA: Do It Online

It is recommended that you complete the FAFSA online. More help is available online, and you will get a response within 3-5 days, rather than 2-3 weeks by mail.

Before you start, find out what information you need and how to fill out the form. Save time by gathering all the necessary documents and information first. Go to the FAFSA to find out exactly what to do. http://www.fafsa.ed.gov/index.htm

You can also use the *Completing the FAFSA*, a detailed tutorial from the U.S. Department of Education. It's available online and in downloadable form.

FAFSA Worksheets: Get a Head Start

The FAFSA Web site has many resources to help you:

- A list of the documents you will need before beginning your FAFSA. http://www.fafsa.ed.gov/index.htm

- A worksheet to determine your FAFSA - If the FAFSA considers you to be dependent on your parents or family, you will need to provide information about them on the application. The dependency status worksheet helps you figure out whether you're dependent before filling out the FAFSA. http://www.fafsa.ed.gov/index.htm

- Download the FAFSA You can use it to practice filling out the real FAFSA. http://federalstudentaid.ed.gov/index.html

Questions about FAFSA? Find Answers

If you have questions about completing the FAFSA, call the Federal Student Aid Information Center at 1-800-4-FED-AID, or click the "Live Help" link on the Contact Us page of the FAFSA Web site, then click the "CUSTOMER SERVICE LIVE" button.

https://fafsa.ed.gov/contact.htm

FAFSA4Caster: Be Ahead of the Curve

If you are a high school junior or below, use FAFSA4Caster to estimate how much federal assistance you might get. This FREE tool helps you:

http://www.fafsa4caster.ed.gov/F4CApp/index/index.jsf

- Estimate your eligibility for federal student aid

- Reduce the time it takes to complete the FAFSA

- Plan for your future financial needs

Source: U.S. Department of Education

4 - LEARN WHAT'S AVAILABLE — SCHOLARSHIPS, GRANTS, LOANS

Scholarships, grants, loans and more…

One of the best ways to learn about all the available federal loans, grants, and work-study opportunities is in Funding Education Beyond High School: The Guide to Federal Student Aid.

http://studentaid.ed.gov/students/publications/student_guide/index.html

Scholarships: Earn to Learn

Scholarships are gifts. They do not need to be repaid. There are thousands of them, offered by schools, employers, individuals, private companies, nonprofits, religious groups, and professional and social organizations.

Some scholarships are merit-based. You earn them by meeting or exceeding certain standards set by the scholarship-giver. They might be awarded based on academic achievement, or a combination of academics and a special talent, trait, or interest. Other scholarships are based on financial need. Here are some tools to help find yours:

- Federal Student Aid Scholarship Search –
  https://studentaid2.ed.gov/getmoney/scholarship/v3browse.asp

- State Higher Education Agency Listings –
  http://wdcrobcolp01.ed.gov/Programs/EROD/org_list.cfm?category _ID=SHE

Grants: Need and Receive

Grants are also gifts, but they are usually based on financial need.

Most often, grant aid comes from federal and state governments and individual colleges. Available federal grants include:

http://studentaid.ed.gov/PORTALSWebApp/students/english/grants.jsp

- **Pell Grant.** These are federal grants awarded to undergraduate students.

- **ACG.** The Academic Competitiveness Grant is for college freshmen and sophomores who are eligible for Pell Grants and who took "rigorous" classes in high school.

- **FSEOG.** The Federal Supplemental Educational Opportunity Grant is awarded to undergraduate students with exceptional financial need.

- **National SMART Grant.** The National Science and Mathematics Access to Retain Talent Grant is awarded to college juniors and seniors who are eligible for Pell Grants and are majoring in mathematics, technology, engineering, a foreign language critical to national security or physical, life or computer sciences. Students must also have grade point averages of at least 3.0 in their majors to be eligible.

- **TEACH Grant.** The Teacher Education Assistance for College and Higher Education Grant is for students who plan to teach in schools that serve low-income students.

Loans: Borrow for the Future

Loans are contracts that allow a student to borrow money and repay it over time, with interest. In the case of most federal student loans, you do not need to begin repaying them until several months after you leave college or are no longer enrolled at least half time.

Every year, more than $70 billion in federal student aid is given out in the form of low-interest loans.

Some banks and financial institutions offer private student loans. These loans often have variable interest rates, require a credit check, and may not provide the benefits of federal student loans.

If taking out loans makes you feel a little nervous, you are in good company. Many of the students interviewed for this website felt the same way. But looking at loans as an investment in their future helped them get past their fear.

To learn more about federal student loans, read Federal Aid First, an online brochure from the U.S. Department of Education.

http://fsa.ed.gov/federalaidfirst/index.html

Work-Study: Get a Job

The Federal Work-Study (FWS) program provides part-time jobs for students with financial need to help them pay for their education.

The program is administered by participating schools. It's designed to put you to work in the community, or in a job related to your studies, whenever possible.

FAST FACT: More than 3,400 schools participate in the Federal Work-Study program. In 2007, over 800,000 students received work-study aid.

Other Sources of Aid: Find More Funding

Funding Education Beyond High School: The Guide to Federal Student Aid from the U.S. Department of Education features a section called Other Financial Aid Sources. It includes many other ideas to help you pay for your education, like the AmeriCorps community service organization and the U.S. armed forces.

http://studentaid.ed.gov/types

Tools and Tips: Find and Save Money

A little homework can earn you a lot of cash for college. A little common sense can help you use your money wisely. Here are a few tips to get started:

- Use the financial aid and scholarship wizards on the Federal Student Aid Web site. You can search for scholarships based on talents, interests, background and more.
  http://www2.ed.gov/students/college/aid/edpicks.jhtml

- Check the colleges you're considering for merit- or non-need-based scholarships to academically talented students.

- Check with your state education agency to find out if you're eligible for state assistance based on merit.
  http://wdcrobcolp01.ed.gov/Programs/EROD/org_list.cfm?category_ID=SHE

- See if you are eligible for an athletic scholarship, if you are athletically inclined.

- Stick close to home. Most state colleges and universities offer lower tuition to instate residents.

- Go to a lower-cost community college for one or two years; then, transfer to a four-year school.

- Live at home. You could save thousands of dollars.

Get more ideas on finding and saving money on the Federal Student Aid website. http://www2.ed.gov/students/college/aid/edpicks.jhtml

Source: U.S. Department of Education

5 - SCHOLARSHIPS, FELLOWSHIPS...TELL ME MORE!

Undergraduate scholarships and graduate fellowships are forms of aid that help students pay for their education. Unlike student loans, scholarships and fellowships do not have to be repaid. Hundreds of thousands of scholarships and fellowships from several thousand sponsors are awarded each year.

Generally, scholarships and fellowships are reserved for students with special qualifications, such as academic, athletic, or artistic talent. Awards are also available for students who are interested in particular fields of study, who are members of underrepresented groups, who live in certain areas of the country, or who demonstrate financial need.

Most scholarship applications will ask for information such as year in school, citizenship, state of residence, religion, ethnic background, disability, military status, employer, membership organizations, and so forth. An application requires a student to list information on extracurricular activities, sports, leadership, career plans, major plans, and future goals.

Where do I look for scholarships?

- Internet scholarship websites such as Fastweb Scholarship Search, Scholarship Experts, and Mach25 (see list of scholarships at the end)
  http://www.fastweb.com
  http://www.scholarshipexperts.com
  http://www.collegenet.com/mach25/app

- High School Counselors Office

- Public Library

- College's Financial Aid Office

- Bookstores – financial aid guides

- Organizations – religious, military, community service agencies, unions, professional associations

- Employers

- College Financial Aid Offices

- State scholarship programs such as Florida's Bright Futures Scholarships or Georgia's HOPE Program

Steps in your search for money to pay for college:

1. Begin your search early; write down the deadlines, and fill out scholarship applications ahead of time.

2. Use all resources available from the colleges themselves, internet sources, community, regional, and national sources.

3. Know your focus. If you are seeking undergraduate scholarship opportunities, do not focus on the graduate level.

4. Follow all the steps and instructions. Ignoring details could ruin your chances to have your application reviewed. Neatness counts.

5. Write an essay that makes a strong impression about you personally.

6. Check the address to be sure it gets where it needs to go. Keep a backup file in case it is needed.

7. Project yourself as confident and courteous. Reveal the importance of assistance while being respectful.

8. Have a friend, teacher, or parent review it before you mail it. Ask for help if you need it.

6 - HOW DO I AVOID SCHOLARSHIP SCAMS?

Are you asking, "How do I know when a scholarship is really a scam?" There are several ways scams become apparent. Finaid.org (http://www.finaid.org/scholarships/common.phtm) discusses several including:

- Money required before getting scholarship but scholarship never materializes.

- It may look like a scholarship program, but the scholarship company may be a for-profit agency. In other words, it costs to apply for it, and the money the company raises goes towards paying for the award.

- A low interest loan if offered for a fee prior to approval.

- A letter indicates you won a scholarship prize, but you must pay to receive it.

- Scholarship matching services guarantee scholarships.

- A free financial seminar often includes a sales pitch for insurance, annuity, or other investment products.

Scam Indicators

1. If you must pay money to get money, it might be a scam.

2. If it sounds too good to be true, it probably is.

3. Spend the time, not the money.

4. Never invest more than a postage stamp to get information about scholarships.

5. Nobody can guarantee that you'll win a scholarship.

6. Legitimate scholarship foundations do not charge application fees.

7. If you're suspicious of an offer, it's usually with good reason.

7 - HOW CAN I SAVE FOR MY CHILD'S COLLEGE EDUCATION?

Your child is focused on his or her school work, activities, and developing interests while you begin to focus on the end goal, your child's entrance into college. Like, what are your options for saving or for investing and how will you plan to pay for college? Planning for college is a serious matter. Talking to a financial planner at your local bank is a great place to start.

Stocks and Mutual Funds – Many people use stocks to fund college education in the form of mutual funds. Buying and selling, taking a risk versus security, looking for a yield or return, can be used as one investment strategy for college planning. If the investor's shares are worth more than the original cost, progress is made. Talk to your accountant, your banker, or your financial planner for more information about stocks and mutual fund opportunities.

529 Savings Plan – These plans are also known as Qualified State Tuition Programs. Each state sponsors a program and once withdrawal begins, they are tax exempt as long as the funds are used to pay for higher education expenses. Check out State by State Comparison Plans. Be sure to ask your financial planner about anything you do not understand.

Inheritance and Grandparents – Many grandparents would like to be able to assist their grandchildren on their journey to college. A 529 Savings Plan is an excellent way for them to shelter inheritance money from estate taxes while offering support to the student. Grandparents can use the annual gift tax exclusion for a single contribution for as much as $65,000 per beneficiary as long as the contributions are made for the beneficiary for five years. If the account owner dies, the 529 plan balance is not considered part of the estate for tax purposes.

Universal Life Insurance – Universal life offers a great option to help your family prepare for the unexpected. It provides a flexible premium and adjustable benefits so that as your needs change, you have the option to change your coverage. Additionally, as premiums are paid, the policy can accumulate account value which grows tax deferred until you need it. Talk to your insurance agent to get specific information.

Features include:

- Flexibility – decide the amount of life insurance, benefit, and premium payments.

- Security – protects your loved ones from financial hardship should the unexpected occur.

- Death benefit – proceeds are generally income tax free to the beneficiary.

- Guaranteed interest rate – The interest rate at which the account value grows is guaranteed never to drop below a defined level.

- Cash value growth is tax deferred – The growth in cash values is tax-deferred under current federal income tax law.

Certificates of Deposits – Certificates of Deposits or CD's are relatively risk free investments. They are FDIC insured to $250,000 and offer a fixed rate of return, whereas the principal and yield of investment securities will fluctuate with changes in market conditions. The interest earned is taxed as ordinary income. CD's are not very liquid, so if you withdraw money from them early, you may be facing an interest penalty.

Bonds and Zero-coupon Bonds – U.S. government bonds are considered the least risky investments available. They are government guaranteed. Series EE bonds are tax-free to low and middle income families and are used to fund a college education. Zero-coupon bonds are bought at a substantial discount and pay their face value upon maturity. Market fluctuations can affect the interest paid on these bonds. The interest income from zero-coupon bonds is subject to taxes annually as an ordinary income.

Independent College 500-Indexed Certificates of Deposit – IC 500 is the index created by the College Board based on the costs of 500 independent colleges and universities. The rate of return is directly related to this index.

Research your options, start early, plan carefully, and stay focused on your goal. This approach will lead to saving money for college funds.

8 - NEED-BASED VERSUS MERIT-BASED FINANCIAL AID

It is important to understand how to get the most money from the colleges a student is applying to, as aid can be need-based or merit-based.

Need-Based Aid is based on the family's financial need. A family can figure this amount to be the Cost of Attendance (COA) form the Expected Family Income (EFC).

Points to understand about Need-Based Aid:

- Information from the Free Application for Federal School Aid (FAFSA) is needed. Other colleges may require completion of the CSS Financial Profile.

- Grants do not need to be repaid.

- Loans will need to be paid with interest.

- Other types include Work-Study Programs, Perkins Loan and Subsidize Stafford Loan, and the Federal Supplemental Educational Opportunity Grants (FSEOG).

Merit-Based Aid is usually awarded for a student's academic achievement in high school. Other common examples of Merit-Based Aid include:

- Awards for special talents such as musical or athletic skills.

- May be awarded by states, colleges, universities, private groups or individuals.
- Tuition waivers.

9 - KEEP TRACK OF COLLEGE COSTS

Expenses	College 1	College 2	College 3	College 4
Tuition and fees: In-state Out-of-State	$ $	$ $	$ $	$ $
Books and supplies	$	$	$	$
Room and board	$	$	$	$
Transportation	$	$	$	$
Miscellaneous	$	$	$	$
Total Expenses:	$	$	$	$
Funds Available:				
Student and parent contributions	$	$	$	$
Grants: Federal – Stafford Loans; Perkins Loans; Graduate PLUS; Parent PLUS Local: Institutional(College or University)	$ $ $	$ $ $	$ $ $	$ $ $
Scholarships: Athletic, Arts, ROTC, Military 1) 2) 3)	$ $ $	$ $ $	$ $ $	$ $ $
Private Student Loans	$	$	$	$
Summer Earnings	$	$	$	$
Loans	$	$	$	$
529 Savings Plan	$	$	$	$
Total Funds, Grants, Loans, Scholarships, Work-study available	$	$	$	$
Funding Gap between College Costs and Financial Aid	$	$	$	$

Are your "funds available" less than or equal to your total for "expenses?" If not, you have a funding gap which means that you have more expenses than funds available and will need to take out a loan or seek other sources of funds.

10 - SAMPLE AWARD REPORT

Mr. Samuel Sample

123 Sample St.

Sampleville, ST 99999

Dear Samuel:

Congratulations on your admission to Sample University. We in Student Financial Aid look forward to working with you and your family over the next four years. We have reviewed your application for financial aid for the 2011-2012 academic year and are pleased to make this tentative offer of financial aid assistance based on a careful analysis of the information you provided.

Your need was calculated using the Budget and Resources detailed below:

Budget Category	Amount
Tuition and fees	39,212
Room and meals	11,234
Books and personal	2,764
Travel	400

Budget totals	53,610

Resources	Amount
Student contribution	1,900
Parental contribution	9,760

Total Resources	11,660
Need (Budget - Resources)	**41,950**

To meet your need, Sample University offers you the following assistance:

Source	Fall	Spring	Total
Sample U Scholarship	18,225	18,225	36,450
Self Help Offer	2,750	2,750	5,500
	------------	-----------	-----------
Total Awards	20,975	20,975	41,950

The above financial aid award is tentative pending receipt of the following items:

Sample University Student Information Review Form - As a Sample University Scholarship recipient, you must complete the Student Information Review Form before your scholarship can be credited to your student account. The online form is now available on Web at student.sampleu.edu under the "for Students" section in "Financial Record." You must have a current valid certificate on your computer in order to access the form.

The questionnaire helps us determine if you match any of the named scholarships which are used to fund students' Sample U financial aid. The form asks questions about your personal interests, extracurricular activities and work experience, as well as your plans during your time at Sample University. Scholarship aid is made possible by a community of alums and friends whose generosity allows the Institute to maintain a policy of need-blind admissions. The information that you share enables us to show donors the impact of their philanthropy. If you have questions or experience any difficulty with accessing or completing this form, please contact finaid@sampleu.edu.

Please feel free to contact Student Financial Aid at 000/000-0000 with any questions regarding your financial aid award or visit our web site at http://web.sampleu.edu/sfs/.

Sincerely,

Student Financial Services

11 - HOW DO I APPEAL MY FINANCIAL AWARD?

Congratulations, you were admitted to your college of your dreams! Next you receive a letter of notification from the financial aid/scholarships office. If you did not receive the award you expected, you may need to make an appeal for more funds.

Follow these steps to appeal for more funds:

1. Contact the aid office and ask what procedure you should follow to appeal for more financial assistance. Visit the office in person if time is on your side.

2. A "financial appeal" is when you attempt to demonstrate that with your current level of income and assets, you can't afford to pay the total cost of attendance for the first year. Ask the aid counselor to recalculate the initial Expected Family Contribution (EFC). Be sure to share any new information as well as all supporting documents including income verification, an update on asset holdings, a list of unusually high expenses, and a description of special circumstances. This new data could bring your EFC more in line with what you can afford.

3. A "competitive appeal" is based on the rivalry that can exist between schools which are roughly similar in selective admissions requirements. Ask if the school has an institutional policy and sufficient scholarship funds, that "puts them on record" as willing to respond to the aid packages of their rivals. Sharing copies of the other award letter with the intent of improving your original aid award may be a way to substantiate a competitive appeal.

You will not know what is possible until you ask. On one hand, the appeal may not produce a different award. On the other, the college may respond and increase the total amount of aid you receive which will allow you the opportunity to pursue the dream of attending your first choice school.

12 - BE MONEY SMART – GET THE MOST "BANG FOR YOUR BUCK!"

Money Management Tips: Spend with Care

- Make a budget and stick to it. A budget is just a self-imposed guideline for how much money you can spend and what you can spend it on. You will be amazed at how much further your money goes when you have a budget.

- Avoid credit cards. In college, you'll get many credit card offers from banks. Your best move? Shred them. As attractive as they might seem, the interest on credit cards can put you in a very deep financial hole.

- Buy used books. Textbook costs can average $1,000 a year. Most campus bookstores sell used books that can help reduce this cost. You might also save money by buying textbooks online.

- Leave your car at home. Cars consume more than just gas money. There are insurance, parking (and parking tickets!) and repair expenses, too. Walk, use public transportation and/or ride a bike.

- Watch the ATM fees. Choose a bank with free ATMs near your school. ATM fees can add up quickly.

Bad Deals and Scams: Know and Avoid Them

- Fee-based scholarship searches. Bad deal. Commercial financial aid advice services may cost more than $1,000, but you should never have to pay for this information. Here are sources that offer information FREE:

    - The Federal Student Aid Information Center. Call 1-800-4-FED-AID (1-800-433-3243); TTY users can call 1-800-730-8913

    - Your state higher education agency

    - A college or career school financial aid office

    - Your high school counselor

    - Your library's reference section

    - FREE online scholarship searches

    - Foundations and religious or community organizations

    - Ethnicity-based organizations

    - Your employer or your parents' employer

- Fee-based FAFSA assistance. Bad deal. Lots of free help is available to help you fill out the FAFSA. Websites that offer FAFSA help for a fee are NOT affiliated with the U.S. Department of Education. If you are asked for your credit card information, you are NOT at the official FAFSA Web site.

  - Get assistance from these FREE resources:
  - The official FAFSA http://www.fafsa.ed.gov/
  - Financial aid administrators at schools you are considering
  - The Federal Student Aid Information Center. Call 1-800-4-FED-AID (1-800-433-3243); TTY users can call 1-800-730-8913

- Protect your identity. Avoid scams. Protect your identity as you go through the financial aid application process. To reduce risk:

  - After completing your FAFSA online, exit application and close browser.
  - Don't tell anyone your Federal Student Aid PIN, even the person helping you complete the application.
  - Review your financial aid documents and keep track of the amounts you applied for and received.
  - Never give personal information over the phone or Internet unless you made the contact. For questions about a solicitation or your student loan account, call 1-800-4-FED-AID.
  - Shred receipts and documents containing personal information when you are finished with them.
  - Immediately report lost or stolen identification to the issuer and to the police.

- Report fraud and identity theft. For more information about financial aid fraud or to report fraud, visit the Federal Trade Commission's scholarship scams page. If you suspect that your student information has been stolen, contact one of these resources immediately: http://www.ftc.gov/scholarshipscams

  - U.S. Department of Education, 1-800-MIS-USED (1-800-647-8733)
  - Federal Trade Commission, 1-800-ID-THEFT (1-877-438-4338)

Other Considerations

Private loans. Private loans can be useful, but watch out for bad deals. Interest rates can be higher, and repayment terms can be harsher than government loans. Use all federal student loan options first. Investigate the private loan organization; check with the Better Business Bureau; get references and read the fine print. http://www.bbb.org/us/

Source: U.S. Department of Education

13 - THE ULTIMATE BUDGET WORKSHEET FOR COLLEGE STUDENTS

CATEGORY	MONTHLY BUDGET	MONTHLY ACTUAL	SEMESTER BUDGET	SEMESTER ACTUAL	SCHOOL YR BUDGET	SCHOOL YR ACTUAL
INCOME						
From Jobs						
From Parents						
From Student Loans						
From Scholarships						
From Financial Aid						
Miscellaneous Income						
EXPENSES						
Rent or Room & Board						
Utilities						
Telephone						
Groceries						
Car Payment/Transportation						
Insurance						
Gasoline/Oil						
Entertainment						
Eating Out/Vending						
Tuition						
Books						
School Fees						
Computer Expense						
Miscellaneous Expense						
NET INCOME (Income less Expenses)						

If an expense is incurred more or less often than monthly, convert it to a monthly amount when calculating the monthly budget amount. For instance, auto expense that is billed every six months would be converted to monthly by dividing the six month premium by six.

14 - FINANCIAL AID AND SCHOLARSHIPS – LIVE LINKS

Financial Aid Websites

- **529 College Savings Plan** - Putting money into a 529 college savings plan for a child may not be a flashy gift, but over the long run, it may be one of the most valuable. http://www.savingforcollege.com/

- **Adventures in Education** - Interactive services and information about career planning, college selection, and college funding, and a public service from Texas Guaranteed Student Loan Corporation. http://www.adventuresineducation.org/

- **Children's Bureau Express** - A fact sheet on college aid for Foster Youth. http://cbexpress.acf.hhs.gov/index.cfm?event=website.viewArticles&issueid=93&sectionid=5&articleid=1635

- **CollegeBoard: Pay for College** - Offers financial aid services advice, articles, and links for students and parents. http://www.collegeboard.com/pay/

- **CollegeNET** - Provides online applications for colleges in the U.S. and abroad, as well as, college search functions and a scholarship database. http://www.collegenet.com

- **College is Possible** - American Council on Education's K-16 youth development program that motivates middle and high school students from underserved communities to seek a college education. http://www.collegeispossible.org/

- **College Scholarships and Financial Aid Page** - Easy access to information on colleges, scholarships and SAT and ACT test preparation. http://www.college-scholarships.com/

- **Counselors and Mentors Guidebook** - A discussion on the financial aid process including step-by-step instructions on the FAFSA. http://www.fsa4counselors.ed.gov/clcf/attachments/CMH09-10.pdf

- **CSS Profile On-Line** - The CSS Profile is the form many private colleges and universities require, in addition to the FAFSA, for those applying for financial aid. https://profileonline.collegeboard.com/

- **EdWise** - An excellent online financial planning guide. http://www.edwise.org

- **eStudentLoan.com** - Offers comparisons of alternative student loans, scholarship search, financial aid information, and more. http://www.estudentloan.com/

- **Free Application for Federal Student Aid** (FAFSA - The official site for the Department of Education Free Application for Federal Student Aid (FAFSA). It includes an online submission form with necessary documents, deadlines, eligibility, and general student aid information for college students. http://www.fafsa.ed.gov/

- **FAFSA4Caster** - Understanding financial aid. What is federal student aid? Who qualifies? How do you apply? Get an early start on the financial aid process by learning the basics now. It can be as easy as A-B-C! http://www.fafsa4caster.ed.gov/F4CApp/index/index.jsf

- **FastWeb** - Find college financial aid, conduct a scholarship search with our scholarship search engine, and get the money you need to pay for college at FastWeb. http://www.fastweb.com

- **FinAid: The Financial Aid Information Page** - Comprehensive free resource for student financial aid information on the Web. Free scholarship search, financial aid calculators, glossary, and bibliography. http://www.finaid.org/

- **Financial Aid Finder** - Features financial aid information, including student loan programs, government grants, 529 college saving plans, and scholarships. http://www.financialaidfinder.com/

- **Financial Aid Letter** - Read real college financial aid award letters. Decode confusing (and sometimes misleading) loan and scholarship information. Translate financial aid jargon and acronyms into plain English. Get great tips on raising extra college cash, cutting costs, and making that degree more affordable. Find out why you deserve clear and complete cost information, and why colleges aren't delivering it. http://www.financialaidletter.com/

- **Finaid Facts** - Online resource for financial aid information, covering FAFSA, student loans, and regulations. http://www.finaidfacts.org/

- **Department of Education** - Office of Post Secondary Schools - http://www.ed.gov/students/landing.jhtml

- **Georgia School Finance Commission** - The official website of the Georgia Student Finance Commission (GSFC) provides financial aid to help Georgia students realize their higher education dreams. http://www.gsfc.org/gsfcnew/index.cfm

- **Grant Wrangler** - A free-grant listing service that makes it easier for educators to find funding, including grants, gifts, and awards for school and community projects. The website also helps grant-giving organizations promote their award opportunities to counselors and other educators. http://www.grantwrangler.com/

- **ISO** – International Student Organization - A membership organization of international students who are currently studying in the USA and abroad. http://www.isoa.org/list_scholarships.aspx

- **NASFA** - Resource for planning a Financial Aid Workshop with PowerPoint presentation and handouts. http://www.nasfaa.org/home.asp

- **Sallie Mae Financial Aid Information** - Sallie Mae®, the nation's leading provider of student loans and administrator of college savings plans, has helped millions of Americans achieve their dream of a higher education. The company primarily provides federal and private student loans for undergraduate and graduate students and their parents. http://www.salliemae.com/

- **Salliemae Wired Scholar** - How to interpret your acceptance and financial award letters. http://www.collegeanswer.com/index.jsp

- **SimpleTuition** - Is designed to help students and families find their way to the ideal student loan or financing option for educational expenses, and to help them take action. http://www.simpletuition.com/student_loans_home

- **Student Aid** - Financial Aid Resource Publications from the U.S. Department of Education- Funding Education Beyond High School: The Guide to Federal Student Aid is a comprehensive resource on student financial aid from the U.S. Department of Education. Grants, loans, and work-study are the three major forms of aid available through the Department's Federal Student Aid office. Funding Education Beyond High School: the Guide to Federal Student Aid tells you about the programs and how to apply for them.

http://www.studentaid.ed.gov/students/publications/student_guide/index.html

- **Student Finance Domain** - Guide for students, with objective advice on finding everything from the best credit card for students to financial aid and private student loans. http://www.studentfinancedomain.com/

Scholarship Search Websites

Source: Website descriptions are quoted from the individual website.

- American Indian College Fund - The American Indian College Fund provides scholarships and other support for the American Indian students. http://www.collegefund.org/

- **Asian Pacific Islander American Scholarship Fund** - An authoritative, one-stop information resource and sociological exploration of the historical, demographic, political, and cultural issues that make up today's diverse Asian American community. http://apiasf.org/

- **Black Excel** - We've been a "Top 10" BET pick, and called one of the "top 25 educational web sites" in the nation (I-WAY magazine). http://www.blackexcel.org/

- **The American Indian Education Programs** - The American Indian Education Programs are supervised via the Office of Professional Development. http://www.indianeducation.spps.org/Welcome.html

- **Bureau of Indian Education** - Excellent information for Native American students. http://www.bie.edu/

- **Children's Bureau Express** - A fact sheet on college aid for Foster Youth. http://cbexpress.acf.hhs.gov/index.cfm?event=website.viewArticles &issueid=93&sectionid=5&articleid=1635

- **College Scholarships** - Go straight to the scholarships that interest you and begin the application process. Every scholarship in our database is easy and simple to view, just by clicking. http://www.collegescholarships.org/

- **Disaboom** - A scholarship site for students with disabilities. http://www.disaboom.com/Resources/DisabilityScholarships/Default.asp

- **Go College** - Free Scholarship Service is a student's reference to finding money and getting the most out of a college education. http://www.gocollege.com/

- **Hispanic Scholarship Fund** - Provides Hispanic high school and college students with the vision, resources, and mentorship needed to become community leaders and achieve successful careers in business, science, technology, engineering, and math. http://www.hsf.net/

- **First in the Family** - Most people realize the difference a college education can make in their lives. But if you're the first in your family to do so, the impact can be extraordinary. http://www.firstinthefamily.org

- **First Generation** - The following info should give you a better understanding of the post-secondary route and help ease your anxiety of being a first generation college student. http://www.ecampustours.com/collegeplanning/gettingstarted/firstgenerationcollegestudents.htm

- **International Education Financial Aid** - IEFA is the premier resource for financial aid, college scholarship and grant information for US and international students wishing to study abroad. At this site, you will find the most comprehensive college scholarship search and grant listings plus international student loan programs and other information to promote study abroad. http://www.iefa.org/

- **International Student Loans** - InternationalStudentLoan.com is here to help, by offering a range of international student loans and study abroad loans to international students and Canadian students in the USA and for US Students studying around the world. http://www.internationalstudentloans.com/

- **Schools Awarding Aid to International Students** - Your international student and study abroad online portal for those who are looking to further their education overseas. http://www.internationalstudent.com/

- **Latino College Dollars** - Scholarships for Latino students. http://www.latinocollegedollars.org/

- **Mach 25 Free Scholarship service** - Keyword search and profile search is a great place to start if you already know something about the scholarship you are looking for. Enter a series of keywords to find all scholarships that contain those same words in their name or description. http://collegenet.com/mach25/app, http://collegenet.com/mach25/app?service=page/keyword

- **Merit Aid** - Is the first centralized and comprehensive website dedicated to matching students with merit-based scholarships from colleges across the country. http://www.cappex.com/

- **Military Scholarship Finder** - You and your dependents have great military education benefits. Learn about great schools and programs that can help you reach your goals. http://aid.military.com/scholarship/search-for-scholarships.do

- **My Free Degree** - It's FAST and it's FREE. Search our database with billions of dollars of college scholarships and financial aid awards. An amazing database related to majors. http://bit.ly/pjPr41

- **Posse Foundation** - The Posse Foundation identifies public high school students with extraordinary academic and leadership potential who may be overlooked by traditional college selection processes. Posse's partner colleges and universities award Posse Scholars four-year, full-tuition leadership scholarships. These Scholars graduate at a rate of 90 percent and make a visible difference on campus and throughout their professional careers. http://www.possefoundation.org/

- **QuestBridge** - QuestBridge is a non-profit program that links bright, motivated low-income students with educational and scholarship opportunities at some of the nation's best colleges. QuestBridge is the provider of the National College Match Program and the College Prep Scholarship. http://www.questbridge.org

- **Scholarships.com** - The Internet's leading scholarship search service and financial aid information resource, helps students make the decisions that shape their lives: researching and finding college financial aid, choosing a college, and paying for college. And it's all free. http://www.scholarships.com

- **Scholarship Experts** - After several years of development and constant refinement, we are pleased to continue offering ScholarshipExperts.com, a fast, easy and free way to find scholarships on the Internet, delivering accurate and timely search results that have been filtered and customized. http://www.ScholarshipExperts.com

- **Scholarships for Foster Children** - http://www.collegescholarships.org/scholarships/foster.htm

- **Scholarships of Students with Learning Disabilities** - Almost all colleges and universities provide some level of services and/or accommodations for learning disabled students, as mandated by the Americans with Disabilities Act (ADA). The colleges and universities listed on the website go a step further...they offer programs, some quite comprehensive, designed to support students with learning disabilities. http://www.college-scholarships.com/learning_disabilities.htm

- **Scholarship Scams** - Understand how to identify scholarship scams. http://www.finaid.org/scholarships/scams.phtml

- **Scholarships for Students with Learning Differences** - Incight empowers people with disabilities to become contributing members of society. http://www.incight.org/

- **School Soup** - Providing students with the most scholarship and other financial aid options on the internet – over $32 Billion in scholarship awards! http://www.schoolsoup.com/

- **Student Awards** - A scholarship search website. http://www.studentawards.com/

- **Student Finance Domain** - A guide for students, with objective advice on finding everything from the best credit card for students to financial aid and private student loans. http://www.studentfinancedomain.com/

- **United Negro College Fund** - At a time when a college degree is what a high school diploma was to previous generations, the minimum entry-level requirement for almost every well-paying career, UNCF plays a critical role in enabling more than 60,000 students each year to attend college and get the education they want and deserve. To close the educational attainment gap between African Americans and the majority population, UNCF helps promising students attend college and graduate. http://www.uncf.org/

- **Zinch** - A free and reputable scholarship search service. http://www.zinch.com

Minority Scholarships

- AFROTC High School Scholarships - http://www.afrotc.com/

- A Better Chance Scholarships - http://www.abetterchance.org/

- Adventures in Education - http://adventuresineducation.org/

- Alexander Graham Bell Association for the Deaf - http://www.agbell.org/

- Ambassadorial Scholarships - http://bit.ly/rpy2dc

- American Legion Scholarships - http://www.legion.org/

- Ayn Rand Institute - http://www.aynrand.org/contests

- American Rhodes Scholars - http://www.scholarships.com/financial-aid/college-scholarships/scholarships-by-type/corporate-scholarships/american-rhodes-scholars.aspx

- American Assoc. of University Women - http://www.aauw.org/fga/fellowships_grants/index.cfm

- American Chemical Society Scholarships - http://www.cnetweb.org/american_chemical_society_scholarships.htm

- American Fire Sprinkler Scholarship Contest - http://www.afsascholarship.org/

- AISES Google Scholarship - http://bit.ly/oXFCVP

- AmeriCorps - http://www.cns.gov/

- APS Minorities Scholarship Program (Physics) - http://www.aps.org/programs/minorities/honors/scholarship/

- Art and Writing Awards - http://www.artandwriting.org/

- Astronaut Scholarship Foundation - http://www.astronautscholarship.org/

- AXA Achievement Scholarship - http://www.axa-achievement.com/

- Baptist Scholarships - http://www.free-4u.com/baptist_scholarships.htm

- Bank of America Corporate Scholars - http://bit.ly/ptMAiz

- Best Buy of America Scholarships - https://bestbuy.scholarshipamerica.org/index.html

- Black Excel Scholarship Gateway http://www.blackexcel.org/link4.htm

- Black Student Fund - http://www.blackstudentfund.org/index.aspx

- Chicana/Latina Foundation - http://www.chicanalatina.org/scholarship.html

- College Net Scholarship Search - http://mach25.collegenet.com/cgi-bin/M25/index

- Coca Cola Scholars - https://www.coca-colascholars.org/cokeWeb/

- College Board Scholarship Search - http://apps.collegeboard.com/cbsearch_ss/welcome.jsp

- College-Bound High School Seniors - Scholarships - http://scholarships.fatomei.com/scholar13.html

- College Connection Scholarships - http://www.collegescholarships.com/

- Congressional Hispanic Scholarships - http://www.chciyouth.org/

- College View's Scholarship Search - http://www.collegeview.com/financial_aid/schol_directory/

- Collegiate Inventors Competition - http://www.invent.org/collegiate/

- Congressional Black Caucus Scholarships - http://www.cbcfinc.org/cbcf-scholarships.html

- Congressional Hispanic Caucus Institute - http://www.chci.org/

- Coveted National Scholarships - http://bit.ly/nKfqRg

- Daughters of the American Revolution Scholarships - http://www.dar.org/natsociety/edout_scholar.cfm#general

- The David and Dovetta Wilson Scholarship Fund - http://www.wilsonfund.org/

- Dell Scholars Program - http://www.dellscholars.org/public/

- Discover Card Scholarship - http://www.discoverfinancial.com/community/scholarship.shtml

- The Elks National Foundation Scholarships - http://www.elks.org/enf/scholars/ourscholarships.cfm

- Elks Most Valuable Student Scholarship - http://www.elks.org/

- Engineering School Scholarships - http://www.engineeringedu.com/scholars.html

- FAFSA (Free Application for Federal Student Aid) - http://www.fafsa.ed.gov/

- FastWeb Scholarship Search - http://www.fastweb.com

- Federal Employee Education Fund - http://bit.ly/qxFOkf

- Federal Scholarships and Aid - http://www.fedmoney.org/

- Federal Student Aid Portal - http://1.usa.gov/qyZssS

- Finaid: Minority Scholarships - http://www.finaid.org/otheraid/minority.phtml

- Fridell Memorial Scholarship (Dale E.) - http://www.straightforwardmedia.com/fridell/

- Gates Millennium Scholarships (Annual) - http://www.gmsp.org/%28hmrfvje1fdxdi0nwbrpmbd45%29/default.aspx

- Gateway to 10 Free Scholarship Searches - http://www.college-scholarships.com/free_scholarship_searches.htm

- Hispanic Scholarship Fund - http://www.hsf.net/

- Intel Science Talent Search - http://www.intel.com/

- International Students Scholarships & Aid Help - http://www.iefa.org/

- Jackie Robinson Foundation Scholarships - http://www.jackierobinson.org/

- Jewish Scholarships - http://www.free-4u.com/jewish.htm

- Marine Corps Scholarships - http://www.marine-scholars.org/

- Martin Luther King Scholarships - http://www.sanantonio.gov/mlk/?res=1024&ver=true

- Methodist Scholarships - http://www.free-4u.com/methodist_scholarships.htm

- Microsoft Scholarships - http://www.microsoft.com/college/ss_overview.mspx

- Minority Scholarships - http://www.free-4u.com/minority.htm

- Minority Undergraduate Fellows Program - http://www.naspa.org/resources/mufp/

- Music For The Blind - http://www.nfmc-music.org/

- NAACP Scholarships - http://www.naacp.org/pages/naacp-scholarships

- National Merit Scholarships - http://www.nationalmerit.org/

- Nursing Scholarships - http://www.blackexcel.org/nursing-scholarships.html

- National Black Nurses' Assoc. Scholarships - http://www.nbna.org/

- National Black Police Assoc. Scholarships - http://www.blackpolice.org/

- National Scholarships at All Levels - http://scholarships.fatomei.com/

- Orphan Foundation of America - http://www.orphan.org/

- Paralegal Scholarships - http://www.paralegals.org/displaycommon.cfm?an=13

- Posse Foundation - http://www.possefoundation.org/

- Presidential Freedom Scholarships - http://www.nationalservice.org/scholarships

- Princeton Review Scholarships & Aid - http://www.princetonreview.com/college/finance

- Princeton Review Internships - http://www.princetonreview.com/cte/search/internshipAdvSearch.asp

- Private Scholarships For Seniors - http://www.phs.d211.org/stsvc/college/scholarships.asp

- Project Excellence Scholarships - http://www.wmscholars.org/

- Prudential Spirit of Community Award - http://spirit.prudential.com/view/page/soc

- Questbridge - http://www.questbridge.orgRon Brown Scholarships - http://www.ronbrown.org/

- The Roothbert Fund Scholarships - http://www.roothbertfund.org/scholarships.php

- Scholarship & Financial Aid Help - http://www.blackexcel.org/fin-sch.htm

- Scholarships Based on Ethnicity - http://www.college.ucla.edu/UP/SRC/ethnic.htm

- Scholarships For Hispanics - http://www.scholarshipsforhispanics.org/

- Scholarships List and Search - http://www.adventuresineducation.org/sbase/

- Scholarships on the Net (1500 Links) - http://whatsonthe.net/scholarmks.htm

- Scholarship News - http://www.free-4u.com/

- Scholarships for Minority Accounting Students - http://www.aicpa.org/Career/DiversityInitiatives/Pages/smas.aspx

- Scholarships Pathways - http://scholarshipssite.blogspot.com/

- Scholarship Scams - http://www.ftc.gov/scholarshipscams

- ScienceNet Scholarship Listing - http://www.sciencenet.emory.edu/undergrad/scholarships.html

- September 11th Scholarship Funds - http://www.nasfaa.org/linklists/911scholarship.asp

- Siemens Foundation Competition - http://www.siemens-foundation.org/

- Sports Scholarships and Internships - http://bit.ly/nYVeTQ

- State Farm Insurance Hispanic Scholarships - http://www.statefarm.com/foundati/hispanic.htm

- Students of Color Scholarships - http://www.financialaid4you.com/index.php/scholarships

- Student Inventors Scholarships - http://www.invent.org/collegiate/

- Super College Scholarships - http://www.supercollege.com/

- Thurgood Marshall Scholarship Fund - http://www.thurgoodmarshallfund.org/

- Tylenol Scholarships - http://scholarship.tylenol.com/

- UNCF Google Scholarship - http://www.uncf.org/forstudents/scholarDetailSGA.asp?id=304

- Undesignated Scholarships (Engineering) - http://students.sae.org/awdscholar/scholarships/undesignated/

- United Negro College Fund Scholarships - http://www.uncf.org/forstudents/scholarship.asp

- United States National Peace Essay Contest - http://www.usip.org/ed/npec/index.html

- USA Access Education Scholarships - http://www.raconline.org/funding/funding_details.php?funding_id=225

- Wal-Mart Community Scholarship - http://www.walmartfoundation.org/

- Wal-Mart Scholarship Programs - http://walmartstores.com/CommunityGiving/8736.aspx?p=236

- War Memorial Fund - http://www.usjaycees.org/

- Wells Fargo Scholarships - http://www.wellsfargo.com/collegesteps

Disability-Related Scholarships and Awards

General

- Lime Scholarship - Google & Lime - http://googleblog.blogspot.com/2009/04/introducing-google-lime-scholarship.html

- Paul G. Hearne Leadership Award - http://www.aapd-dc.org/DMD/PaulHearneAward.html

- Proyecto Vision - http://www.proyectovision.net/english/opportunities/scholarships.html

- Undergraduate Scholarship Program Central Intelligence Agency - https://www.cia.gov/careers/student-opportunities/index.html#undergradscholar

Hearing Loss/Deafness

- AG Bell Financial Aid and Scholarship Program Alexander Graham Bell Association for the Deaf and Hard of Hearing - http://nc.agbell.org/NetCommunity/Page.aspx?pid=493

- Graduate Fellowship Fund Gallaudet University Alumni Association - http://financialaid.gallaudet.edu/Financial_Aid/Scholarships.html

- Hard of Hearing and Deaf Scholarship Sertoma International - http://www.sertoma.org/NETCOMMUNITY/Page.aspx?pid=344&srcid=190

- Minnie Pearl Scholarship Program The EAR Foundation - http://www.earfoundation.org/

- William C. Stokoe Scholarship National Association of the Deaf: Stokoe - http://www.nad.org/

Visual Impairments

- ACB Scholarship American Council of the Blind - http://www.acb.org/

- AFB Scholarships American Foundation for the Blind - http://www.afb.org/scholarships.asp

- CCLVI Scholarships Council of Citizens with Low Vision International - http://www.cclvi.org/

- CRS Scholarship Christian Record Services for the Blind -
  http://services.christianrecord.org/scholarships/index.php

- Ferrell Scholarship Assoc. for Education & Rehabilitation of the Blind
  & Visually Impaired -
  http://www.aerbvi.org/modules.php?name=Content&pa=showpag
  e&pid=77

- Guild Scholar Award Jewish Guild for the Blind -
  http://www.jgb.org/guildscholar.asp

- Lighthouse Scholarships Lighthouse International -
  http://www.lighthouse.org/services-and-assistance/scholarship-
  award-programs

- Mary P. Oenslager Scholastic Achievement Award Recording for the
  Blind and Dyslexic - http://www.rfbd.org/About-RFB-D/19/

Physical/Mobility Impairments

- 1800Wheelchair.com -
  http://www.1800wheelchair.com/Scholarship/

- AmeriGlide Achiever Scholarship AmeriGlide -
  http://www.ameriglide.com/scholarship/

- National MS Society Scholarship Program National Multiple
  Sclerosis Society - http://www.nationalmssociety.org/living-with-
  multiple-sclerosis/society-programs-and-
  services/scholarship/index.aspx

- SBA Scholarship Program Spina Bifida Association of America -
  http://www.spinabifidaassociation.org/

Health Impairments

- HFA Educational Scholarship Hemophilia Federation of America -
  http://hemophiliafed.org/%20programs-and-services/educational-
  scholarships/

- Kevin Child Scholarship National Hemophilia Foundation -
  http://www.hemophilia.org/NHFWeb/MainPgs/MainNHF.aspx?men
  uid=53&contentid=35

- Pfizer Epilepsy Scholarship Award Intra Med Educational Group -
  http://www.epilepsy-scholarship.com/

- Scholarships for Survivors Program Patient Advocate Foundation - http://www.patientadvocate.org/events.php?p=69

- Solvay Cares Scholarship Solvay Pharmaceuticals - http://www.solvaycaresscholarship.com/

- Ulman Cancer Fund for Young Adults - http://www.ulmanfund.org/Services/Scholarship/20092010ScholarshipProgram/tabid/565/Default.aspx

Learning Disabilities

- Anne & Matt Harbison Scholarship P. Buckley Moss Society - http://www.mosssociety.org/page.php?id=30

- Learning Through Listening Award Recording for the Blind and Dyslexic - http://www.rfbd.org/applications_awards.htm

Mental Health

- Lilly Reintegration Scholarship - http://www.reintegration.com/

Lesbian, Gay, Bisexual, and Transgender Financial Aid and Scholarship Resources

- The Advocate Guide For LGBT Students - http://www.campuspride.org/advocatecollegeguide/

- Campus Pride - http://www.campuspride.org/finding_scholarships.asp

- Finaid - http://www.finaid.org/otheraid/gay.phtml

- The Gay and Lesbian Guide to Colleges - http://amzn.to/q9Gv3A

- Human Rights Campaign - http://www.hrc.org/issues/youth_and_campus_activism/8644.htm

- Inside College - http://www.insidecollege.com/reno/GayFriendly-Colleges/451/list.do

- Point Foundation - http://www.pointfoundation.org/

- Scholarships for LGBT Students - http://www.collegescholarships.org/scholarships/lgbt-students.htm

15 - TOP 21 FINANCIAL AID TWEETERS

1. HOT PICK! @drchristinehand – College Planning Tips from College-Path.com! https://twitter.com/drchristinehand

243

2. @Fafsahelp – Tips on everything related to the Free Application for Federal Student Aid (FAFSA), and the latest news concerning student loans and scholarships. http://twitter.com/fafsahelp

3. @studentloaninfo – This "Student Loan Ninja" updates readers with articles she discovered while surfing the web, all of which discuss student loans and financial tips for students. http://twitter.com/studentloaninfo

4. @BethWalker_CFC – Beth Walker is a "college funding expert" who posts numerous links to articles each day which provide various tips on scholarships, and how to save and/or apply for college. http://twitter.com/BethWalker_CFC

5. @Student_Loan_US – Specifically for college students in America, these links cover the latest in private student loans, the Student Loan Consolidation Program, and politics.
http://twitter.com/Student_Loan_US

6. @MoneyCollege – These tweets provide links to other articles about student loan horror stories, credit card debt, student employment, and even free music downloads. Users can also send in their own "college financial survival" tips to the author. http://twitter.com/MoneyCollege

7. @CollegeBlogs – The financial aid guru Lynn O'Shaughnessy discusses the latest in educational and financial news for college students; many of the tweets reference articles published on her blog, the College Solution. http://twitter.com/collegeblogs

8. @securestudent – Read up on the latest in financial literacy news that is circulating around the web. Some tweets link to articles which provide tips on how students can avoid debt and maintain their bank account balances. http://twitter.com/securestudent

9. @StudentLoanNews – Some of these posts discuss student scams and loan repayment rates, but the majority of the tweets cover the latest political issues and events which are affecting the cost of higher education. http://twitter.com/StudentLoanNews

10. @educationmoney – Read up on the most frequently asked questions regarding student loans and bad credit, as well as tips for

high school graduates and the latest in educational politics. http://twitter.com/educationmoney

11. @GraduateCheap – These tweets cover numerous scholarship contests and opportunities for low or middle-income families, Pell Grants, and financial aid for minority students and single mothers. http://twitter.com/GraduateCheap

12. @CollegeGamePlan – This humorous twitterer updates followers with articles he found which discuss tips on student debt and taxes, college applications, financial survival, and student loans. http://twitter.com/CollegeGamePlan

13. @College_Experts – Get advice from college advisers and counselors who provide information on student loan debt, how to get accepted into college, or how to "ace" your exams. https://twitter.com/College_Experts

14. @planettuition – This twitter account provides up-to-date news on financial aid, statistics on student loans and employment, as well as information and facts on the future of higher education. http://twitter.com/plannettuition

15. @DodgeCollege – From textbook rentals, salaries, to college costs and student loan debt, followers of this account get updated on the latest in tuition costs, scholarships, and educational news. http://twitter.com/DodgeCollege

16. @MYFinc – Learn how to "map your future" and your finances by reading articles on identity theft, tuition costs, raising your credit score, and employment after graduation.
http://twitter.com/MYFinc

17. @nasfaa – From the National Association of Student Financial Aid Administrators (NASFAA), read up on the latest in American politics and how it affects your education. http://twitter.com/nasfaa

18. @GradGuard – These tweets cover numerous complex issues every college student should be aware of, such as tuition and renters insurance, refund policies, and health care. http://twitter.com/GradGuard

19. @intstudentloans – International students or students interested in studying abroad could learn a thing or two from these tweets. Stay up-to-date on the types of student loans that are available in different countries. http://twitter.com/intstudentloans

20. @CheapScholar – Doug Schantz works as a college administrator, and his goal is to help others find ways to make education more affordable for college students. His posts discuss the cost of textbooks, tuition discounts, and health insurance tips. http://twitter.com/CheapScholar

21. @Green_Panda – College students/graduates can check out this twitter account to read up on personal finance, student scams, cheap travel options for students, and "what is cool on the web" regarding the latest in student loans and education.

    http://twitter.com/Green_Panda

Heading Off to College – the Transition

1. Packing the Essentials

2. Dorm Room Decorating – Conquer the Budget; Small Space; and Ugly, Standard Furniture!

3. Save on Textbooks – Search Sites

4. Hi-tech Tools – Gadgets Galore!

5. Saying Goodbye to High School and Hello to College Life

6. Websites for Transitioning to College

7. Finding the Balance: Study Skills and Time Management Tips

8. Understanding Your Learning Style

9. Staying Safe While on Campus

Heading off to college is exciting and nerve-wracking at the same time! So many questions may be whirling through a student's brain. Did I make the right choice, choose the right college? Did I pick the "right" dorm in which to live? What if I don't get along with my roommate? Do I have any idea how to sign up for classes? What do I need to pack for school? And lastly, how will I say "goodbye" to family and friends? This chapter will supply information to make the transition a smooth one. It will be important to find a balance between studies and social life. Students will have to adjust to a new time schedule, learn each professor's style of teaching, set up their rooms to meet their needs, and say "goodbye" to the old times and "welcome" in the new experiences.

1 - PACKING THE ESSENTIALS

It's never too early to start shopping for the essentials. You can start early by getting any seasonal items as soon as possible. Know the layout of your room. Find out what you can bring and what you can't bring. Some schools allow small refrigerators but not microwaves. Call your roommate ahead of time so you do not duplicate items. Buy in bulk when you can. Bring your own "munchies."

What to Take

- Twin size sheets, mattress pad, towels, pillow, and comforters

- Bathroom supplies—shampoo, deodorant, soap, toothpaste and brush, flip-flops, other personal toiletries, and cleaning supplies

- Bean bags, futons, rug, curtains, lighting and bulbs, alarm clock

- Small storage containers, backpack, a bucket, bulletin board with pins; desk items - stapler, pens, pencils, paper, binders, paper clips; message board, ruler, notebooks, trash can, binders, book ends, calculator, index cards

- First aid kit, medicines, "munchies," coffee cups, travel mugs

- Laundry basket, laundry detergent, stain remover, fabric softener, Goo-Gone, rolls of quarters, sewing kit, portable vacuum, iron and board, and lint brush

- TV, microwave, small refrigerators, batteries, iron, flashlight, dinnerware, cups, glasses and utensils, fan

- A tool kit – duct tape, flashlight, flat head screwdriver, hammer with claw, nails, Philip's head screwdriver, pliers, wire cutters, putty knife, screws, tape measure, utility knife

- Cell phones and calling cards to keep in contact with friends and family

- Clothes for all seasons— if you don't have room, switch them out over the holidays on your visits home— appropriate shoes and boots as needed.

- Family and friends contact list for emergencies

What Not to Take…

- If freshmen are not allowed to have cars on campus at your school, you should leave your car at home. It's not always necessary to have a car on campus. Many colleges have their own shuttle buses if you are on a large campus. If you do bring a car, be aware of tow zones, or you will find it a costly venture (around $90) to get your car back. Leave the personalized license plate home—you don't want to give strangers information about yourself.

- Hot plate burner and candles…you don't want a fire.

- All pets, high school memorabilia, full size refrigerator,

- Expensive clothing and accessories (unfortunately it is the real world, and theft does occur).

- Jewelry you don't wear often.

- Of course, no fireworks, guns or explosives. School should be safe for all.

2 - DORM ROOM DECORATING – CONQUER THE BUDGET; SMALL SPACE; AND UGLY, STANDARD FURNITURE!

What are the three biggest concerns facing college freshmen when it comes to setting up a dorm room? Working within a budget, coping with a small space, and learning how to manipulate the standard, ugly dorm room furniture can be a challenge. So, what can you do to a room which you aren't allowed to paint, with walls you can't nail objects into, and two-of-a kind beds, dressers and desks? Learn more about how to make your space comfortable, bring a little bit of home with you, and create storage area which is essential.

Quick Tips for Those on a Budget!

- Can't paint? Use chalk to draw on the walls – you can erase it later with baby wipes or a dry eraser.

- Try fabric on the walls by using corn starch mixed with water. Apply the mixture to wall, smooth it out and watch how the fabric sticks to it. It's all natural and comes right off without removing paint. This is an easy way to get color and texture in your room.

- Check your local thrift stores or pick up items at a yard sale.

- Be sure your furniture is multi-functional. For example, a portable stool may double as an end table.

- For drapes without using screws – use small hooks with adhesive that pulls off the walls when you are ready to move.

- Dress up your table or desk with wall-paper, wrapping paper, or place mats, and cover it with plexiglass – this allows you to switch images out and stay fresh.

- Want a unique bedspread? Buy a plain white comforter and use fabric paint to design your focal point.

- Instead of staples, use dorm tape to adhere photos to walls or hang a series of clipboards and switch out the pictures as events change.

- Art work – use recycled items. Be creative with toilet paper rolls to design wall artwork.

- Make unique shelves by screwing old drawers together and giving them a coat of paint.

- Decorate your walls by checking out the Dollar Stores for cheap frames.

- Communicate with your roommate ahead of time so you don't bring duplicates.

It's a Small Space!

A lot smaller than what you are used to. So, how do you cope with this?

- Use items that reflect – mirrors can make the room look larger.

- Consolidate by watching TV on a laptop instead of a large screen.

- Make a bed a couch when not sleeping on it – add a throw blanket and some pillows.

- Organize your space by using bins, shoe trees, and stack storage boxes.

- Buy some bed risers to create space under your bed or loft-up your bed to create more space.

- Try moving the furniture around.

- A rolling cart can double as a towel rack.

- Hide clutter if you don't have a closet door by hanging a drape that can be pulled closed.

- Use wall space - go up and out and under to create space

- Use small rolling storage drawers under desk – they can be easily moved.

- Laundry basket or shoe rack that hangs can double for storage units.

- Keep your colors to three- any more will make your space too busy.

- Layer colors at ground, mid, and eye level.

- Check out cool pictures of dorm rooms on the Internet.

Dealing with ugly, standard furniture – any suggestions?

- Want a good night's sleep? Try adding a pillow-top to your dorm mattress.

- Since all dorm rooms tend to look the same, make them more exciting by making the bed stand out with throw blanket and colorful pillows.

- Buy a vintage office chair to replace your standard one.

- What about a cool rug? If you don't have a rug, consider using floor tiles – they stick together, but not to floor.

- Try moving your dresser into the closet to give you more space for a featured item, like a comfortable chair.

3 - SAVE ON TEXTBOOKS – SEARCH SITES

Books are not cheap. You may want to shop around if you know what books are needed for the courses you plan to take. Here is a list of websites that might help you with this task.

- **AddAll** - Book search and price comparison http://addall.com

- **Alibris.com** - Save big on high-quality books. http://www.alibris.com/

- **Amazon** is the place where you can save on new textbooks and up to 90 percent on used textbooks. You can also sell your textbooks online. http://www.amazon.com/s/ref=nb_sb_noss?url=search-alias%3Dbooks&field-keywords=textbooks&x=0&y=0

- **BarnesandNoble.com** - If you order over $25 in textbooks from this site you will not be charged for shipping, but this does not qualify for rented or used textbooks. http://www.barnesandnoble.com/u/textbooks-college-textbooks/379002366/

- **BetterWorldBooks.com** - Still the site is promoting a "Bargain Bin Blowout" which allows users to purchase five used books for $15. http://www.betterworldbooks.com/

- **BigWords.com** - This site gathers information from various textbook sites and calculates each price as well as the total shipping amount. http://www.bigwords.com/

- **Bookbyte.com** - All textbooks are 100% guaranteed. http://www.bookbyte.com/returnpolicy.aspx

- **Books Without Barriers** - Bookshare® is free for all U.S. students with qualifying disabilities. http://www.bookshare.org/

- **Bookfinder** - Check out the new and used textbook price comparisons. http://www.bookfinder.com/textbooks

- **BookRenter.com** - Another site that offers free shipping both ways. http://www.bookrenter.com/

- **Bookshare** - Accessible books and periodicals for readers with print disabilities — it is also free for all U.S. students with qualifying disabilities. http://www.bookshare.org/

- **CampusBookRentals.com** - There are no shipping fees, and once you receive your textbook you will be provided with a prepaid UPS shipping label. You can rent your book for the Semester (130 days), Quarter (85 days), or Summer (55 days), but they also offer 15 or 30 day extensions. http://www.campusbookrentals.com/

- **CampusBooks4Less** - Find and compare prices on new and used textbooks at online booksellers, Includes promotional discounts from sellers. http://www.campusbooks4less.com

- **Cheap Textbooks** - http://www.cheaptextbooks.com

- **CollegeBookRenter.com** - You can rent books off this site for 60, 90, or 190 days, and you are provided with a pre¬paid return label upon delivery. http://www.collegebookrenter.com/

- **ecampus.com** - Shipping costs approximately $3 depending on where you live and how fast you want it shipped to you, and you will also be given a free UPS return shipping label with your textbook. http://www.ecampus.com/

- **Follett New & Used Textbooks** - The place where you can search by course, by book, or by category including a database of over 800 campuses. Fifty percent guaranteed buy back on selected titles. http://www.efollett.com/

- **Half.com** - Unlike other textbook websites, the seller of the textbook decides how long you have to return an item to get a refund. http://www.half.ebay.com/

- **Renting Textbooks by Chegg** - http://www.chegg.com

- **Textbooks for Cash** - Book buyback service that pays premium prices for used textbooks. http://www.textbooks4cash.com

- **Textbookx** - New and used college textbooks with significant discounts. Also provides a textbook buyback book swap. Search by title, ISBN, or author. http://www.textbookx.com

- **TextbookHound** - Search by title, author and ISBN in 20 online college bookstores. http://www.textbookhound.com

- **TextbookLand** - Compares prices of new and used textbooks. http://www.textbookland.com

- **TextbookStop.com** - When you order a book off this site you will be provided with a prepaid return shipping label, and you are eligible for a full refund if you return the book 10 days after you received it. http://textbookstop.com/home.jsf

- **ValoreBooks.com** - This site has a "Free Textbook Giveaway" so students could be eligible to win free textbooks for a year. http://www.valorebooks.com/

4 - HI -TECH TOOLS – GADGETS GALORE!

Have you been thinking about what you want or need to take to college to make your life easier? Here are a few ideas of "hi-tech" gadgets.

- Desktop or Laptop? Without a doubt, most students will choose a laptop. You may need to think about what computer capabilities you will need. Are you a language major or focusing on engineering or architecture? Will you need special programs like an AutoCAD or Photoshop? Be sure your computer needs meet the appropriateness of your choice of studies. How much memory is important to you? Does your school require a laptop? Will you need a docking station in your dorm room? What size monitor do you need?

- Printers may be something you will want to invest in for homework, term papers, finals, and online data. There are many types available, though Inkjets are more affordable than laser. There are multi-purpose printers that scan, fax, email as well as make copies. Think about ink and toner cartridge replacements, paper, and portable design if space is a factor.

- Netbooks, laptops, mini notebooks, and tablets come in all ranges and colors. They are light, easy to pack and carry. Most of them weigh approximately 2.8 lbs., and they have a fairly long battery life—approximately 10 hours.

- What about music? Do you have an iPod, Shuffle, Nano, Touch, or Zune? Do you like to download music, videos, and pictures? Think about the capacity of each item, and whether you need speakers. How about a digital recorder?

- Do you need to back up your hard drives? You may want to use a portable hard-drive to back-up your data. Use flash drives (USB thumb drives) for organizing course work.

- Power Strips and Surge Protectors may be on your packing list. Dorm rooms may have limited outlets for plug-ins. Be sure to check with your Resident Assistant (RA) to see what your capacity is for such items. You don't want to pose a hazard to others.

- And don't forget the basics such as camera, extension cords, power strips, CD-Rs, back-up software, batteries, Ethernet cord, jump drive, mouse pad, wireless card, surge protectors, tools, extra-long TV cable, cell phone and charger, alarm clock, and lamps.

25 Tips for Incoming Freshmen

College not only poses a need for academic adjustment, but an adjustment to a new lifestyle. Juggling a new schedule and expectations that go along with it can affect freshmen emotionally, physically, and academically. Many colleges are attuned to this transition and offer support to freshmen in a variety of ways.

Dorms have trained personnel called resident assistants or RA's assigned to help students with everyday issues including roommate issues, school rules and guidelines, activities, and other school community issues. "Meltdowns" or emotional distress can occur due to grade pressure.

Mental health centers on campus offer counseling services from licensed psychologists and psychiatrists for counseling issues such as depression, eating disorders, anxiety, chemical dependency, and so on. If students need medical attention, the medical centers on campus can handle those requests. There are a variety of spiritual centers that can also offer support to students who wants to continue involvement in their faith life, attending retreats, and volunteering for community service opportunities. Career Centers are open to students interested in career exploration, internships, resume building, study abroad opportunities, and applications to graduate school.

The following list includes a collection of suggestions made by upper classmen for incoming freshmen.

1. Moving-in day can be stressful. Don't yell at your parents; they are trying to help you. Pack light!

2. If your dorm does not have air conditioning, bring fans!

3. Attend orientation activities; you will have plenty of times to do other activities later.

4. Maintain contact with family and friends via email, texting, or phone calls. This will reduce his or her anxiety and fears.

5. Find a balance between keeping contact with the friends from home and new friends at college.

6. Don't go home every weekend. You need to establish a life on campus.

7.   Relationships take work to keep them going; share events to keep each other up-to-date with your lives.

8.   Make a good first impression and remember names.

9.   Find a group to sit with at lunch; get to know people in your classes; join a study group.

10. Network with people; you may need a recommendation for an internship or need to interview for a job in the future.

11. Get to know your academic advisor to discuss your major; meet with your professors so you understand class expectations; see your RA (resident assistant) for everyday life issues; ask the registrar for help in signing up for classes and business office (bursar) for paying your bills.

12. Take responsibility for your own learning.

13. Study, study, study! Find a comfortable place to do your studying where you will not be disturbed.

14. Ward off procrastinating when it comes to school work; attend class daily and keep organized notes. You never know what the professors will focus on in class or on exams.

15. Get involved in activities— you never know whom you will meet or what you will enjoy. Become a leader on campus.

16. Enjoy your weekends; you may need a break from your studies, but remember to eat right, get your exercise, get enough sleep, and stick to a calendar to meet your deadlines and appointments.

17. Girls and Guys— stay safe, respect each other, and take care of your reputation—you are responsible for your actions.

18. Avoid peer pressure; don't worry about what others think about you.

19. Learn to accept change— in yourself, in others, and in situations.

20. Maintain contact— use Facebook, Skype, or other social networking methods, but remember to be safe when interacting with strangers. Choose privacy settings carefully, change passwords often, and think before you post.

21. Avoid "drama," gossip, and confront issues before they get too big. A word on roommates – set rules you can agree on, communicate, be considerate, be flexible, and be respectful.

22. Don't do drugs or use alcohol illegally; they will ruin your future!

23. Monitor spending— keep yourself on a budget—know the cost of your living, give yourself an allowance, organize receipts, be frugal, understand your debt load, avoid credit cards, and watch out for identity theft.

24. Remember, when you go home for that first visit, you will need to talk with your parents about their expectations.

25. Ask for help! You don't have to "go it alone." Use the power of positive thinking to accomplish your goals.

6 - WEBSITES FOR TRANSITIONING TO COLLEGE

- **AfterCollege** is an online professional platform that connects college students, alumni and employers through customized career networks at colleges and professional organizations across the country. We started AfterCollege with a simple goal: To create a better way for job seeking students and alumni to connect with the right employers. Today, AfterCollege powers the largest number of career networks on the internet, using its patented process to deliver thousands of exclusive opportunities to students and alumni each day. http://www.aftercollege.com

- **Campus Security** - Check out College Statistics - On-campus security information. http://ope.ed.gov/security/

- **College Tips of College Life** - Tips on surviving college life in your dorm. http://www.collegetips.com/college-life/dorm-tips.php

- **College Drinking Prevention** - This snapshot of annual high-risk college drinking consequences includes a concise list of facts outlining the effects of alcohol abuse on college campuses, communities, and students. http://www.collegedrinkingprevention.gov/CollegeStudents/

- **Studying in College** - Time management, prioritizing tasks, creating a budget and so on. http://www.studygs.net/schedule/

- **Transition to College for Parents** - No matter how prepared students think they are, starting college is the beginning of something new. Understanding your student's new way of life, and being available to listen and make suggestions, if asked, is important to your student's new way of life. Your continued support is important to your student's adaptation to the college experience. http://www.mnsu.edu/fye/parents/familyguidebook/collegetransiti on.html

- **An Unabridged List of Counseling Topics** - Topics range from ADD to Test Anxiety and more. http://www.dr-bob.org/vpc/virtulets.html

- **You Can Deal With It** - A public service of American Education Services (AES) provides college graduates and students with important information on money management, student loans, budgeting and the benefits and dangers of credit cards. Each section provides information, techniques, tools and practical advice on how to approach many of the common financial situations facing today's college graduates and students. http://www.youcandealwithit.com/

- **Young Money** - Tips on Money Management http://www.youngmoney.com/money_management

7 - FINDING A BALANCE: STUDY SKILLS AND TIME MANAGEMENT TIPS

It is important to find a balance between classes, work, and campus activities. Remember to take your health seriously and to set realistic expectations for yourself. If you're attending classes full-time, try not to work more than 20 hours a week.

Showing up for class and having your work done on time is a great way to start your college career. There a many ways to approach the task of studying, preparing for class, and taking tests.

Study Tips

- Develop a schedule that meets your needs and will keep you from wandering off to other tasks.

- Make every hour count … so create a 24 hour a day schedule, account for sleep, class, lab time, meals, hours for study, and hours for socializing with friends and family.

- Keep your workspace organized so you don't spend time looking for items.

- Begin 30-90 minutes after a meal and never within 30 minutes of going to sleep.

- Study when you are alert and ready focus.

- Prioritize what you want to study first— rank your classes according to the assignments.

- Study in chunks— for 30-40 minutes at a stretch.

- Review your lecture notes soon after they were given to add any extra information you may remember but did not write down in your notes— take breaks at your desk so you won't get distracted. Ask yourself questions and discuss topics with peers and professors.

- Improve your critical thinking skills.

- Be the best writer you can be — most colleges have writing labs to help you with papers.

For Class

- Pay attention to the syllabus.

- Sit where you will not be distracted.

- For classes with recitation, i.e. foreign language, practice to sharpen skills.

- You can study anywhere that suits you — the library, the student lounge, your room, as long as it is conducive to learning.

- When reading, get the main idea, extract important details, take notes, outline text.

- Develop a method for note-taking — listen to lecture, formulate questions, review and revise, and research notes.

- Choose teachers who actively involve you in learning.

- See your instructors outside of class.

- Find an academic or faculty advisor to help you with your choice of courses.

Taking Tests

- Taking exams—glance at the test and then always read the directions.

- Answer the easy questions first; pick out key words for true false statements like "always" and "never;" in multiple choice questions, eliminate the obvious wrong answers first and choose from the rest.

- Essay questions— pay attention to the instructor's words such as "list," "describe, or "compare and contrast." Do a quick outline on some scratch paper including the points you want to include.

- Pay attention to your handwriting, grammar, punctuation, and spelling.

8 - UNDERSTANDING YOUR LEARNING STYLE

Have you ever thought about how you learn? Your learning style has nothing to do with intelligence; it has to do with how your brain works. There are auditory learners, tactile or kinesthetic learners, and visual learners.

Auditory learners learn best by:

- Explaining material they are learning

- Reading out loud

- Making up a song about what they are learning or making up rhymes

- Using audio tapes to listen to information

- Stating the problem out loud and working through it

- Studying in groups

Tactile or kinesthetic learners:

- "Let's try and see how it works!"

- Should use the book while talking

- Write while reading or talking about topic

- Sit near the front as to not be distracted by others

- Use the computer to continue use of touch

- Write lists repeatedly

- Stand while explaining things and use gestures

- Use audio tapes as you walk or exercise

- Make flashcards – test yourself

Visual learners:

- Take notes while listening to lectures

- Use color to highlight notes

- Use graph paper for diagrams, flow charts, etc.

- Use a computer to organize information

- Use visual analogies, photographs, images

- Make flashcards to help remember images

Take North Carolina State's Index of Learning Styles Questionnaire to understand more about your own learning style!"

http://www.engr.ncsu.edu/learningstyles/ilsweb.html

9 - STAYING SAFE WHILE ON CAMPUS

Read the paper, watch the news, or listen to the radio. This will alert you to crime in cities, suburbs, or in the country. No town or campus is immune from crime, so understanding what you can do to stay safe is paramount.

Many college security offices have call boxes around campus, evening escort services, and a staff that patrols day and night. Others have developed emergency alert systems that call students' cell phones. Each campus has its own reporting system.

Here are some quick tips to help ensure your safety while on campus:

- Walk in groups or at least with one other person – there is safety in numbers.

- Be aware of your surroundings—do not walk in unlit areas at night and avoid those seldom-traveled shortcuts.

- Do not prop open entrances of residence halls – use door pass keys for safety.

- Keep your dorm room door locked while you are sleeping.

- Use door peepholes before opening your door.

- Vary your route if you walk every day to and from class, your job, or meals.

- If you are at a party, never let a stranger get a drink for you and never leave a drink unattended.

- Do not accept rides from people you don't know; a stranger may have a different agenda than you.

- Be aware of people loitering in hallways; take note of their clothes, their faces, jewelry, and unique features such as tattoos.

- Never lend your keys or identification to anyone.

- Do not leave your backpack and personal belongings unattended.

- Make sure someone knows where you are and when you expect to return.

- Consider carrying a personal alarm device, like a whistle and keep your cell phone charged.

- If you have a "gut-feeling" about a stranger, a fellow student, or a situation you find yourself in, trust your instinct and remove yourself from that situation as soon as possible.

- Do not listen to music wearing earphones while walking on campus at night. You will not hear a possible attacker approaching.

- The same goes for talking on a cell phone while walking across campus at night. You may be distracted and unaware of your surroundings.

Just for Parents

Your children are filled with excitement as they open their letters of acceptance to the college of their dreams. You are happy for them, but you realize they are about to enter the adult world. Are they ready for what they are about to face? Have you taught them how to problem solve? Will they make good choices? This transition can be difficult for parents as well as the child. This chapter will address ways to support your children as they navigate through the application process, ways to support your children as they make the transition to college, and ways to adjust to the "empty nest."

1 - WHAT PARENTS NEED TO KNOW ABOUT HANDLING THE ADMISSIONS PROCESS

It is important to understand your role in the admissions process as well as your child's and his or her counselor's roles.

Parent/Guardian Support is Important in the College Planning Process

- Understand that each child is unique.

- Recognize that students live in a complex time that is often highly competitive.

- Respect your child's choices and listen with an open mind.

- Provide helpful, encouraging, and constructive feedback.

- Model appropriate behavior; they copy what they observe.

- Encourage children to communicate with the colleges directly; try not to take over the process or the responsibilities that belong to the applicants.

- Remember that college counselors are professionals who have unique experiences in this field.

- If you are perplexed by a counselor's suggestion – ask the person to clarify the recommendations.

- Do not assume that online blogs and social networks have accurate admission information.

What to Expect from Your Child

- Your children should develop their skills to research, to make their own decisions by understanding their values, interests, and work ethic.

- Timely attention to tasks and deadlines through the college application cycle.

- Honest and open communication; open-mindedness; a willingness to be assertive, and ask questions.

- Openness to allowing parents and guardians to assist them in owning the search and application process.

What to Expect from Counselors Who Are Professionals in this Field

- Expert guidance and support through the admissions process.

- Assistance in creating a thoughtful and balanced application list.

- Clearly identified tasks for parents and students to complete.

- Thoughtful consideration of counselor recommendation comments

- A willingness for the parent or guardian to assist the child in owning the process by helping him or her learn to be self-reliant and self-sufficient.

2 - FIRST IN THE FAMILY

Should They Go? How Will I Cope With the Transition?

Parents of first generation college students may ask themselves several questions: Is my child smart enough? Is college for more privileged students? How will the child change when he or she goes off to school? How will I cope with them leaving?

Going to college can open the doors to new jobs, increases in pay, more pleasant work conditions, and a sense of satisfaction. As the students go through their search of careers, major area of study and college possibilities, you can support them along the way.

Parents can:

- Be part of the team in the process.
- Help them meet with their guidance counselor and other mentors like teachers or coaches at the school. Speak up for what classes they need to take.
- Ask about standardized testing exams needed for college entrance.
- Assist their children with a quiet, organized study area.
- Encourage their children to get involved in activities at school or work.
- Research colleges and financial aid/ scholarship options with their children.

Once your child is admitted, and makes his/her final decision where to attend, you can help with the transition. This time can be difficult as emotions come to the surface. Remember these important points:

- If you trust your child, he/she will have more self-confidence, stand up for what he/she believes, feel he/she is supported back home and is more likely to say "no" to tough situations.
- You will get to know your child on a different level, develop a bond over new conversations, and begin an "adult" relationship with them.

- Your child will need to figure some things out for him or herself and may make some mistakes. Help your child understand this is a part of life.

- Be sure your child knows you believe in him or her and walk the fine line of not appearing too intrusive.

- Help your child manage emotions by modeling your reactions and intervene as necessary.

3 - "HELICOPTER" PARENTS GO TO COLLEGE

Do you remember the little yellow signs that would hang in the window of a car that read, "Baby on Board"? These were created by concerned parents of the millennial age. Are you the "Safety Expert" who thinks ahead and who knows the lock down and security plans of the college campus your child will attend? Or maybe you are the "Traffic Expert" who gets calls from or calls your child as if he or she were still home. These parents often listen to their children's concerns offering advice, but leaving the decision-making up to the child. The "Rescue Helicopter Parent" rushes in with supplies such as articles for a class project or a new outfit to make a broken heart feel better. The "Consumer Advocates" demand their money's worth like a guarantee of a new job upon graduation. Lastly, the "Black Hawk" parents come in with guns blazing demanding action, and they start at the top no matter what the issue.

One definition of a "helicopter parent" is a person who micromanages every aspect of his or her child's life. Sure, parents should advocate and protect their children, but it is important to look at the far reaching consequences.

While overprotective parents may want the best for their children, they can cause more harm than good. Parents should ask themselves these questions:

- Is it okay for children to make mistakes?

- Do I feel the need to rescue them when they are addressing a problem?

- How will my child learn to grow and be self-reliant?

- How can I train them to exist in the adult world without allowing them to experience problems so they can develop their problem-solving skills?

Dangers of Being a Helicopter Parent:

- Undermining their children's confidence
- Instilling fear of failure
- Stunting growth and development
- Raising anxiety levels

Teach your children the value of negotiation. Encourage communication, and listen to their thoughts, opinions and feelings as they try to sort through solutions. While it is important for parents to have a healthy and positive interest in their children and their education, it is also important for parents not to undermine the children's self-confidence or autonomy.

4 - STAYING ORGANIZED

It will be important to stay organized as you proceed through the college application process. Here are some tips to make life easier:

- Create a filing system that works for you.
- Purchase folders and labels to hold information on applications, bank accounts, copies of checks and payment stubs, important college information, correspondence, housing data, insurance (car and medical), expenses including travel and tuition.
- Keep track of contacts at each institution.

Making a calendar that spans the school year will keep you focused on important dates such as orientation, the start of classes, Parent's Weekend, holiday breaks, the start of the next semester, the end of the school year, and tuition due dates.

Keep track of the following pertinent data:

- Health forms
- Date of physical
- Vaccinations
- Nearest pharmacy – address and phone number
- Phone number of Health Center at College
- Address and phone of hospital closest to college

- Child's blood type

- Eyeglass prescription

- Other medication prescriptions

- Medical Waiver

- Housing Forms – questionnaire, housing preference

- Tuition bills and New Student Orientation – books, supplies, and other miscellaneous expenses

- Bank information – address, account number, ABA routing number, transfer information, credit card expectations

- Power of Attorney and Other Written Consents in case of emergencies such as hospitalization, insurance needs, and/or treatment by physicians

5 - HEALTH AND INSURANCE

Be sure to check with your insurance company to insure your child has coverage while away from home. Can prescriptions be filled out of state?

Your child should be prepared to handle the basics of first aid. Be sure he or she has the following on hand:

- Acetaminophen or ibuprofen for aches, pains, and fever

- Rubbing Alcohol and hydrogen peroxide

- Antibacterial and antibiotic ointments

- Bandages or all sizes – first aid tape and scissors

- Cough drops and syrup

- Eye drops

- Hot and cold packs

- Medicine for allergies, colds, diarrhea

- Thermometer

- Tweezers

- Antacids for upset stomach

Be sure your child knows how to avoid staph and other infections by:

- Frequently washing his or her hands

- Not sharing personal items

- Keeping cuts and scrapes covered by clean bandages

Insurance documentation should be on record including health policy numbers, car insurance policy numbers, as well as Homeowner's or Renter's Insurance to cover losses due to damage from water, smoke, theft, or mechanical breakdown. Be sure to take an inventory of property taken to college.

6 - THE MONEY DISCUSSION

It is important to discuss finances with your child. Is your child ready for responsible spending within a budget?

Make a budget, open a credit card of emergencies, and open a checking account. Be sure your child knows how to write a check, to make a deposit, to keep a register, to reconcile statements, and to address risks of identity theft. Find out if a direct deposit or money transfer can occur at a bank near or on campus. Does the bank have an ATM, and does it charge a fee to use it? Explain the difference between a debit and credit card. Discuss monthly service charges, fees for "bounced" checks from the bank. Keeping receipts and deposit slips in a safe place is important so they can balance their checkbooks. Do they need access to a savings account? Can transfers be made online? Are students aware of other types of accounts such as Money Markets or Certificates of Deposits?

What are the hidden bank fees for using an ATM, dropping below a set check balance, writing too many checks, past due payments on credit cards, annual card fees, cash advances, balance transfers, and exceeding the credit limit. These can affect their credit score in the future.

Review financial aid and scholarship, and student budget information in the previous chapter.

7 - NEW STUDENT ORIENTATION

Has your child received his or her new student orientation information? Do you need to register, respond or make a payment? Are hotel reservations made and dorm rooms ready for moving in? Have you arranged for transportation to college?

There are many benefits for students who attend orientation programs put on by the college and universities. They are designed to:

- Assist students in the transition into college.

- Provide the students with opportunities to familiarize themselves with the campus, dorm rooms, classrooms, dining halls, library, bookstores, computer services, laundry facilities, publications, stores, etc.

- Help students understand what support services are available such as the infirmary, counseling and career services, writing centers, and religious centers.

- Meeting their roommate(s).

- Meet other students in their classes as well as upper-classmen.

- Discuss students' accounts and register for classes.

- Explain students' online accounts.

- Meet academic advisors to discuss goals and aspirations.

- Provide students with information about courses, curriculum, majors, minors, and requirements for graduation.

- Discuss extracurricular opportunities on and off campus.

- There are programs for parents to understand their children's new college life.

- These same programs give parents the opportunity to meet the President, the Deans, and administration and ask questions about college programming.

8 - OFF TO COLLEGE WE GO!

The drive to college leaves each person filled with anticipation and excitement. But, before anyone can unpack the car, you will need to pick up the keys and other important information. Most schools will have individuals available to help you and your child unpack upon arrival. You will most likely unload your boxes, carry them to the dorm, move your car, and then unpack.

- Take note of any damages or problems in the room. Note these on the form that may be given to you by college personnel.

- Be creative with organization and storage space such as under the bed, on bookshelves, and in closets.

- Help your child create his or her workspace.

- Discuss dorm safety like locking doors and windows even when going to restroom.

- Don't overload extension cords or power outlets.

- Keep cell phone charged in case of emergency.

Are cars allowed on campus? Find out before your child takes a car to school. Ask yourself:

- Is it practical to have a car?

- How will you handle routine maintenance?

- Do you have a copy of the registration, insurance cards, and registration items?

- Do you have a road service plan for emergency situations?

- How about a second set of car keys?

- Does your insurance company have stipulations regarding taking the car to another state for a certain period of time?

- Have you located the nearest certified mechanic?

What is in an emergency roadside kit?

- Car jack

- Cell phone charger

- Emergency flares, warning triangles or cones

- Fire extinguisher

- Flashlight

- Jumper cables

- Insurance and emergency numbers

- Tire inflator

- Washer fluid

- Scraper and brush for snow and ice

- Kitty litter for traction in mud and a mini shovel for snow

What about parking? Are there parking lots? Is there a cost? Can the car be left on campus over holidays? Know your child's travel plans: car, plane, or train.

Travel tips for your child:

- Photo ID

- Keep tickets in hand

- Carry keys

- Unplug electrical equipment

- Empty refrigerator of food that will spoil

- Give family itinerary

- Get spare prescriptions

- Confirm plans, flights, seat assignments

- Dress comfortably, bring food, and drink plenty of fluids

- Carry-on case no larger than 22 inches – pack light and in layers

Parents often drive off campus feeling empty. Remember, you can still send mail and "care packages," join parent groups, attend athletic events and parent weekend events, make weekly phone calls, and text!

9 - SAYING GOODBYE TO YOUR HIGH SCHOOL SENIOR

Seniors are counting down the days until the end of the school year. They are waiting in anticipation of packing up the car and heading down the road to their new life at college. Everything seems to be the last – the last dance, the last pep rally, the last set of finals, and lastly, saying goodbye to friends and family.

During the summer they will be busy packing, texting their new roommate to coordinate what to bring, registering for classes, and spending time with close friends. Meanwhile, parents are starting to feel neglected. This time is bittersweet for them. Though parents are happy to see the child pursuing their dreams, they can't imagine their home without him or her.

Knowing the bird has to leave the nest, there are a few things the child and parent can do to help each other during this time of transition. Let one another know you love each other and that each will be missed; let them know the relationship has been meaningful, and the transition to the next stage of life will be weathered; and let them know you are only a phone call or text message away.

So, here are some guidelines for the making the most of your time together before the great departure:

- Acknowledge your mixed emotions.
- Talk about this new stage of life.
- Trust your parenting skills and trust in your child's ability.
- Know there will be challenges and successes.
- Spending time with friends is natural.
- Tension and disagreements might arise the closer you get to the separation.
- Set up times to connect; parents don't always expect answers to your emails.
- You have given each other a great gift – the development of a responsible, young adult.
- Deal with the money talk.
- Buy tissues.

Parents may need to get reacquainted with each other. Remember to rest, exercise, and reconnect with friends. Follow your passion. Set a schedule for communication with your child. Take a deep breath, and start to enjoy the next phase of YOUR life!

10 - TIPS FOR ADJUSTING TO AN EMPTY NEST

Do you find yourself headed down memory lane when your child's excitement builds as he or she packs the car heading off to college, starting a military career, or getting a first apartment? You may feel shaky, sad, confused, or relieved. Parents react differently to an empty nest. It is a time of change, a time to look at your child's needs and your needs. It can be a fresh beginning. Here are several tips to help you cope:

Rest. Take time for yourself while you adjust to the change and try to figure out how you really feel. Drastic changes may only cause regret later, so hold off on the redecorating.

Exercise. If you find yourself sad or depressed, exercise is a way to lift your mood. Find a friend or a workout buddy to help you start a new routine. Avoid those fatty foods, chocolate and cocktails. Opt for a round of yoga, aerobics, weight training, and healthy eating.

Reconnect with others. Revisit your relationships. If you are single, you may want to get out and mingle. If you are married and you have spent decades focusing on your children, find new energy to reconnect with your loved one.

Follow your passion. Do you like to volunteer? What about going back to school? Think about taking on some new life-enriching activities. Now may be the perfect time to write that book.

Set a schedule for communication. Many parents worry that they will lose contact with their child. Set a regular phone date with your child once a week. This will ease your mind and give them some sense of freedom.

Sources for more Information:

- Angel, Sherry. "When Your Young Birds Have All Flown. Letting go of that last youngster can be a jarring experience, but there are ways to weather it." *Los Angeles Times*. Sept. 12, 1990.

- Association for Psychological Science. "Is Empty Nest Best? Changes in Marital Satisfaction in Late Middle Age." *ScienceDaily*. Dec. 12, 2008

- Belkin, Lisa. "When Children Leave." *New York Times*. Sept. 18, 2008.

- Conan, Neal. "Experiences with Empty Nest Syndrome." *NPR Talk of the Nation*. Dec. 5, 2001.

- Cushman, Fiery, rev. "Empty Nest Syndrome." *Psychology Today*. April 15, 2005.

- Demere, Tom. "Nests and Nest-building Animals." *Field Notes*; San Diego Natural History Museum. Spring 2002.

- Forman, Gail. "Rethinking the Empty Nest Syndrome." *Washington Post*. Sept. 6, 1988.

- Hartocollis, Anemona. "Early Pangs of Empty Nest Syndrome When the Children Leave Home for College." *New York Times*. Sept. 4, 2005.

- Levine, Bettijane. "Empty nest? Now keep it like that." *Los Angeles Times.* June 29, 2006.

- Lyon, Lindsay. "Is Empty-Nest Syndrome Nothing but an Empty Myth?" *U.S. News and World Report*. March 5, 2008.

- Nakao, Annie. "They can (and do) go home again. Empty Nest syndrome? Parents of 'boomerang' children should be so lucky." *San Francisco Chronicle*. May 30, 2004.

- Parker-Pope, Tara. "Your Nest is Empty? Enjoy Each Other." *New York Times.* Jan. 20, 2009.

- Raup, Jana L. and Jane E. Myers. "The Empty Nest Syndrome: Myth or Reality?" *Journal of Counseling and Development*. November/December 1989.

- Rosen, Daniel. "The Empty Nest Syndrome." *RelayHealth*.

- Span, Paula. "When the kids move out, the parents move on. Or at least they try." *Washington Post*. Aug. 27, 2000.

- University of Missouri-Columbia. "Empty Nest Syndrome May Not Be Bad After All, Study Finds." *ScienceDaily.* Feb. 24, 2008.

- Yara, Susan. "Father's Empty Nest." *Forbes*. Aug. 23, 2006.

NOTES

A Final Note

"Knowledge is Power"

You did it! You took a giant first step to understand more about the college admissions process. No matter where you are in your high school career, the information you just read should vastly increase your odds of getting into the college that is the best fit for you.

The rules are constantly changing in regards to college admissions, and the process of gaining entrance has become more competitive. I hope this book has helped answer questions asked by you and your parents regarding career, major and college search, vital strategies for standardized testing, preparing for the interview, navigating the financial aid process, and much more.

If you are need of more information, feel free to visit http://www.college-path.com, and do not forget to tell your friends about "College Bound" so they can get their own copy. I think you will find they will thank you.

I wish you all the very best!

Dr. Chris

P. S. Remember: There is also a 2013-14 Edition of "My College Bound Plan" – the companion workbook to College Bound with forms and checklists, and is available at College-Path.com - http://www.college-path.com/college-path-store.

To follow my College Planning Blog via Facebook, Twitter and RSS Feed.

Friend the College Path Fan Page on Facebook:

http://www.facebook.com/pages/College-Pathcom/74842441589

Follow Dr. Chris on Twitter ID: http://twitter.com/drchristinehand

Subscribe to the College-Path.com RSS Feed: http://feeds.feedburner.com/CollegePath

INDEX

Made in the USA
San Bernardino, CA
19 December 2013